Romantic Immanence

SUNY series, Studies in the Long Nineteenth Century

Pamela K. Gilbert, editor

Romantic Immanence
Interventions in Alterity, 1780–1840

Elizabeth A. Fay

Published by State University of New York Press, Albany

© 2023 State University of New York

All rights reserved

Printed in the United States of America

No part of this book may be used or reproduced in any manner whatsoever without written permission. No part of this book may be stored in a retrieval system or transmitted in any form or by any means including electronic, electrostatic, magnetic tape, mechanical, photocopying, recording, or otherwise without the prior permission in writing of the publisher.

For information, contact State University of New York Press, Albany, NY
www.sunypress.edu

Library of Congress Cataloging-in-Publication Data

Name: Fay, Elizabeth A., 1957– author.
Title: Romantic immanence : interventions in alterity, 1780–1840 / Elizabeth A. Fay.
Description: Albany, NY : State University of New York Press, [2023] | Includes bibliographical references and index.
Identifiers: LCCN 2022059405 | ISBN 9781438494746 (hardcover : alk. paper) | ISBN 9781438494760 (ebook)
Subjects: LCSH: Romanticism—Great Britain. | English literature—18th century—History and criticism. | English literature—19th century—History and criticism. | Immanence (Philosophy) in literature. | Other (Philosophy) in literature. | LCGFT: Literary criticism.
Classification: LCC PR447 .F396 2023 | DDC 820.9/145—dc23/eng/20230503
LC record available at https://lccn.loc.gov/2022059405

10 9 8 7 6 5 4 3 2 1

Contents

Acknowledgments   vii

Spinozist Alterity and British Romanticism   1

Section I
Corporeals: Embodied Egos

Chapter 1   Blake's Mythical Interval   25

Chapter 2   Coleridge's Wilding   67

Section II
Corporeals: Embodied Difference

Chapter 3   Barbauld's Sisters: Immanent Bodies   107

Section III
Incorporeals: Dream Visions and Nightmares

Chapter 4   Percy Shelley's Immanent Language   149

Chapter 5   De Quincey's Eventful Dreams   185

Section IV
Corporeal Bias: Bodies as Incorporeals

Epilogue Immanence and Racial Alterity	225
Notes	231
Works Cited	247
Index	257

Acknowledgments

I would like to thank *The Wordsworth Circle* for permission to use part of "Coleridge Finds Spinoza's Dharma Nature," appearing in volume 47 (Summer 2017), © 2017 by The University of Chicago. Reproduced by permission of The University of Chicago Press. All rights reserved. And I would like to thank *Romantic Circles Praxis* for permission to use a portion of "Rhymes of Wonder: Otherness without Distortion," *Praxis* volume "The Futures of Shelley's *Triumph*" (August 2019). I would also like to thank my husband, Chuck Meyer, for living with me through the long gestation of this book, and my daughter Eleanor for being the inspiration for so much in my life. Finally, I can't thank my editor, Rebecca Colesworthy, enough for all her support, handholding, and editorial acumen.

Spinozist Alterity and British Romanticism

Alterity is a subjective experience with the capacity to transform human beingness and sense of reality. It destabilizes identity, time, and place within a perceptual disorientation often accompanied by a sense of non-movement and beatitude or overwhelming terror. It can last a few seconds but feel infinite. And it demands the ethical response of recognizing its truth. My own literary introduction to alterity was through William Wordsworth's encounters with the sublime as represented in his epic *The Prelude* (c. 1805) and the odes. The haunting "Intimations of Immortality" ode (1807) exemplifies language's incapacity to render the sublime experience fully. Only metaphor, poetic rhythm, and rhyme can do even partial justice to the experience of alterity. Reading Longinus's tract on the rhetorical relation between poetic language and sublime affect helped inform how I understood the power of Wordsworth's poetry on me; Edmund Burke's and Immanuel Kant's theories of the sublime contextualized the Romantics' centering of the sublime despite their interest in other forms of alterity. These alternative modes of Otherness, although subordinated by the period's investment in the sublime, are present in Romantic literature and represented in the scholarship to varying degrees. *Romantic Immanence* explores one of the least recognized or discussed: Spinozist alterity, which I refer to throughout as "immanence," a term that recalls Spinoza's indebtedness to Greek Stoic thought.

Samuel Taylor Coleridge's "opium dream" poem "Kubla Khan" (c. 1797) provides a good example of Romantic recognition of a quite different mode of the absolute from the sublime: immanence. As Coleridge's footnote explains, the poem produced by the dream encodes alterity by recounting the visionary dream while gesturing toward the uncaptured, unrepresentable excess of the experience. Interrupted during his opium-fueled dream, he afterward "retained some vague and dim recollection of the general purport of the vision, yet, with the exception of some eight or ten scattered lines and images, all the rest had passed away."[1] Those lines are like bodies, scattered but interconnected and gesturing toward a larger vision of an alterity that is neither sublime nor Gothic, neither religious nor rhetorical. It is an Otherness more attuned to the rhythms of the universe, to the affective interrelation of things and ideas, and concerned with what is expressible as bodily felt sense but beyond language. Coleridge's poem attempts repeatedly to regain the dream's insight concerning a deep interconnection and interbeing of substance shared by bodies and ideas, dreams and things. Attempts to capture this universal truth of immanent life in poetic language is the focus of the present study.

All experiences of Otherness including immanence, all experiences of unrepresentable, untimely excess, convey a promise that the vision is true and that its truth is transformative. Also included is a felt mandate: the experience must be shared. Genres other than epic or lyric poetry, such as Gothic novels or essays insofar as they use imagistic and rhythmic language, can express an engagement with this excess, disseminating the experience to a variety of audiences. Whatever the genre, to render alterity verbally requires a use of language that suggests the bodily rhythms and imaginative figurations of a nonrepresentable and excessive encounter. In the sublime, by contrast, the bodily is transcended as the ego-mind merges with a higher, transcendental power such as God. Unlike the sublime, immanence accords well with the poetic or with chanting because harmony, whether that of language or of actants, is revealed through and as expressive, breathing, and moving bodies, bodies that articulate and affect each other. The very essence of the poetic is that its rhythms move us, its images affect us. It breathes as we do. It is therefore the art best suited to sharing immanence revealed in its truth.

As indebted as the Romantic period is to Enlightenment thought, and particularly to Enlightenment explorations of reason that find their apogee perhaps in the skepticism of David Hume and the critiques of Immanuel Kant, Romantics also found the counter-strains of Spinozism to be generative, more accessible, and more adaptable. Spinozist immanence, which relies on the principal notion that God and nature are the same—so that there is no separation between the mundane and the sacred—provides a variant of Otherness that contrasts with the sublime, in which the mundane is stripped away so that only the divine or transcendental appears. I am describing the sublime as Romantic odes depict it or yearn for it to appear, rather than its effects catalogued by Edmund Burke and Kant.

If the sublime is the most recognizable form of alterity in the Romantic period, representing the terrifying, existential experience of Otherness that tears the human self out of its carefully tended territory, there are also less violent and less terrific forms of Otherness familiar to readers of Romantic literature such as the Gothic and religious expression (as in Coleridge's "Religious Musings," with its apostrophic cry "Believe though, O my soul . . . !" [*Coleridge's Poetry* 33]). These literary treatments of alterity offer various ways for readers to access affective experiences that lent a persuasive solemnity to the existential angst produced by revolutionary crisis. But there were other world-changing phenomena that made people want their uneasiness voiced about how fast things around them were changing, and then assuaged through revelatory works of art. The period generally was one of heightened awareness of human difference stemming from an increasingly global commerce and an emerging theory of human raciality arising with the fractures arising in the Atlantic triangle trade. Additional factors were the defamiliarizing effects of increasingly visual microscopic and telescopic worlds; experimentation with opioids, especially laudanum; and the estranging yet alluring qualities of human and material representatives of cultures beyond British and continental borders. In *Sublime Understanding*, Kirk Pillow has made the argument that a major importance of the sublime was how it orients interpretation of indeterminacy and fragmented knowledge beyond the normal scope of understanding. As Pillow makes clear, however, Kant's theorization of the sublime, and then Hegel's (which Pillow argues expands on Kant's), aestheticizes this interpretive model: that is, the sublime distances the experiencer from the indeterminacy just as a painting of a sublime landscape does. The resurgent interest in earlier philosophies such as that of Baruch Spinoza as well as antinomian religious traditions were indications that alterity in forms other than the sublime, forms that made the indeterminacy of Otherness sensorily immanent rather than aesthetically distant, could provide a more proximate and pliable relief from a too-rapidly changing and expanding world.

What interest in Spinoza yielded, along with the Greek Stoic philosophy that influenced him, was a mode of alterity that had gone underground along with antinomianism during the Enlightenment. Its claims are antithetical to reason and science, and far distant from Deist explanations. Although Spinozism does bear some resemblance to the secret knowledge of Freemasonry, it is far removed from symbolic rituals and other nods to arcane wisdom embedded in Masonic practices. Whereas Enlightenment interest in Freemasonry lay in its claims to ancient knowledge, Spinozism offered the nonrepresentable and nontranslatable experience of immanence, less appealing to the rationalist mentality. This sudden but gentler experience of alterity than the sublime is characterized by a sense of unity and inclusivity. It is the antipode to the sublime's eradication of anything outside its terrible presence, but precisely for this its appeal was to the Romantic rather than Enlightenment sensibility. Together immanence, the sublime, the Gothic, antinomianism, and Unitarianism were all ways to experience Otherness without absolute terror.

Moreover, what immanence offers is that excess and nonrepresentability in an immanent encounter do not eviscerate the self, emptying it out as does the sublime, but rather open the self into the infinite vastness of nondivision, of radical inclusivity. In this it has allegiance to antinomian thought, which had remained under cover since the end of the English Civil Wars. Like antinomianism, immanence is the experience of internal rather than external authority. The wholeness that includes everything and everyone is internal down to the lowest level of the opened-up self, which is no longer partitioned off but is integrally bound to all else. That "all" is Nature itself, in Spinozist terms, or in Stoic terms (by which Spinoza was highly influenced), the All as One. In this, immanence offers a possible antidote to the eighteenth-century's scientistic categorizing of human and natural bodies into classes separate from the "universal subject" of white, male, Anglo privilege. We recognize this "antidote" in the project of Romantic nature poetry, which expresses in various ways the many in the one and radical inclusivity.

Romantic Immanence focuses on Spinozist alterity, arguing that although scholars have studied various forms of Otherness during the Romantic period, immanence has rarely been identified as such even when the texts it appears in are well-known. Yet immanence was a pervasive strand of intellectual and imaginative thought in Romanticism, appealing to the republican, idealist, and radical alike. Despite this, the political, even utopian promise of immanence was all but drowned out in the revolutionary failures of the Reign of Terror's aftermath. Even the Gothic lost much of its huge appeal after the 1790s. The sublime may have seemed a more potent source of spiritual and imaginative defense against the reactionary times of the Napoleonic Wars. But whereas the sublime singles out the individual, immanence holds a more communal promise, and certain artists held on to that promise. Tracing its effects on the Romantic imagination—with its promise of a new world order (chapters 1 through 3) and threat of its loss (chapters 4 and 5)—will enable us to better understand how the first- and second-generation Romantics imagined possible immanent futures for their troubled times.

How do we locate immanence in Romantic thought and art, and how do we know when we see it? Writing of Spinoza's conception of *Deus sive Natura*, the divine as nature, Gilles Deleuze explains that Spinozist philosophy is predicated on the interconnectedness of all things at the deepest level.[2] In *The Ethics* (1677), Spinoza himself discusses this essential quality as the affective relation between bodies in motion, whether thoughts or things. These bodies share a deep affection through their shared substance, so that the interconnection is thoroughly integrated. Both of these descriptions of immanence contrast sharply with the oppositional self-Other structure of the sublime, and with its tearing, disruptive force rather than affective movement. Another distinction is the sublime's polarity of infinity versus perceived space and time; in immanent alterity that polarity is replaced by a simultaneity of infinity and here-now. The sublime is characterized by violence and fear of death, a thunderclap of nonbeing; immanence reveals life itself as an infinite intra-relation of movement and being that also incorporates stillness and negation into its continuous expression. It is the absolute's expression that reveals itself anywhere, in the material world or in dreams, in foreign lands or next door. By contrast, the sublime's absolute has physical requirements such as the vast height of the alpine mountaintop or the death-filled terror of a storm at sea, a raging battlefield or an immense glacier. Sometimes representations of sublime and immanent alterity bump up against each other in the same literary work, or immanence and the Gothic collide, as if the poet or author were comparing kinds of alterity. Midway through Coleridge's "Rime of the Ancient Mariner," the Mariner views an approaching ship, soon revealed as a Gothic apparition inhabited by spectral figures; these are gambling to decide the fate of all onboard. Here Gothic alterity overwhelms with its hallucinatory presence, but almost immediately the Mariner has an intense epiphany in which the slimy sea redacts itself and the terrifying water-snakes appear to him in their immanent perfection. As I demonstrate in chapter 2, Coleridge's treatment of immanence dominates the poem's investments. Similarly, in her *Letters Written During a Short*

Residence in Sweden, Norway and Denmark (1796), discussed in chapter 3, Mary Wollstonecraft frequently toggles between the scenic sublime she has learned to view from treatises like Burke's, and an immanence opening up before her whose absorptive pull she feels effortlessly.

Immanence emphasizes how delusory "mastery" is. For the sublime and the Gothic, mastery by the Other is the primal effect on the human mind, but in immanence mastery is mere appearance. If the sublime swallows up the human and the Gothic imprisons it, both thereby staging mastery in its infinite power to overwhelm and reduce the human to the alienated self, immanence overwhelms with its leveling force and horizontal distribution. Immanence involves (as in involution) human experience by revealing an integration and deep intimacy that already inhere but go unrecognized until the immanent encounter. As experiences of alterity, the sublime, the Gothic, and immanence are comparable to other modes of alterity: direct revelation of God; the expansive illumination brought on by hallucinogenic drugs; the defamiliarizing estrangement of racial Otherness; the mathematical calculation of infinitude. Each mode of alterity involves either terror, fear of self-loss, intense wonderment, epiphany, transcendence, non-separation, or deep interbeing. Several of these effects describe immanence, especially wonderment and deep interbeing. These present a thorough dissolution of Cartesian dualism and Enlightenment reason so that the experience is instead a non-separation, an integral unity even between corporeal and noncorporeal. Thoughts and dreams are as much a part of the radical inclusiveness of immanence as physical bodies. The sublime emphasizes category; Burke's account registers this effect through his anatomy of sublime qualities such as vastness, darkness, and force: the table of contents lists ninety-six different topics for analyzing the sublime in contrast to the beautiful. Immanence emphasizes a radical oneness, all things are at bottom the same in their thusness, all things are at once the sacral thing.

While the Romantic period saw what might appear to be the superseding of the sublime over immanence, in fact Spinozist immanence continued to influence artists through the nineteenth century, especially after George Eliot's translation of Spinoza's *Ethics*. Even so, the sublime as a model for understanding eternity was more recognizable for those returning to a Christian faith as political radicalism lost popularity. By contrast, immanence is itself radical, and has been considered so all the way back to Spinoza himself. Immanence does not oppose itself to human limitations but rather dissolves boundaries between subjective and objective: eternity and here-now are the same, and, as Blake points out, vast space and a grain of sand too are the same. "To see a World in a Grain of Sand . . . Hold Infinity in the palm of your hand / And Eternity in an hour" ("Auguries of Innocence," 1–4). Even binarism itself disappears; space and time dissolve into the present now. Nondualism, the dissolution of binarism, addresses what Barbara Johnson calls "the imperatives of the not-self" by switching emphasis from egotistical frameworks to the vibrancy of all that which is not self.[3] Difference does not come back as repetition of the self-same but as the same difference that is the One. Knowledge does not come back as self-mirroring, as delusion, but as intimate knowing of another thing, of all things. Any experience of Otherness has lasting effect, some more transformative and inspirational, some half-forgotten soon after; but all give evidence of a suprahuman force of which occasionally we have intimations. During the Romantic period, artists, poets, and prophets appeared to have more of these experiences, as Blake's prophetic and Illuminated Books testify, or at least the Romantics were particularly interested in documenting and sharing them.

How to document, how to share such experiences is always problematic. Perhaps because of Longinus's rhetorical analysis of the sublime in Homer's and Sappho's poetry, the sublime has come to be associated with certain genres of poetry: the epic as in Homer and the meditative lyric as in Sappho. But it can also be found in poetic prose, and scholars have argued for it appearing in novels and other prose forms; indeed, we need only think of John Donne's sermons to realize that poetic language has affiliation with the sublime whether we are reading poetry or prose. Not just the sublime but all literary forms treating alterity require poetic language. Tropes alone cannot do justice to the violent experience of the sublime or the intimate inter-beingness of immanence; there is something that also or especially requires the musicality of the poetic with its meter, its pauses, its sharp stops or abrupt shifts, its sonorousness. This may be why Longinus's *On the Sublime*, a rhetorical treatment of the sublime, initiated a tradition that, more than any other category of alterity such as the divine or the supernatural, treated the sublime as a category of the aesthetic. Not just Burke's, but also Immanuel Kant's aesthetic analysis concretized the historical reception of the sublime as an aesthetic one in a tradition running from Longinus through to Boileau (Nicolas Boileau-Despréaux), Shaftesbury, John Dennis, Addison, and others. Intriguingly, Kant's *Critique of the Power of Judgment* (1790) argues that it is the spectator who judges whether an experience is sublime, and who does so from a distance. Distance is critical to aesthetic experience in aiding an affective and imaginative response to the heightened experience of terror, illumination, awakening, or enlightenment. Kant's analysis transforms sublime alterity into an effect of mind without the body's input, reinforcing a mind-world division. His transcendental reason goes hand in hand with the aesthetic distance he puts between the judging subject and the judged object, the beautiful and the sublime. Hegel goes further; his end goal of the dialectic is absolute knowledge. Therefore his treatment of the sublime in the *Aesthetics* is in terms of the dialectic, treatable through reason's process. This, too, is an important distinction from immanence, which involves the body in a world-making experience and understanding that cannot be distilled by the reason.

Because Spinoza rejected Descartes's rationalism, devising his system in order to contest the Cartesian one, it's important to my project to recognize Kant and Hegel as indebted to Descartes in a way that the German Idealists (Schelling, the Schlegels, and the early Hegel especially) rejected because of, or harmonized with, their embrace of Spinoza and immanence. Like Spinoza, then, and although more poetically just as immersively, the Romantics resist the transcendental model of Enlightenment reason and Cartesian principles. Further, immanence works for them as an alternative alterity to the sublime, which is a model of transcendence that denies immersion. But again, Spinozist immanence is radical through and through. Writers like Coleridge embraced immanence during the early revolutionary enthusiasm of utopian goals but then felt the allure of Christian faith, turning to it as the age eventually strove for political stability after military and colonial unrest. And at the end of the period, writers like De Quincey felt deeply ambivalent about both bodily immanence and a transcendental sublime; the first seemed unbearably present while the second seemed unreachable. The loss of any illusion of control was now not a blessing, as for Coleridge, but a curse derived from industrial and colonial excesses. This marks the turn into a Victorian frame of mind and the end of Romantic ideals as mainstream. However, the embrace of immanence by nineteenth- and early twentieth-century women writers like George Eliot and Virginia Woolf—the fact that Romantic immanence does not disappear—reveals that it was not a momentary spasm in aesthetic processes but that it is affectively compliant to counter projects of artists working against mainstream norms and open to alternative ways of understanding what is larger than any one form of human knowing.

One treatment of the sublime that comes close at times to how I am examining immanence is what Barbara Claire Freeman terms the "feminine sublime."[4] Freeman's definition of the feminine sublime rests on an alterity she locates in women's writing that eschews the violent, patriarchal qualities traditionally assigned to the sublime. Her effort to identify the feminine sublime have implications for my own project in that Freeman examines texts not usually associated with sublime experience, such as women's domestic fiction; in my case I examine texts not normally associated with Spinozist nature. Moreover, her analysis of women writers reveals an avoidance of the "more or less explicit mode of domination" associated with Longinus when those writers engage with the sublime's "crisis in relation to language and representation" (Freeman 2). The feminine sublime, like Romantic immanence, occurs in experiences of alterity such as the sense of self-dispersal that eclipses and overrides schemes of domination even in verbal descriptions of the encounter. A strong example of this is George Eliot's description of "that roar that lies on the other side of silence" (*Middlemarch*, qtd. in Freeman 1). The crisis in language's ability to represent what lies on the other side of silence provides an interval, in my terms, an expansive or stretched space-time, in which Otherness can reveal itself beyond the subject's compulsion to objectify and dominate. This is also the definition of immanence. In chapter 3 I return to the problem of whether what Eliot's "roar" refers to is the feminine sublime or Romantic immanence, and whether there might be a feminine version of immanence.

As Freeman explains, the sublime is conceived of as transcendence, as "a struggle for mastery between opposing powers, as the self's attempt to appropriate and contain whatever would exceed, and thereby undermine it." Furthermore, "Within the tradition of romantic aesthetics that sees the sublime as the elevation of the self over an object or experience that threatens it, the sublime becomes a strategy of appropriation" (2-3). Romantic immanence is, by this definition, a counter-sublime that lets go of domination and transcendence for absorption into Otherness as capacious, even infinite, inclusion. But whereas the feminine sublime "does not attempt to master its objects of rapture" (3), immanence has no objects of rapture. The interrelationality of entities or bodies includes the human experiencer, whose subjective boundaries dissolve. The felt sense of this is beyond bodily limitations of perception and intuition, loosening into an incommunicable expressiveness that later, on reflection, can find representation through poetic language as the articulative form most analogous to immanent experience.

Freeman's examination of Longinus, Burke, and Kant on the sublime reveals that their theories catalog the variety of ways excess resists sensory requirements (immeasurable vastness, gloomy depths, intolerable sound) in order to illustrate how excess always resists symbolization in language. However, Freeman explains, the standard or masculine sublime can only be defined through its difference from the feminine, which provides a locatable, domesticated base or ground for transforming unsymbolized excess into masculine transcendence and mastery.[5] By contrast, Romantic speculation about the divine in nature, for example, as in William Wordsworth's "Nutting," discovers a feminine presence that has more resonance with Romantic immanence through Spinoza's *Deus sive Natura*, "God or Nature." This is no mere pantheism, as Romantic nature poetry is often reductively understood, but rather the imaginative engagement with Spinozist concepts. As Marjorie Levinson notes, Wordsworth's poetry is rife with Spinozist terms such as "joy, nature, affection, appetite, and motion," and with the "unmediated body knowledge" and attention to the body in motion that bespeak more than passing knowledge of Spinozist concepts.[6] That Wordsworth could never convincingly treat immanence as nature-spirit—needing always to give it a hint of threat or vengeance toward man—may be due to his exaltation of the sublime and his need for a gendered account of transcendence. However, his poetic representations of alterity in nature are closer to Spinoza's conception of the deep interconnection of all things in the *Ethics* and to the Oneness or nonduality of immanence. Furthermore, the threat that informs so much of Wordsworth's nature poetry is always directed at the delusion caused by human egocentrism.

A return to the past's dominant and also less remembered philosophical innovations, from Neoplatonist to Spinozist thought, was part of Romantic intellectuals' exploration of how the present could be felt more thickly and intensely, and the future imagined more complexly. The present registers how fast and deeply things are changing, and a way to pause the rapidity of a pressing time seems provident; the future holds a promissory note that is nevertheless precarious. How one imagines that future depends on how Otherness reveals itself in an epiphanic experience of the present as right here now. An immanent experience.

I. Oneness and Otherness in Spinozism

Alterity has to do with an inexplicable excess; a surplus that eviscerates boundaries and centers, ground, and identity in the sublime, or dissolves them as mere barriers to true sight in immanence. Although Otherness seems opposed to everyday doing—surely one has to travel to Mont Blanc to experience the sublime?—Romantic literature shows how quotidian circumstances can be when alterity strikes. De Quincey's encounter with the Malay traveler at his cottage door is a case in point. Or the circumstances can be extraordinary and world-changing, as in revolution. War can give a particularly visceral encounter with alterity, war's horrifying effects producing either sublime or Gothic experiences: fear of death, loud explosions, bloodshed, and large-scale panic. All of these increase the desire for mastery; the sublime is a mode of alterity that demonstrates absolute mastery and promises a share in that mastery through transcendent experience. But if Romantic fascination with the sublime was at least partially a response to the turmoil of the years most traumatically represented by the Reign of Terror, what did a more colloquial form of Otherly encounter look like to those same Romantics? A sudden illumination among trees or with a starry sky; a dream or nightmare; too much laudanum: all of these produced extraordinary revelations evoked in poetic language. All of them rival accounts of the sublime.

Romantic Immanence singles out this more intimate mode, examining poets and poetic writers whose works express experiences not captured by the cataloging of alterity limited to the sublime, Gothic, religious, or racial Otherness. Immanence was theorized in Greek Stoicism concerning corporeal and incorporeal bodies, and in Spinoza's correspondence between ideas and matter. Spinoza's investment in democracy was worked through the deep interrelation of bodies in his philosophy, making Spinozism politically radical from the beginning. Because Spinoza incorporated Stoic thought, his philosophy alone could provide the Romantics with the implications of immanent life for their own dreams of a democratic futurity. Recuperating Spinozist philosophy from its historical marginalization helped the Romantics think through what revolution might mean, and further, what true democracy might look like. It is alterity as horizontal rather than vertical.

We now have a strong body of work on the importance of Spinoza's philosophy to Enlightenment and Romantic thought; we have less on the importance of early Stoic philosophy, especially its theory of immanence, or of the interrelation of the two for the Romantics, or even on how heavily Spinoza was influenced by Stoic philosophy.[7] The young Hegel, as well as Schelling and Nietzsche, were students of Spinozist thought, weaving it into their theories of the negative as a site of potentiation. Importantly, Spinoza was considered a dangerously radical thinker from his own lifetime up through the Romantic period; the charge of Spinozism was the charge of heresy. In *Radical Enlightenment* (2001), Jonathan Israel has mapped out Spinoza's importance to radical thought in the French Enlightenment, a movement that opposed what Israel defines as the "moderate" Enlightenment. Whereas the moderate intellectuals took Cartesianism as their model for how subjects comprehend their world as a mind-world division, radicals such as Diderot were "nouveaux spinozists" who related mind or soul with sensory experience and bodies as what moves, whether human or nonhuman. Levinson explains how threatening Spinoza was to establishment thought in Britain: "Characterized as both materialist and idealist, atheist and pantheist, rationalist and nominalist—branded as scholastic, Epicurean, Stoic, and Kabalistic—Spinoza was until fairly recently the great outlier in the history of philosophy" (Levinson 373). His thought, however, had never gone completely underground, just as the early Stoics' philosophy never fully disappeared. In *The Romantic Imperative*, Frederick Beiser includes Spinoza with the German Romantics in his discussion of them as a whole (Beiser 2–5). French Enlightenment and German Romantic interest in Spinoza reached Britain through the increasing networks for publications and public debate. As Levinson notes, "knowledge of Spinoza and of the political salience of his thought was not only available to but unavoidable" for the Romantics (Levinson 376).

Spinoza's philosophy was also incredibly fruitful for revolutionary thought because it undermines institutional power, which he was determined to work against. His concept of "conatus," an individual's power to persist, is especially revolutionary in that it applies not just to all social classes, but to all being, human and nonhuman, sentient and nonsentient. This revamps the way we understand the necessity of institutional control, revealing the artificial and harmful character of laws and institutions that constrain conatus, the individual's life force. It also points to the way in which bodies, human or not, are inclined toward a celebration of life and away from its stalling or decease. As such, Spinoza's philosophy points directly to a celebration of immanent life, of the shared substance of all bodies sentient or nonsentient, and away from anything like "mastery."[8] All bodies incline toward motion, and all bodies affect other bodies they contact: thus we have conatus (persistence as movement) and community. The dynamic flow of life in interrelated connection is exactly what immanent encounter reveals and realizes. This is true of ideas as well as bodies. Like the early Stoics, Spinoza understood incorporeals such as ideas, the soul, and the mind to be bodies just as corporeal bodies are. Incorporeals, including language, also move and affect other bodies: the soul engages in sensory perception; idea and body are analogs of the same thing and can affect each other. The Romantic breeze can inspire poetry of genius.

So why isn't Spinozist immanence more recognized in Romantic literature? Otherly encounters in Romantic texts that appear different from the sublime and Gothic have largely been either ignored by modern critics or shoehorned into a different recognizable category: for example, the agential aspect of thought and dream in Percy Shelley's political poetry is classified as idealism, and De Quincey's shape-changing hallucinations are interpreted as xenophobic anxiety. *Romantic Immanence* explores what I view as a stronger interpretation of these two examples. Immanence is in and of bodies, but also in and of thought, and in and of the world and universe. It bridges thought and thing, the ideal and the real, in revealing them to be fundamentally of the same substance with the same efficacy. It is present in Shelley's idealism and De Quincey's dreams, radically revisiting what "enlightenment" can mean and do.

All modes of alterity do the same work of exposing human thought as limited by what the mind can conceive and imagine, at the same time opening into truths that shatter egocentric "truths." They all provide an antidote to eighteenth-century Enlightenment, which examines and theorizes the world in terms of a "universal" subject who stands in for a model for understanding the world and experience through what is self-identical and what is "other." However, how modes of alterity are theorized does alter how Otherness is experienced, translated into experience, or into the remembered encounter. In immanence the "subject" is not universal but particular—this self right here, whose ego-boundaries dissolve in the immanent event. Immanence intrigued the Romantics in Britain and Germany because it is the mode of alterity most opposed to Enlightenment reason and science. It is primarily an experience of the nondual: a non–self-identical ontology providing insight into the possibility of an entire epistemology predicated on nondualism. Alterity in general might be best summed up as radical unknowableness: it is unnamable, unscriptable, illegible, and therefore any poetic or visual rendering of an experience of it is necessarily gestural. Immanence insists on not-knowing by integrating the unknowable into the illuming experience: not-knowing is the immanent version of the sublime's transcendent knowledge.

In Germany, Lessing provided a motto, "One and All," from the Greek *"hen kai pan"* for imagining and representing an experiential encounter with unknowable immanence. The concept allowed artists and intellectuals to experiment with it as a counter to Enlightenment formal and imaginative restraints. The motto is one Lessing derived from the pre-Socratics that was kept alive by the Neoplatonists, but Lessing associated it more with Spinoza, whose philosophy helped advance a speculative-materialist approach that deepens the mind's potential. Although Spinoza distinguished matter and thought as two separate forms of activity, they have a causal connection in terms of substance: they are both God's expression. His philosophy was developed in opposition to Descartes's, his contemporary, whose distinctions between divine and human substance, mind and world substance, are essential for his theory of the cogito.[9] Spinoza offered the Romantics a revivifying contrast to the Cartesian viewpoint, initiating widespread popular debate about Spinozism in Germany, although Spinozist philosophy there was identified with pantheism. This also caused real antagonism, as the "Pantheism Controversy" between the philosophers Moses Mendelssohn and Friedrich Henrich Jacobi showed,[10] and Spinoza's presumed atheism is another reason immanence lost its appeal later in the period. Nevertheless, it was this heated struggle over ideas that popularized the "One and All" creed. *Hen kai pan* refers to the concept of there being no singular and stable entity; all beings are part of and participate in the absolute One, yet their diversity and difference are not eliminated by the One. Coleridge famously translates the concept as "multeity in unity"; identity in difference is another formulation. Both express the idea that all manifestations of being are always both particular and participate in the One's radical inclusion. If we think of the atom (a Greek concept), atoms make up our bodies, our possessions, dirt, and insects, yet the very same atoms also transcend history in that they originated in world creation. Human bodies and dust, as the Old Testament writers also knew, are of the same fundamental substance: "for dust thou art, and unto dust shalt thou return" (King James, Genesis 3:19). Identity in difference, One and All.

This One is a dynamic cosmic entirety that contains the nonsentient as well as the sentient, and without parameters in terms of time and space. Yet human cognition has difficulty with what German idealism terms the conceptless concept, the absolute or One. The human mind experiences the absolute as a paused or stretched "now" in temporal terms, and spatially as "just here" in this now. The One characterizes the experience of revelation before it can be reduced to one or another theorized mode of alterity: it is the instantaneous experience of the dissolution of self in the overwhelming awareness of an Otherness that cannot be thought or comprehended but is deeply sensed. One has no choice: revelation is an event that occurs, by which one is involuntarily drawn and thrown as both witness and the affected, altered as the event enfolds and unfolds. It is this experience that, in varying degrees of intensity or trauma, connects all modes of alterity, but immanence differs in making vividly alive things functioning in one great cosmic network of energy. The One and All is a presage of our current understanding of the cosmos as an energy system.

What philosophers such as Schelling and Hegel, and poets like Coleridge and Shelley, saw in Spinoza was a potential for a new direction in art. Immanent revelation is one in which joy or beauty—what Coleridge's Ancient Mariner associates with "blessedness"—predominates. This is the "All" that both the Stoics and Spinoza showed is both singular and differentiated, both intimate and infinite. It is the empowering affect that Spinoza calls "joy." Nature is, in this sense, the cosmic entity that is both the living world and the Logos that organizes and informs this world; it is both divine and material, but also both material and immaterial, both bodies and thought inseparably together. Logos is the expression of immanence, the co-identity of idea and thing that Spinoza theorizes. Nature *is* poetry in this sense, for it is poetic, figurative language that best grapples with what cannot be pinned down by rational discourse or mere description.

In the chapters that follow, I unpack the relation of Stoic ethics, particularly its concept of incorporeals as bodies, in combination with Spinoza's ethics of bodies and ideas to show how everyday life and immanent ontology cohere. Although for Spinoza as well as the Stoics "ethics" refers to how bodies interact, the Romantics understood encounter with alterity to produce enlightenment, facilitating the ethical life in which bodies of all kinds, and their interrelation, are valued. Using significant German interventions in this trajectory, I trace literary engagements with these ideas in Blake, Coleridge, Barbauld, Wollstonecraft, Radcliffe, Dorothy Wordsworth, Coleridge, Percy Shelley, and finally De Quincey. De Quincey's hallucinations provide a variant form of immanence in that it is both domestically and mentally interior, privileging the immediacy of hallucinations that undo form to reveal that all sentient and non-sentient beings are entangled and enmeshed, participating in each other's expression. I use De Quincey's tormented response to bodily immanence as evidence of a failed sublime transcendence in the final chapter as a counter to Blake's delight in radical immanence in chapter 1. At the core, all forms of immanence are variants of the cosmic substance, as is the dream itself. How each author expresses immanence differs substantially, but the similarities cannot be denied, nor can they be recategorized. Coleridge's depiction of Spinozist nature in "Rime of the Ancient Mariner" cannot be reduced to Christian mysticism, and Dorothy Wordsworth's poetic journal entries are irreducible to the aestheticized mode of "nature writing." For each of the British writers I treat, alterity in the sense of Romantic immanence plays out differently, although always as a revelatory experience in which time and space, ego and selfhood, drop away. Although twentieth- and twenty-first-century interpretations of these works have largely ignored immanent alterity, redirecting how we read these texts opens them up to what may be a more Romantic understanding of them.

II. Immanent Ethics

Another goal of *Romantic Immanence* is to bring Romantic ethical life into play. Romantic poetry typically treats the everyday or local character of immanent encounter as an ethical one. That form and poetic language are primarily used to hold such experience makes sense; both "express" in that one is bodily or real, and one reveals thought or the ideal. The two together produce a harmony and rhythm that, in the case of immanent experience, also expresses a cosmic truth and therefore an ethics. According to Stoic philosophy, human-cosmic harmony occurs through the practice of virtue and the harmony of virtuous ethical life, therefore, resembles lines of iambic verse. According to Cleanthes, one's actions "are like half lines of iambic verse; hence, if they remain incomplete they are base, but if they are completed, they are virtuous."[11] This poetic harmony as conceived by the Stoics was not, by the time of the Romantics, understood as something pursued through virtue and reason alone. Several centuries before, Spinoza had already shown that the passions intrude on and interfere with reason's capacity to direct and enforce an ethical life. Affective life must be in harmony with virtues for ethical life to proceed; for the Romantics, this meant expressing one's life as "lines of iambic verse." But where verse and affect come together in a manner that reveals cosmic harmony and the integration of all things is in the experience of immanence. Affect, both in the Spinozist sense of how bodies affect each other through contact and in the sense of emotional vulnerability, is integral to immanent encounters. The heart and mind are equally affected in immanent revelation.

Immanent encounter, best understand as an event, leads to ethical action. The encounter's incorporeal effect of enmeshed ideas, sensations, emotions, and desire produces a realignment of values through an understanding of diversity and unity as simultaneous and shared. The whole comes into focus, so that the future and past of the immanent event "are evaluated only with respect to this definitive present," as Deleuze explains, "and from the point of view of that which embodies it."[12] Moreover, if the tense is paused or halted in the immanent interval ("now" is all that presents itself), past and future don't drop away so much as become the same as "now," the same as "is." In this way, Shelley's dream of futurity in *The Triumph of Life* is enfolded into the dream of the past and the present, each projecting the other in a kind of metalepsis. The presentness of temporalities, with past and future identical with now, is an inheritance from the pre-Socratics: time is dynamic, circular, or enfolding rather than linear. Therefore the present moment is already enfolded by and enfolds the past and future. The future, then, is immanent. This conception offers the possibility not only of a new direction for art, but of a new art.

In Romantic terms, Hegel's vocabulary of ground and grounded is a useful way to think about ethics in terms of the present moment, and therefore the future.[13] The One is the ground of the particular forms of thought and object-bodies that participate in our experience with the external world. In normal subjective experience, form covers over ground: we see trees and dogs and people, not a common substance that informs them and all else. But during an immanent encounter, ground and grounded disambiguate, pull apart, and yet hover over each other, as in pulsations, or groundedness falls away completely, leaving only Spinozist substance and an experience of the Stoic One. The One is Romantic Nature or the living, breathing, ensouled world (as in William Wordsworth's "Nutting" and similar poems). But the realization of ground as that which is our true identity is not entirely blissful "truth." The One is all-inclusive and neutral: it contains dark as well as light, for it is the human and not the cosmos that assigns "evil" and "goodness." Light and dark are versions of each other, highly entangled in the sense of Hegel's term "reflection": each is in the other, immanent to it and reflecting the other. Coleridge understands this when the Ancient Mariner realizes the water-snakes are beautiful (the albatross and the water-snakes as coidentified), but also sees the specter ship of ghastly death figures. As readers we think the Mariner's own death ship and his "punishment" as survivor are the negative lens, with his realization concerning the water-snakes as the positive lens. The specter ship in relation to that realization seems wrong, a Gothically horrific imposition, but the poem is meaningful when we see the pulsation of dark to light to dark as variants of each other, ground and grounded in turn as one and then the other takes form. They are both true to the One, since it holds that all things have recognizable identities apart from that one essential unity without form. The non-separation of light and dark, blessed and spectral is the truth that the Mariner must understand and relay.

Romantic engagement with immanence and its truths is fostered by an ethical pull toward the everyday: the albatross and the wedding, not the specter ship or water-snakes. Each immanent encounter presented in writing holds open the possibility that the inconceivable future is responsive to ethical practice; that individual action matters, not in the heroic sense but in the rhythms and virtues that inhere in all things, from water-snakes and serpents to fallible humans like the Wedding Guest. What the Romantics pondered was how art might intervene in bringing about a future different from the past and present. New kinds of art might also be new ways of approaching what is unknowable, whether this is futurity or alterity itself. Something hovers over immanent encounters that is in excess of that event; this is what poetic language can suggest. Because alterity is irreducible to language, this suggestive capture must rely on rhythm, rhyme, and other bodily responses to that experience: the very matter of poetry and poetic prose. The poetic works focusing each of the following chapters are attempts at just such new kinds of art, each providing a new formal response to an irreducible experience, and each recognizing the harmonic relations between cosmic order and human virtue that both the Stoics and Spinoza saw as inherent in our common materiality. Each argues for a transformation of the present through ethical action in a new way. This is quite distinct from the revelatory outcome of the sublime, a mode of alterity so deeply entrenched in our understanding of Romanticism that its nontranslatability and the inaction it produces has formed our sense of the Romantics as obsessed with what language and the poetic *can't* do, rather than what people and their passions do or fail at doing. But poems of immanent encounters reveal a different story. *Romantic Immanence* traces this story, which includes narratives of failing along with those of doing.

The chapters (detailed descriptions follow below) are organized into the following sections. Chapters 1 and 2 constitute "Corporeals: Embodied Egos." These chapters are essentially case studies of Romantic versions of immanent encounter. Both deal with the problem of the resistant, self-enclosing ego: the first chapter, which examines Blake's creation myth in his illuminated books, determines that only by sacrificing the ego can immanent life be realized; the second, taking Coleridge's "Rime of the Ancient Mariner" for its exemplary text, focuses on the necessity of dissolving ego before immanence can be realized. In the next section, "Corporeals: Embodied Difference," the third chapter functions as a pivot, troubling the versions of ego resistance in Blake's and Coleridge's works as "representative" by turning from the male bodies of the first two chapters to female bodily experience. Taking a different tact, this chapter treats four women writers in whose works various degrees of immanent encounter occur to determine whether gender makes a difference in how immanence is experienced or realized. The last two chapters, representing second-generation Romantics, comprise the third section, "Incorporeals: Dream Visions and Nightmares": chapter 4 studies Percy Shelley's dream vision in *The Triumph of Life*, and chapter 5 traces the hallucinatory immanence of De Quincy's opium confessions. The final section, "Corporeal Bias: Bodies as Incorporeals," contains an epilogue on racial alterity and how this bodily awareness arose parallel to that of immanent alterity.

In chapter 1, "Blake's Mythical Interval," I treat Blake's mythic conception of the four zoas, who represent human attributes and who are controlled by passions and human ego, as Spinozist bodies whose movement, along with that of their incorporeal emotions and thoughts, affects each other as bodies. The space in which their mythic development occurs is the interval, a generative space of struggle between blinding ego and prophetic sight. Developed through his major poems is the realization of the One and All, achieved in his masterpiece *Jerusalem* through Los's self-sacrifice, which is the sacrifice of his egotism. In losing ego, Los the poet-zoa demonstrates what is necessary to open oneself up to the interval's illumination of infinite Spinozist substance and its expression.

Chapter 2, "Coleridge's Wilding," provides a key text for thinking about Romantic immanence, "The Rime of the Ancient Mariner." I show how the Mariner's encounter with the water-snakes is an immanent encounter that leads to his enlightenment, a realization of the need for virtue and an ethical life. It is an experience of the raw power of nature as well as the plenitude of Spinoza's *Deus sive Natura*. The poetic force of the

"Rime" is its use of repetition rhythmically and semantically; repetition as the "burden" or chorus of a ballad is metaphorically transformed into the Mariner's insistent repetition of his tale as an ethical act. Significantly, in the post-encounter ethical practice of poetic recitation the Mariner invokes the rhythms of the universe and immanent life.

Chapter 3, "Barbauld's Sisters: Immanent Bodies," examines four women writers whose works reflect a concern with the beingness of sentient and nonsentient bodies and the ethical consistency of immanent encounter. The writings of Anna Lætitia Barbauld, Mary Wollstonecraft, Ann Radcliffe, and Dorothy Wordsworth represent immanent experiences and encounters in different ways while revealing a similar attitude toward the beingness of the world and the ethical relation woven deep into its ontological expression. For each writer, the problem becomes how to suggest this expression. After engaging a key text of each writer, I then turn to exploring why and how Dorothy Wordsworth's engagement with immanence is the most sustained and developed of the four writers. At the same time, I consider whether these writers exhibit an engagement with immanence that reflects a gendered understanding of embodiedness in terms of the One and All.

Chapter 4, "Percy Shelley's Immanent Language," demonstrates that *The Triumph of Life* is a formal argument for how the dominant philosophical tradition as it coalesced in the Enlightenment had so distorted human experience that language proves inadequate to its undoing. As a consequence, both reasoned thought and human language are alienated from the bodies they belong to. The poet's only course of ethical action is to break language in order to free it as a form of speaking the nondual. The broken-off last lines suggestively point to an immanent future of a democracy yet to be expressed. I argue that it is the impossibility of representing immanent language that causes Shelley to break off composition; the ellipses in the last section of the poem indicate where he was at a loss for words.

In the final chapter, "De Quincey's Eventful Dreams," De Quincey's exploration of opiate hallucination in the *Confessions of an English Opium-Eater* and other key texts reveals the capacity for mind-altering substances to restore comprehension of Nature's Spinozist substance. Furniture, a phantasmatic East, and the dreamer are all one substance. If opium dependence seems to be an abuse of nature, it also stimulates immanent encounter and so also begins the turn toward an ethical life practice that is revealed in De Quincey's Edenic dream vision ending the

Confessions. However, De Quincey's own xenophobic attitudes turn these dreams to nightmares, and his hallucinations to egotistical but humiliative visions as well as insights into the Spinozist substance of things in themselves, such as furniture and mail coaches.

Finally, the epilogue, "Immanence and Racial Alterity," yokes together the Romantic issues of radicality and racialization as they mediate human Otherness. Although chapter 5 addresses the period's absorption of the East into an aestheticized and commodified concept (opium stands in for "the Orient" for De Quincey), it doesn't address the conflict between immanent life and an immanence denied to real African persons who were enslaved and commodified. I briefly explore the combination of corporeal and incorporeal uses of Blackness during the period and how this denaturalization of the Black Other was used to smooth over Romanticism's conflicted relation with racial alterity. My sense is that racialization, which was invented and used to justify slavery within capitalism and expanding trade networks, also supported the sublime as a more authorizing mode of alterity for those benefiting from capitalism. Within that contest, Spinozist immanence once again had to become a subordinated, even subversive mode of alterity following Romanticism's decline.

Section I

Corporeals: Embodied Egos

1

Blake's Mythical Interval

Universality, the necessary requirement of all poesy, is in our contemporary age possible only for the person who is himself able to create from his own limited condition a mythology, a self-enclosed circle of poesy.[1]

—F. W. J. Schelling, *The Philosophy of Art*

If by eternity is understood not endless temporal duration but timelessness, then he lives eternally who lives in the present. Our life is endless in the way that our visual field is without limits.[2]

—Ludwig Wittgenstein, *Tractatus Logico-Philosophicus*

To see a World in a Grain of Sand
And a Heaven in a Wild Flower
Hold Infinity in the palm of your hand
And Eternity in an hour[3]

—William Blake, "Auguries of Innocence"

In William Blake's world vision ethics always involves a politics, a vital point. Duty and pity and sentiment separate self and other, denying another's very being as well as their dignity: "Pity would be no more, / If we did not make somebody Poor: / And Mercy no more could be, / If all were as happy as we" ("The Human Abstract" 1–4).[4] By contrast, the ethical involves doing as a way of becoming, as involved in the dynamic becomings of the world whether bodies, ideas, or things. For Blake, a way to demonstrate rather than merely critique the difference is mythopoetics, in which stories created around these becomings and interbeing compose a cosmic vision of becoming figured as human. Mythopoetics is the ideal subject matter of Blake's idiosyncratic "Illuminated" or visionary art. Each character in the mythic series is both recognizably human and figures the ego's inherent divisiveness simultaneously with the psyche's yearning for unity. Unity and divisive separation both creatively produce or destructively constrain; they are not contrary to each other but are instead two directions energy takes, though one is an ethical, outward-directed movement and the other delusively self-centered. How they are harnessed produces the various ways the Spinozist energy barometer of joy and suffering affect persons and things, bodies and thoughts. "As all men are alike in outward form, So (and with the same infinite variety) all are alike in the Poetic Genius," Blake announces in "All Religions are One" (pl. 5: 2–9). Poetic genius is the enlightened vision of the awakened nature of all being, that which opens into realization of immanent life. It is visionary insight and awakened life.

I will be focusing on Blake's illuminated books that together provide his mythopoetic cosmos (especially *The Marriage of Heaven and Hell*, 1790; *America a Prophecy*, 1793; *The First Book of Urizen*, 1794; *The Book of Los*, 1795; *Milton a Poem*, 1804–1811; and *Jerusalem*, 1804–1820) to examine how these prophetic poems make use of the interval of stretched time that is the space of potential and actualized awakening, the realization of immanence. For Blake, this interval is not one of inactivity; instead of nonmovement there is a restlessness, a pre-movement. My argument is that Blake's creation story takes place in the interval, a space in which a restless shuttle between egotistical resistance (division, embodied by Urizen) and an opening up to realization (unity, figured by Los) leads to the prophesied, awakened life (Jerusalem). Awakened or immanent life is always already available, but as an expression of the absolute, it can only be perceived in the opening up of epiphany and prophetic insight. As both painterly and poetic visions, the illuminated books demonstrate how a shift in perspective can transform delusion into insight, egocentric certainty into enlightenment: the interval is not only where pulling back and opening up tug at each other, but also where seeing differently leads to an enlightened perspective. Illuminated books, enlightenment, and prophecy are all a matter of struggle and perspective, and together are the great matter of Urizen's and Los's evolving relationship. These poems are not in themselves prophecies in the sense of illocutionary force or declarative performances as are Swedenborg's prophecies.[5] Instead, when taken together, Blake's prophecies depict a fully illumined universe, complete in its immanence with the sacred fully in the mundane. They are his own kind of politics, his own revolutionary vision.

Blake's particular brand of revolutionary politics differs from the radicalism of Thomas Paine (*Rights of Man*, 1791) and Mary Wollstonecraft (*Vindication of the Rights of Men*, 1790), as Saree Makdisi makes clear in his book on Blake during the 1790s.[6] However, contra Makdisi, I interpret Blake's politics as owing to an insistence on immanence, on the dynamic interrelation of bodies and ideas, diurnal and eternal. I find support for this view in Blake scholarship that examines eighteenth-century covert networks of antinomian thought and politics, such as Jon Mee's *Dangerous Enthusiasm*, and research that uncovers deeper levels of Anglo-German intellectual networks such as Alexander Regier explores in *Exorbitant Enlightenment*. In *Marriage of Heaven and Hell* (1790), for instance, Blake focuses on deep interrelation as a thesis and teaches the reader to see devils as angels and hell as paradise in order to understand the immanent, participatory nature of all things from a nondual perspective. It is an ontopolitics that is thoroughly enmeshed in the aesthetic and style of his art, as this reflects "life" (being and world) to be both idea and substance. Ontopolitics is based in bodily experience, in the insistence of the body and its felt sense. That insistence—as both the attentive regard and the body's persistence in being—is yoked to the ethical nature of life itself. As D. M. Yaeger argues, Blake uses the poetic imaginary to blast Christian religious prophecy with an ethics far richer than the promised Good.[7] In agreeing, I would also rephrase this as an ontoethics that is far richer than the promised Good, and a prophecy that announces the immanent now rather than an envisioned future. Blake's ethical ontopolitical art accords well with Wittgenstein's aphorism that "ethics and aesthetics are one," with Wittgenstein's understanding of ethics as belonging to ontopolitical life.[8] In *Jerusalem: The Emanation of the Giant Albion*, Blake's rewriting of the Book of Revelation that took sixteen years to create, he demonstrates the process by which the All is ontopolitical life, revealed as infinite Spinozist substance whose expression awaits its revelation. This life of the eternal present moment is immanent life.

In regarding Blake as a Spinozist thinker, and through Spinoza a Stoic one as well, I rely on previous scholarship demonstrating the strong connections between antinomian thought, radical thought, and Hermeticism (revivified in Freemasonry lodges throughout Europe and the colonies as well as in lower-class radicalism). As I have demonstrated elsewhere, the legacy of Giordano Bruno's Hermetic thought and Ficino's translation of the Hermetic texts (*Corpus Hermetica*), Spinozist thought, and Jakob Böhme's teachings in Britain remained strong in the Romantic period.[9] Schelling's *Bruno, or On the Natural and the Divine Principle of Things* (1802) indicates the strength of Bruno's influence on the period. Scholars like A. L. Morton, Mee, Regier, and Makdisi have specifically linked this submerged tradition with Blake.

In Blake's vision, there is an original oneness before division: a passive eternal oneness that contrasts with the All of immanent life. In his account, oneness permitted division, which, once begun, produces a devolution rather than evolution of life. Oneness as the Eternals embody it devolves through difference, and entanglements in and through difference are part of the origin story. But the Eternals' passivity is the problem, not the division that creates particulars per se. Oneness in immanence is constant motion, as Spinoza demonstrates: God is the constant motion of bodies affecting each other. The Eternals' oneness, instead of being elaborated by division, is cut by newly developing egos whose self-production will redound on all smaller, future divisions. This is the fall from grace: the four zoas represent division into particularity, but also into the differentiated viewpoints that make it impossible to see the whole picture, the structure of oneness. The divisive fall distorts vision and perspective, so that separateness seems self-willed isolation, but this seeming can only be a false vision: Urizen's darkened and crippled seeing. Blake's developing creation myth, and what Tilottama Rajan following Blake calls his "system," begins with Urizen's distortions. Rajan argues that Urizen's (d)evolution into the crippled figure he represents in Blake's system follows the body's nervous, circulatory, fleshly regimes that convolute rather than resolve into a perceptually replete organism.[10] Rather than an autogenesis of skeleton encased by the hardened defenses of his ego, as I tend to interpret Urizen's story of self-becoming, Rajan reads Urizen as Blake's response to anatomist John Hunter's physiological discoveries at the time. Rajan's work helps me read Urizen as developing from the inside-out, nervous and digestive systems before bone and skin, but, I would add, at the same time encasing himself in his internal ego world of impulses and contractions. He therefore projects onto everything external his own digestive and circulatory blockages and foldings/infoldings (a theme I return to in chapter 4). These refoldings or "feedback loops" are Urizen's autoimmune responses (Rajan, "Blakes' Bodies" 358); in my reading, the convolutions, blockages, and folds persecute the external world, turning immanent life into something hidden from view, which the poet-zoa Los must take as his quest: to reveal again what had been persecuted and hidden in life itself.

Life itself requires more than the mono-self or monad, Urizen or otherwise. Therefore, each zoa—presented as male—has his female side, cut off but wedded to him just as Adam's rib was taken to form his mate Eve. The zoa-emanation pairs represent the four main aspects of the human mind-body experience (mind, heart, creativity, sexuality), each emanation divided from yet complementing the zoa's attribute: Enitharmon's musicality to Los's poetic creation; Ahania's intellectuality to Urizen's reason; Enion's sexual desire to Tharmas's physicality; Vala as Nature to Luvah's affect, especially love. The giant Albion, allegorizing primeval man, also has his emanation, Jersualem, who must be reunited with Albion before awakened life can be realized. With the female side separated off, at times in contestation with him, each zoa falls more fully from the integrated harmony of the Eternals.

In the world-making that takes place as the four zoas move through their particular transformations and convolutions, the dynamic energy between each zoa and emanation pair can antagonize or harmonize but is always in movement. Separated, zoas and emanations can thwart each other's goals or happiness, their own egotistic concerns blocking their ability to see clearly. But even deluded life is life, and is in stark contrast to figures of nonmovement that block revolutionary transformation such as the hermaphrodite and Covering Cherub, both figures of dread in *Jerusalem*. Such deadening figures are themselves warped, and warp others' ability to see revolutionary change as what opens up to the ontoethical and immanent life. They are Blake's version of Spinoza's conception of "human bondage," in which negative affects like jealousy and hate deplete, block, and stall. By contrast, positive affects like joy energize, motivating individuals toward an ethical life precisely because joy is associated with insight and love of life's sacredness.[11] By contrast, distorted vision and delusion produced by ego-resistance are not deadening but part of the restless movement of life itself. Their positive attribute is that both can be corrected through insight gained in epiphanies, producing a redemptive restoration of the individual to the world that is also a healing of the materialized world. This correction is most fully disclosed through

Los's interventions in *Jerusalem*. Blake's poetic masterpiece concerns the realization of immanent life through corrected vision, wherein separation and contest dissolve into unity and harmony.

Blake's epic *Jerusalem* is central to my argument because in it the world is finally revealed to be always also an unfallen world, always immanent given undeluded seeing. As he puts it in "Auguries of Innocence," "We are led to Believe a Lie / When we see not Thro the Eye" (Pickering Ms., pl. 18: 19–20). Although the everyday world is separated from the primal groundlessness of the Eternals, in it the difference between a fallen and immanent, fully integrated world is a matter of register, of vision, of ethics. Hence, ethics as a political tool for building utopian states has everything to do with Blake's visionary project, as it does for the Stoics' ontology of sentient bodies cohering with insentient ideas, thoughts, visions. In "The Revolutionary Vision of William Blake," Thomas Altizer treats Blake's historical precedents in the early Christian apocalyptic faith, in which God and the body are not antithetical. Blake's return to the early Church's understanding of Christ as God incarnate, as nondual embodiment, is a renewal of Christian ethics, Altizer argues. It is fully Spinozist as well. For Spinoza, versed in both Christian and Jewish gnostic traditions, bodies and ideas are equivalently God's expression; for the Greek Stoics, both corporeal and incorporeal bodies (ideas, emotions, dreams) are expression itself.

Paying attention to self-expressive bodies is an ethical act because it means honoring other beings as necessary participants in the totality of which one is also a part. This tradition of ontoethics and Blake's mythopoetics reveal that the division of the One from the All, the ideal from the real, and the corporeal from the incorporeal, is illusory. These states, Blake tells us, layer over each other: Eden, Beulah, Generation, and Ulro. In Spinozist terms, each state beginning with Eden has a decreasing speed of bodies associated with it so that Ulro is a state of stalled, nearly deadened existence. Eden and Ulro (the fallen world) inhabit the same space just as the redemptive Jerusalem sits within a corrosive London in *Jerusalem*. Learning to see that what we "see" is a deluded version of what is immanently there is the political message Blake conveys. For the zoa poet Los, to tell the difference between delusion and true vision by recounting the history of division is the major artistic project; through it the immanent future of an achieved oneness or harmony of difference can be crafted. Telling and doing are the same thing; this is Blake's central message orchestrating his mythic oeuvre.

Blake's oeuvre exceeds definition as an immanent mode of art, its verbal and/as visual excess working to undo our expectations and neat categories just as immanence is so saturated with life that we normally can only perceive its excess in distilled bits. His mythopoetics describe a becoming of the human that is outside normative time and space as the zoas and emanations strive to achieve a reintegration of the lost harmony. Just as the zoas' female aspect is split off, its destructively critical part is also split off as its inner "spectre." What Blake recognized is that the human is not only an intermixture of feminine and masculine traits, but also that the traits themselves have been divided, categorized, judged along evaluative lines of better and worse. Anthropomorphizing these human traits and dramatizing how they impede progress toward an enlightened life allows Blake to create a universe of human psychological being, demonstrating how we become isolated in our egos and distorted in our perceptions of the world. But it is also both a universal story and a cosmic one, a mapping of the mind onto the universe. Most importantly, it is a story of constant struggle, and if the enlightened state of Eden is available through the twist of the lens in busy, violent London (as in *Jerusalem*), another lens twist can take you right down through Generation and Beulah to Ulro. We are always in the restless space of delusion vying with insight, a space that hums with the vibrancy of becoming, of entering into immanence—and falling back into deluded egotism. Spinoza analyzes it as the movement of bodies as they are pressed on by other corporeal and incorporeal bodies, so that each slows down and speeds up according to its despair (negative affects) and joy (positive affects). In his preface to Part IV of the *Ethics*, Spinoza explains: "Man's power to moderate and restrain the affects I call Bondage" (Curley 543), and in IVP17S he announces, "With this I believe I have shown the cause why men are moved more by opinion than by true reason . . . it is necessary to come to know both our nature's power and its lack of power." This restless space of becoming, of more and less speed (that is increased or decreased power to know) is what I refer to as the interval.

As a totality, Blake's works envision what it means to be immersed in a state that is the interval between ego and nondualism, or between delusion and insight. Ego is a potentially stalled state, whereas insight reveals "becoming" as a creative dynamism, an openness to immanence. The interval is the pause in time-space that opens to alterity through an insight into substance as the atomic-level element that all bodies and incorporeals share: immanent substance. In the realization of shared substance, the interval is the pause that heals difference and out of which the vision it imparts can have force. But if for Blake the interval is dynamic, it is also restless and can be characterized by irritability and struggle. The irritable ego, unwilling to give up mastery, resists the creative openness available in the pause, in which body and mind, thing and thought, inhere and commune. The verbal-visual aesthetic that is Blake's specialty portrays the interval as one of the egoistic struggle for mastery in tension with the eternal coherence of immanence always already there. For Spinoza this is a matter of power, which he calls "conatus": "the force of a Desire that arises from Joy must be defined both by human power and the power of the external cause [Nature/God], whereas the force of a Desire that arises from Sadness must be defined by human power alone" (IVP18Dem). Immanent life as Nature is always there: moving toward joy or toward "lust," as Spinoza calls it, or toward self-interest and human "inconstancy." Inconstancy is another term for the pulling-back movement in the interval. In one sense, the entire mythic cycle of the illuminated books take place in this interval, with *Jerusalem* culminating the narrative of becoming enlightened. This is not to say that *Jerusalem* ends with beatitude, since the Eden gained there is not the One; Blake's Eden is the attainment of realized immanent life, the All in/as the One.

If Descartes formulated the Western psychic state of split-consciousness as a mind-world dualism, for Blake, consciousness is split by ego and desire. For him, this is direct evidence of a fall from a non-Cartesian, nondualistic understanding of the cosmos and the world. The path back to Oneness, the Eternals, is blocked by the first fall of Urizen, but movement toward immanent life *is* possible, made so through spaces of struggle—primarily the void and the abyss—that are also intervals as spaces of paused diurnal time or clock time, intervals in which immanence can come into sight. If the ego wins the struggle, there is a further fall into delusion and suffering, as when Urizen, the zoa of alienated reason, falls catastrophically. If the ego gives up, insight and self-actualization occur, as they do for Los in *Jerusalem*.

This interval, Blake's equivalent of the Greek concept of *chora*, the nontemporal space of creative energy, is restless because it is an account of the psyche's struggle between ego and the insight that lies beyond perception. In *The First Book of Urizen*, it is clear that the interval can divide into further dualism rather than heal it, the ego walling off all but its own delusive darkness: "Times on times he divided, and measur'd / Space by space in his ninefold darkness" (*Urizen*, Copy C, pl. 4: 10).

Arising in the *chora* or interval, Urizen creates his own version of it as a vacuum, airless and "unprolific":

> LO, a Shadow of horror is risen
> In Eternity! unknown, unprolific,
> Self-clos'd, all-repelling. What Demon
> Hath form'd this abominable Void,
> This soul-shudd'ring Vacuum? Some said
> It is Urizen. (pl. 4: 2–8)

Here we can also see that in a larger sense, Blake's entire creation myth unfolds in the *chora*, the space of becoming. Urizen's divisive ego has made this choric space an "abominable Void" that is "unprolific," the very opposite of the generative *chora* of Greek thought. Blake composes his mythic cycle around the major plot point of whether the Cartesian Urizen will succeed in shutting down true enlightenment with his "all-repelling" and "self-clos'd" void, or his brother zoa Los will use his poetic genius to turn toward the interval, the generative space of infinite Spinozist substance awaiting its revealed expression. Immanence is there if one has the eyes to see it; this is what Blake's own visions of the prophet Ezekiel, angels in a tree, and his dead brother Robert reveal.

For Blake, the interval is not a Platonic space of the idea becoming materialized but is instead focused on a struggle between the ego's mastery and opening up to realization of/as immanence. In this sense, the interval can also be imagined as a hovering, in the sense of an opportunity for free play, or of teasing the reader out of thought. The concept of interval or potentiated pause opens up ways to read Blake's use of the abyss and void to vividly figure spaces in which temporalized impasses shift onto a spatial plane that allows for re-seeing and even reconfiguration. It is a spaciousness that allows for conjoint productivity in the most radical sense: the self and the other, the corporeal body and incorporeal idea, struggling to understand their co-production. *The Marriage* demonstrates Blake's insistence on such co-production; it is a work in which the enantiodromia of each set of oppositions (heaven-hell, angel-devil, idyll-abyss, truth-hypocrisy) allegorizes the essential movement of a self-positing with its negation that appears dialectical but remains in tension. As in immanence, there is no resolution because the two terms are already each other, seen through a different lens. The All is the One; the One is all differentiated bodies and ideas, hell is heaven. For Blake, dynamic movement prevents stoppage—the essential evil—and blockage is what keeps us seeing only one side, only dualism, so that we rest in delusion: Urizen but not also Los. The realization that can arise from dynamic opposition, Urizen *and* Los, is that their difference is similitude: everyday life is actually eternity, the abyss is actually Eden; reason becomes poetry.

Intervals most typically appear in Blake's poetry as the cosmic void, or the abyss as its darker psychical manifestation, or Los's despair—as images of what has the potential to become an encounter with alterity. His thinking about the void, his most intriguing figuration of the interval, is deeply influenced by Milton's Satan and his adventures in void space as much as it is by antinomian and millenarian thought. As Blake saw it, Milton's mistake in *Paradise Lost* was not to let Satan free to fly though the space of the void as the archangel he was, but instead to constrain him to ego-driven motives, forcing him to inhabit dark abysses of his own making. This is the same negative use of void that fills the *First Book of Urizen*, where "void" is most often depicted as Satan's hell: "Los wept, howling around the dark Demon [Urizen] . . . a fathomless Void for his feet" (Copy C, pl. 7: 3,7). But a shift in vision and Milton's void has the creative pulsation that enhances Satan's becoming. It is in keeping with this version of the interval that Blake's Milton soars through the void, redressing Satan's error by reimagining his becoming as a curative rather than toxic mission in *Milton, A Poem in Two Books* (1811). Blake's mythic mapping of the world encodes this sense of *Paradise Lost* as a lost opportunity to make use of the interval as an intervention in stultifying and oppressive world systems. The reworking of the myths that articulate his cosmology, as well as the differentiated colorings of the plates (each copy of a work its own palette and vibrancy), both evince an attention to this restless activity of the interval and its promise.

Before a character or realization comes into being, Blake posits an interval, one that has the quality of a thought-space in which the subjective mind suspends itself and so experiences free fall in a neutral (nondelineated, noncolored) space. This space may posit a liberatory direction to the becoming, but it could equally posit the negating quality of the "self-clos'd, all repelling" reason. It may be helpful to think of the interval or void as a mind-space located between the ideal and physical being that corresponds to a spectral realm, one in which life and death are co-constitutional, inanimate matter finding expression through mortal life.[12] That expression as both Spinozist substance and longing as a kind of incorporeal but animated thing opens the future up to unpredictable alternatives.

The imagery most apt for this urgent interval might be the back-and-forth restlessness the fetus experiences during maternal contractions just before the womb jettisons it; such an image is the obverse of Urizen's becoming a skeletalized body in the *Book of Urizen*, where he closes down on his potentiating energy by encasing it in bone. This is a perversion of the void, because Urizen attempts to both stop time and still movement into stasis: life as stillbirth. After Urizen's attempt to separate the void-interval from its creative function, Los takes on the challenge of recuperating its positive energies. The void-interval in transition, as Los and his son Orc struggle against Urizen's static insistence, is free fall rather than the purposeful back-and-forth of Hegelian dialectical movement. Free fall may seem less purposive, and certainly Los entertains what Spinoza calls "confused" and "inadequate ideas" (deluded thought) while he is in it, but it is nevertheless aligned with the restlessness of the void, its urgency, and its resistance to any schema of order and directionality. The void in this sense contains the mobility that allows energy to flow in any number of directions though always toward the life at hand and always with the double movement—the back-and-forth, inside-and-outside, or pulling inward and seeking outward—of the generative interval. In this sense the void-interval is a clear expression of a nature or reality that is God's expression, *Deus sive Natura*. The void is completely full of substance, generative and generous, realizable with a shift in vision.

In an important way, the illuminated books reveal how free fall in the interval is the only perspective from which to see Blake's four worlds or states of existence (Ulro, Generation, Beulah, Eternity). These states are both corporeal or existential, and incorporeal or psychic. Generation and Beulah always contain the possibility of being interval spaces, whether void, abyss, or other *chora*-like space. Because the interval pauses or stretches time, it provides the opening from one state of existence onto another. It also provides a restless space where psychic drives have room to wrestle with and balance each other, becoming either motivating or self-destructive.

I. The Restless Interval

Each writer I investigate for this study imagines the interval of timelessness or paused clock time differently. For Blake, it is a restless space of conflict between the human urge to turn inward, away from what is different, but with the possibility of opening up to difference and the not-self—an opening that can burst into an Otherness that has its own infinite time. And Wittgenstein's description of the present moment in the chapter epigraph illustrates how Blake's interval is essential to his understanding of immanence as both sacred and eternal, yet in the here and now: "If we take eternity to mean not infinite temporal duration but timelessness, then eternal life belongs to those who live in the present." Makdisi, who also considers Spinoza's importance to Blake's understanding that "every thing that lives is holy," repeated throughout the illuminated books, spends a great deal of his book on Blake's conception of time (Makdisi 250). Blake's prophetic poems "blast a hole" in progressive history, "bringing that narrative . . . to a sudden and grinding halt," or rather, "a moment of clarity is achieved . . . by bringing the flow of empty, homogeneous time to a momentary pause" (156). Not a grinding halt so much as a moment of clarity and realization, so that what is already "empty, homogeneous" is paused as diurnal or clock time while stretched into infinity. This is the work of the interval: the disruption of clock time and conception of history as progressively achieving its goal, the pause of stretched time, the realization achieved. As Makdisi notes, the undoing of time occurs through Blake's "emphasis on the moment." Where I take issue with this understanding is Makdisi's claim that "empty time is a mode of thought and of discourse that has no way of reconciling itself with its others, no way of accounting for difference other than in its own terms" (156). Instead, I view Blake's treatment of emptiness as having everything to do with its others; it is what leads to the understanding of "the common essential unity of humankind" as opposed to imperialist agendas of ethnic and racial differences and abilities (251). An emphasis on the moment, which characterizes the interval experience, involves a double movement that resists "a grinding halt" and nonreconciliation. The emptiness of time and of the interval are both the emptiness/plenitude of the *chora*, potentiated energy that is restless and then generative, moving between confused ideas toward "a moment of clarity," a prophetic vision.

The interval has been considered philosophically in ways that are pertinent to Blake's own exploration of it. Plato discusses the productive, generative qualities of the interval between integers (between one and two lies a space—is it empty or full?) in the *Timaeus*, a text that interested Romantic philosophers such as Schelling and Hegel. But Plato more famously discusses the generative *chora* in the *Timaeus*, which might be understood as an interval, a gestational space that is also both empty and full. Derrida, who was also very interested in Plato's *chora*, was intrigued by Plato's interval as well. The interval, his work reveals, should not be thought of as the present moment insofar as that presumes a subject to assess presence in terms of a past and the coming present of the future, or in terms of presence versus absence. To understand the interval as not already divided into all the points between one and two, or not the absence of presence, is to view it as outside the metaphysics of original presence. Blake would agree with this: the interval is not where consciousness or subjectivity is in control, and it does not depend on a transcendental perspective. Immersed in the here and now of the moment, it is where the struggle between Urizen and Los, ego and imagination, constraint and enlightenment take place. Wittgenstein's description of the timelessness of the present moment as a way to view eternity exactly describes the interval in which immanence manifests. The eternal now, which is replete with dynamic life activity, is what the self-struggle between constraint and enlightenment seeks to realize. This is not the act of creation but of illumination.

For Blake, then, the interval's generative quality includes the irritability of back-and-forthing, a double movement between the integers of nothing and some corporeal or incorporeal form. It is important for Blake that the interval is timeless, a redefinition of eternity away from the static nature of the Eternals and toward the negative and positive energies that fuel life. In *Hegel: The Restlessness of the Negative*, Jean-Luc Nancy describes the state of restlessness as essential to the becoming of the world. His description of the world as the space of dialectical becoming is essentially the description of the interval as a generative present moment. For both Nancy and Blake, the interval is an unwilled but essential tarrying, in which different outcomes are possible; unwilled, the pausing opens itself up to potential in the Spinozist sense, *potentia*. Potentiating power for Blake resides in the realization of what Nancy calls being singular plural, but with a stronger sense of the One and All as Spinoza outlines it: each singular entity expresses the totality, which in turn expresses each singular entity, being singular plural, being plural singularly. For Spinoza, there is nothing outside, no transcendence of the multiple that is the totality, for this creation—Nature—*is* God. There is also no ego-centered consciousness that is not delusion: "The Mind," Spinoza writes, "does not know itself, except insofar as it perceives the ideas of the affections of the Body," and the "idea of any affection of the human Body does not involve adequate knowledge of any external body" (II, P23, P25). Moreover, the mind is easily directed by the passions into false ideas, as discussed above.

The interval is where false ideas fall away. Immanence announces itself in the interval in which ego's self-presencing and ego-time are suspended. That suspension—call it void, call it abyss—is not that between what was and what will be, so much as that between what is known and what is not knowable, between what seemed presence and what seemed absence. Immanence is not pure presence revealing itself in the gap between knowing and unknowability; it is the revelation that there is no lack in the always full present moment that the interval allows one to experience. Because this plentitude, not otherwise available to experience except in the interval's revelation, is always there, it has no origin, no originary presence in the metaphysical sense of a first cause. The difference between immanent life and the division into presence/absence is that immanence is unmediated by ego, self-consciousness, and the need to supplement the original thing. Mediation is the ego's attempts to control what can be understood from perception and known from experience, and the ego's need to reduce its own pain at perceived lack. The interval offers the possibility of an unmediated space of unanticipated experience.

If we think of the interval in metaphysical terms, it is entirely mediated by the points between integers or between the past present and the future present. Mediations that divide subject and object, present and absence, voice and writing, science and art, rely on the schema of an originary full thing (such as language) that nevertheless has some lack that is filled by a supplement (such as speech). There is never one supplement, but as Derrida shows (most pertinently to this discussion in his anatomy of Rousseau's oeuvre in *Of Grammatology*), a series of supplements whose mediations cover over the fact that there is no original thing: language is supplemented by speech, speech by writing, writing by footnotes and appendices, texts by marginalia.[13] In the metaphysical interval constructed by a presence supplemented by absence, the interval is a gap that works to prove presence a delusion. What Derrida proves is that immediacy is a construct derived from the supplemental chain: nothing is immediate because that would mean needing no sensory or intellectual reception of it, no moment of recognition or cognition. What we think is presence is something we reconstruct in the milliseconds after perceiving it, or if it is like language, which we reconstruct from particulars of idiomatic and grammatical speech, generalizing after the fact to a language, and then to languages. Presence in this sense is delusionary; immanent life, the plenitude of the moment, is its opposite. Presence cannot be found, but immanence is everywhere.

This is why Blake rejects metaphysics, finding its insistence on presence misleading and its categories (as in Swedenborg's depiction of heaven as divided into mappable terrain) wrong-headed. Blake's creation myth explores the void and abyss as intervals where the ego can resist plenitude or open up to its experience. Urizen closes down on possibility and plentitude, Los struggles and then in *Jerusalem* gives up his ego to embrace immanent life. Instead of metaphysical presence, immanence recognizes binaries as false polarities, and deferral (of meaning, of presence) as a blindness to what is already here. Just as Urizen blinds himself to the fruitful plentitude of life, closing down on it with endless restraints, Los opens up his eyes to insight, seeing the eternal within the mundane. The mundane is not the absence of the eternal, or its supplement, or its deferral; in immanence the mundane is exactly the eternal, exactly the sacred, exactly plentitude, but cutting through endless mediations and supplemental chains. More traditionally, it is revelation.

If the interval as void or abyss signifies possible revelation for Blake, what space signifies democracy for him, that hoped-for utopian community? *America a Prophecy* (1793) shows that the mediations and deferrals that condition how we think and experience the world are hard to remove to make way for political change. The new land is much like the old, although it holds out hope for a revolutionary energy, allegorized as Orc, to burst through old ways of seeing and thinking. For Derrida, it is not the interval, but the much smaller pausing points of ellipsis that trope the space in which political change might be brought on. "Ellipsis" is the term he chooses to image the space of betweenness that is not the interval but "between the 'minus one' and the 'more than one'" (*Rogues* 1). This being "between" is what Blake calls Generation and Beulah, the states between Ulro's minus one and Eternity. "Between these set limits, democracy perhaps has an essential affinity with this turn or trope that we call the ellipsis," for only it can give "*the time there is not*," which is essential to what Derrida calls the "*democracy to come.*" In a sense, by "spacing itself beyond being and even beyond ontological difference," the democracy-to-come images immanence, the All and One of corporeal and incorporeal coproduction (38). This is Blake's understanding of democratic *potentia*, Spinoza's term for the strength of the multitude, that rising force in *America* that Orc enjoins. Orc himself is the figure of revolutionary force as a Spinozist body at its highest level of energy; the energy expresses joy in its politicized fervor, the joy of Orc and the Shadowy female in lustful embrace as a revolutionary bursting forth. Leo Damrosch describes Orc as "buoyed up by flames," noting that Blake associated fire and its energy with delight, and that "revolution is fed by energy" (110).

For Blake and Nancy, the world is constituted by an immanent power that can, like Orc, rupture the bonds of institutionalized control. The Stoics give this immanence a quieter power, that of the body's potential: "a people can revolt" is already the proposition in place necessary for revolution to occur. This understanding of the two kinds of power analyzed by Spinoza—inalienable individual power (*potentia*) and transferable institutional authority (*potestas*; transferable from the state to the people through democratic manifestation)—as what *could* be expressed is very much in evidence in Blake's works. His *First Book of Urizen* in particular dramatizes the struggle on a cosmic level, while *America: A Prophecy* allegorizes it on a mundane one. Spinoza's *Theological-Political Treatise* (1670) and Romantic readings of Spinoza, especially the *Ethics*, resonate strongly with Derrida's democracy-to-come. Blake, too, imagines the time-to-come, but as a condensation of historical time, a rejoining of what had been sundered in the mundane world. In *Jerusalem*, the four states of existence are a simultaneity that can be envisioned as substance expressed in bodies at different rates of speed, with the highest state at the speed of joy.

In the dynamic, restless movement of the interval, the subject must recognize itself as part of Otherly activity, as Orc does in *America: A Prophecy*: 'I am Orc . . . / The times are ended; shadows pass, the morning' gins to break" (Copy A, pl. 10: 59–60). The subject as world spirit, like Orc, "is in no way the *self all to itself*. It is . . . what (or the one who) dissolves all substance" (Nancy 5), just as Orc stamps "That stony Law [of Urizen's ten commandments] . . . to dust" (*America*, Copy A, pl. 10: 63). Like Orc in his ordeal of imprisoned restlessness, during which he can roam the world in imagination by participating in the Oneness that is also the All, the subject *is* what it does: "its doing is the experience of . . . the loss of references and of the ordering of a 'world' in general (*cosmos, mundus*), but also and thereby, its becoming-world in a new sense. It becomes immanent, and it becomes infinite" (Nancy 5). There can be no better description of Blake's chaotic America, and of Orc's position at the end of the poem, his fires having "consum'd" the five gates of religion's "law-built heaven," "their bolts and hinges melted / And the fierce flames burnt round the heavens, and round the abodes of men" (*America*, Copy A, pl. 18: 19, 22).

But as Blake knew all too well in this poetic prophecy after the fact, the American War for Independence was not the liberation of the subject but its stalling in the continued ordeal of not-knowing and not-becoming. The time-to-come can be brought on by the "fiery Demon" Orc, but not by mere men limited by their egocentric delusions. Even the "fierce rushing of th' inhabitants together" (*America*, Copy A, pl. 16:14, 13) was only an actualization of Orc's self-realization, his self relating to itself in Hegelian fashion. Orc's revolutionary energy is itself delusory, because he has not yet learned that the immanent future of democracy is entangled with immanent life. And that life is both eternal and relative. Kant explains that eternity is "a time proceeding to infinity" in which "a person . . . would always progress only from one time into another."[14] Although not a Spinozist, Kant's explanation reveals a property of immanence: death does not end time, nor is eternity outside of time. In immanence the absolute is also the relative, infinity also time passing. If the interval pauses or stretches time, its restless struggle is worth enduring because we believe the healing of perspective will come and delusion drop away.

Nevertheless, "This thought has something horrifying about it because it leads us as it were to the edge of an abyss: for anyone who sinks into it no return is possible," Kant writes in "The End of All Things" (221). For Blake, the abyss holds fear only for angels, who are the guardians of reason, but for poets the abyssal void allows for imaginable transformations along the lines of a time-to-come. The phrase "the infinite abyss" occurs twenty times in Blake's illuminated books and prose texts; "the abyss" occurs several times as well. The potentiality of the abyss is perhaps most clearly dramatized in *The Marriage of Heaven and Hell* (1790) when black and white become reversed once the angel has returned to his mill and the poet's vision has clarified. "The infinite Abyss, fiery as the smoke of a burning city," that is, obscurity rendered palpable, is terrorized by the leviathan in the "nether" black of "the infinite deep" of the abyss (Copy G, pl. 18: 3–4, 16, 8), but once the angel has left this horrifying scene it transforms into a pastoral one inhabited by a harper. This scene reversal allows the poet to understand that the hellish abyss is only an appearing of the restless void-interval, rendered as the angel's deadening "Analytics"; viewed differently, or held in balance with its opposite, it enables the poet, having "suddenly caught him [the Angel] in my arms," to fly to the sun, and then to "lea[p] into the void between Saturn and the fixed stars" (pl. 19: 18, 25–26). Blake's abyssal mediation parallels

Schelling's "speculative physics" as a "non-eliminative Idealism."[15] It is in this sense also consonant with Derrida's conception of the void as the non-emptiness of infinite possibility in the entanglement of matter and yearning. In *The Marriage*, abyss and void are clearly differentiated. The abyss is the analytic's underside; it is despair at the "nothingness" that is the negation of the empirical self and the transcendental self, according to Maurice Blanchot (*Space of Literature* 37). It is also the staving off of stalled time that is an impasse, not a restless interval. By contrast, the void is pure potential, even if its potencies terrorize, as Urizen's horrify the Eternals. The void's potencies can bring forth utopian harmonies or reason's divisiveness and rationales, dividing subject from object, singularity from totality, and justifying both as natural and true. The void is open to either perspective and as such offers an analogue for the imagination's freedom in which both delusive division (as for Urizen) and insight (as for Los) are possible. In *The Marriage*, the poem's speaker-I, clothed in white and holding Swedenborg's books, leaps into the void somewhere in the vicinity of Saturn, the angry planet. There he enacts his realization to the angel he has dragged with him by rejecting the angel's sophistry ("All that we saw was owing to your metaphysics," he explains to the angel earlier after the horrific abyss reveals itself as Edenic, 140). Blake's liberatory void in which the unreason of reason can be shaken off is the imagination's antidote to the static time that is the lowest world of ceaseless ordeal, Ulro. But the void cannot effect change in the world; this must come from a realization of Spinozist expression, the self's relation and interrelation to all other things.

For Blake, liberation from Ulro pertains to the void's generative potential to prepare the ground for the democracy-to-come that for Blake should have been America had human ego not derailed it. For Derrida, it is the unforeseeable event of the rogue, and Blake's Orc is the rogue par excellence. His revolutionary force transforms what for Blake was the failure of the American Revolution into revelation: the collusion of a few founding fathers into a true democracy. Revelation and immanence require different coordinates, different forms of mapping. Only by reorganizing mythic time and space can the time of prophecy appear.

II. Mapping and Coloring the World

Blake mapped his mythic cosmos in several ways, most famously in plate 32 of *Milton* depicting the Mundane Egg, and in plate 12 of *Jerusalem*, which describes the floor plan of Golgonooza, Los's city of "Art & Manufacture." The first is a map of the *cosmos* but as it exists beneath the limiting shell of the Mundane Egg, the materialized world; the second is a map of the *mundus*, but as a mundane building/city that is also where the zoas, emanations, and their progeny conduct their infinite work. The cosmos and materialized world coexist as the Veil of Vala (Nature) in the Spinozist sense of *Deus sive Nature*, the cosmic within the phenomenal mirroring each other. When this is invisible to the deluded eye we have the opposite: "What is visible in the Vegetable Earth, the same is visible in the Mundane Shell reversd" (*Jerusalem* pl. 72: 49). That is, substance exists in all four states of existence at once, but is perceived differently according to the psychic limitation of each state. At its most mundane, the deluded mirrors delusion. Forms of mapping, in which *cosmos* and *mundus* interconnect between planes of spiritual and psychic vibrancy, are constantly at work as Blake constructs his mobile and revisionary system. Its essential schematic and spiritual history undergoes dynamic reworkings with each new poem. This mapping effort is suggestively revealed in various depictions of the celestial and terrestrial in which additional surrounding, interleaving, or topmost figures dominate the mundane world. They suggest and emotionally evoke the plenitude that is in between earth and heaven. In this in-between state of being, the figurations allegorize Kant's theory of the imagination in § 22–23 of *The Critique of Judgment*. For Kant, human freedom is possible only in the arbitrary nature of the conceptual faculty's ability to create possible ideas and forms from sensory objects. Blake's pictorial details and figures jostle the reader's imagination in exactly this liberatory way, forcing an emotional restlessness that will open the mind up to the hard truths of the text.

But Blake's texts and forms are not bound to objects of sense: they are meant to push the reader into the measurelessness of the void. What Hegel calls the restlessness of sense,[16] integral to the world's self-becoming (the world spirit effectuating itself), must for Blake be reconfigured as the human imagination realizing itself. One way in which Blake evokes readerly emotion for the imagination to actualize itself in this far more liberatory way is through the use of color and light effects, with the light often heightened by dark lines detailing and outlining the forms. Here Newton's promiscuity of light that he detected in his experiments with the prism can serve to locate a theoretical difficulty with how to see that extends beyond any appropriate viewing of aesthetics into an impinging on sightedness by theory.[17] In participating in the debate about whether light is made up of corporeal, or corpuscular, bodies, Newton used the bodily trait of promiscuity to explain how light colors intermingle, particularly when they all combine to produce white, the One ("of such a confused aggregate . . . is generated Whiteness," *Newton* 177). Promiscuity as Blake exercises it suggests a fertile ground, an opening into disparate fields of color and meaning that can make art out of the restless activity of the negative. In *The Marriage of Heaven and Hell*, for example, the black of the abyss of hell when viewed without ideological mediation reveals itself as the blues and greens of pastoral, the minerals of the paint colors made of the same Spinozist substance as the poetic lines. Black and blue-green are revealed as the same thing. This works more prismatically, in the sense of light's aftereffect in Blake's aquatint method. If Goethe theorized aftereffects as the play of colors on the retinal apparatus, he also believed that colors "demand" their opposite and "reciprocally evoke each other" in an alternative explanation of immanent nondualism.[18]

Although optics was a subject of interest to the Lunar Society, and Erasmus Darwin conducted his own experiments on optical illusions and aftereffects in the late 1780s, Blake would not have been basing his challenges to color theory on scientific experimentation or on Goethe's color wheel of primary and complementary hues (not published until 1810).[19] Yet Goethe's contributions to the psychological experience of colors are valuable for understanding Blake's color-world and his use of different palettes for printings of the same works. One way to think about it is that individual plate colorations use less a prismatic or Newtonian set of hues than a vibrating, dynamic, or interactive coloring of the type that interested Goethe. A similarity can be drawn between Blake's interest in the living qualities of color and Goethe's concern not only for human receptivity to color's dynamic tendencies but also for the fluctuation of mineral and plant-based colors that painters and dyers relied on. Blake created a method in which no palette is authorized, no vision could be colored the same way twice; all seeing is interactive, dynamic, in flux.[20] Seeing is only circumscribed when it is reduced by mediations of light to merely white and black, as in the abyss encountered in *Marriage of Heaven and Hell* by way of the guiding angel's obstructive vision. But seeing is what is constrained or freed, not substance, whose underlying truth is only *as* its expression. It is the perceiver who must open themselves up to the nondual seeing Blake's art of visual-verbal play demands.

There is therefore a mystical vein in Blake's use of color that aids him in mapping the restlessness of the interval. Varying color palettes attest to the variety, changefulness, and promiscuity of material appearance. Variational coloring, in other words, both expresses resistance to contractual color schemes and resists conscripted understandings of alterity as, in the end, one thing alone. For Blake, dualistic philosophies that account for others and Otherness produce a scientism that is a real threat to the creative imagination and true enlightenment. Descartes and Newton both represent the divisive, ego-centered form of thought that controls what is seen, simultaneously disallowing insight or enlightened sight. Blake's mythology implies a systematic working out of how to break free of divisive seeing that resonates with Friedrich Schlegel's view in his 1790s *Athenaeum* period: that "system" means not scientism but the productive working of the absolute as it is present in the particular. Blake's mythos is similarly an absolute whole of which fragments or particulars can be envisioned and articulated but which can never be more than fragmentedly known; this is an immanent art. Within each of Blake's particular works, immanence can only appear in its dynamism, never as a static, finalized thing. Therefore, each plate must be printed and colored afterward, causing each print pull to have the opportunity for varying colorations and palettes in order to embody the living fragment that itself resounds with the immanent absolute.

Schlegel's theory of the fragment as an integral part of the whole or All, and focus on *poiesis*, is evocative for Blake's verbal-visual art in its concept of the fragment as a living interface *and* its production. This is what Schlegel terms "an absolute 'combinatory art' " of philosophy and poetry that escapes the material accidents of time, place, or genius.[21] This is not to say that Blake's own genius and identity as Milton's heir does not contribute to his artistic vision, but that the philosophy in which he participates is expressive of the " 'energy' or . . . 'energetic man' " through whom "infinitely flexible . . . universal power" moves, not to capture the absolute whole but to be capable of "an infinite capacity for form, for the absolute of form" (*Literary Absolute* 57). As Schlegel notes in *Athenaeum Fragment* 249, "The poetizing philosopher, the philosophizing poet, is a prophet. A didactic poem should be and tends to become prophetic."[22] It was his brother Auguste Schlegel who was most concerned with visual art, especially art history and aesthetics. But Auguste's work was focused on *historical* particulars, on the material creation of art and formal beauty rather than on the "infinitely flexible . . . universal power" that Friedrich theorizes. Schelling, who was an important member of the Schlegel group, took the universal even further, using it for his focus in his lectures on the philosophy of art. There Schelling is concerned not with art history or art theory, but with how art is a coexpression of the real and ideal.[23] Like Friedrich Schlegel and Blake, Schelling embraced Neoplatonism not in its dualism but rather in the conception of the materialized artwork as an absolute expression of the Platonic Idea. His contribution is how he theorizes particular artworks as "simultaneous universes,"[24] thus allowing him to consider the universal rather than historical in art.

For Friedrich Schlegel, philosophy and poetry must be coterminous, but for Schelling, philosophy's most important charge was not to think nature but to think the work of art because the One Idea was the Idea of Platonic Beauty.[25] However, putting Schlegel's combinatory art of poetry and philosophy together with Schelling's One Idea opens a lens on Blake's artworks. Additionally, Schelling's *Philosophy of Art* includes an important study of mythology, an art form significant not only for the German Romantics but of perhaps even higher importance for Blake. As David Simpson notes, mythology for Schelling means "the body of ideas and practices holding together a culture," which, at least for the ancients, funds religion.[26] Possibly Schelling's thinking about art might also be a working through of Friedrich Schlegel's *Athenaeum Fragment* 252, in which poetry could substitute for art more generally: "A real aesthetic theory of poetry would begin with the absolute antithesis of the eternally unbridgeable gulf between art and raw beauty. It would describe their struggle and conclude with the perfect harmony of artistic and natural poetry. This is to be found only among the ancients." (53). Similarly, Schelling believes that mythology was only productive of religion with the ancients; with the institution of Christianity, however, it could only be productive of mystery and allegory, both of which further estrange man from spirit. In this Blake vehemently concurs: the Church's drive toward mystification—with allegory and mystery being especially anathema for Blake—is destructive of the privileged relation of man to the natural world, obscuring man's inherent divinity—a conception of the human divine that Schelling shared. Like Friedrich Schlegel, Blake sought to render the living form of his poetry-art.

Blake was not reading either of the Schlegels or Schelling, having begun his philosophy of a poetic-art prior to any of them, but he shared several important sources of inspiration with them: all of these artists and philosophers of art were heavily influenced by the medieval alchemists such as Paracelsus, whose concept of the vegetative soul he borrows, and by the great German mystic Jakob Böhme. Böhme believed that God held the seven source spirits in *potentia* as *Ungrund*, related to Schelling's later theory of the potencies in his *Ages of the World* (another mythopoetic creation that valuably compares to Blake's) and F. Schlegel's conception of philosophy's "potence." (The seven source spirits are aligned with the seven colors Newton determined to belong to the prism, a number chosen for his alchemical beliefs). Böhme's potencies were arranged dialectically as negative, positive, and a compromise in which love is made manifest.[27] Each potency has the value of a fragment, or dynamic particular of the entire series; each confronts its opposite, resulting finally in a synthesis or co-identity [*Indifferentz*]. This triadic movement of negative, positive, and indifference or unity explains the dialectical dynamism at the heart of Idealist philosophy, but Blake is more interested in the confrontation than in the indifference. It is the seeking out, the movement toward something either combinatory or revelatory, that interests Blake more than dialectical synthesis.

Particularly important for Blake's color are the positive potency (seeking, outward directed) and the negative (the resistance of the self-identical), both forces of Spinozist *potentia*. Here Goethe's alchemical interest in the chemism of coloring intersects most with Blake's color practice: some of Goethe's initial observations explain that colors demand each other, "the simpler colour demand[ing] the compound, and *vice versa*," while even in grayscale the reciprocity of the tones gives a "*simultaneous impression of a whole*," which is by "the organ itself . . . sought, rather than arrived at, in *succession*, and which . . . can never be arrested" (*Theory of Colours* 8). The ongoing interplay of seeking and resisting is not, for Goethe, in the artwork but in the eye's perception of it; however, it is the work itself that causes this seeking out by the eye. This compellingly aligns with Blake's belief that his art will illuminate our understanding by reforming our perception. Moreover, for Goethe, a black and white object will at times cause the eye to perceive an "after-vision [which] is accompanied by an appearance of colour" (9). The seeking out, then, is not just between primary and secondary colors, but between the organ of sight and the illumined artwork.

Alchemical seeking out, which can never be arrested in the empirical world, is the seeking that results in Böhme's eternal love, Blake's *Jerusalem*, and the German Romantics' conception of *poiesis* as the Neoplatonic union of truth in beauty that is philosophy. The seeking-out for Böhme is related to the "flash," or spark that initiates and radiates from the positive-negative movement. In the literary work, it is the "lightening moment," the "dazzling burst of light" caused by "those very words, *it is*," which, according to Mallarmé, is the literary work's being, its own totality of vision.[28] For Blake, it is the electrical spark generated from positive and negative potencies that is the charged awakening. His bold use of reds and yellows sparking from figures like Orc encourage the viewer to feel the revelation of Orc's energy. Enlightenment is not an anodyne experience.

III. Illuminating Works

Blake's lifelong project was to create works of living spirit, of spark intensity, that would teach people how to free themselves by individual revelation from institutional power relations, and from the theft of their *potestas*. But in his understanding of spirit, Blake is not terribly far from Goethe's understanding of *Geist* or world spirit. Blake projects this world of spirit as the cosmogenesis of what we recognize as world and human spirit combined. By relating the transformation and displacements occasioned by the zoas' constant restless movement, Blake instructs the reader in how to view subjectivity and agency differently.

The zoas create their own history, which "steps out of itself into work and into [world] history" only in the interaction between reader and prophetic poem (Blanchot 27). For Blanchot, the work only exists in this interaction between the reader and the "being" of the work, its language and the writer's "echo of what cannot cease speaking," his imposition on "the giant murmuring upon which language opens . . . an indistinct plenitude which is empty," that is, empty of worldness because full of spirit. Blake's instruction, his "uninterrupted affirmation [of] the giant murmuring" in the act of writing, his imposition on the indistinct plenitude that is the being of poetic language, *poiesis* itself, is to draw a line around that spirit and speaking depth, and to trace its restless movement and transformations in the forms (zoas, emanations, their progeny) of the many parts of the originary Man, Adam. These forms are all vulnerable to their inner drives, raw emotions, and needs; at the same time, the amalgam of parts that is the overall subject also contains both the positive and negative principles or potencies of spirit. These principles, the yielding of love and the resistance of selfishness, are in dynamic relation to each other (Los and Urizen), as well as within each part (Los moving through his own negativity): it is in this electrical dynamic that Blake locates life itself. "Without contraries there is no progression" might be the most recognizable way to articulate this idea, if the electricity generated sparks something that defies complacent inertia. Simply harboring oppositional forces does not ensure progression or enlightenment, since it can mire one down in delusive certainty and recycled antagonism. By internalizing the violence of institutional power, Blake reveals the otherness existing within the individual that can be harnessed to drag the subject to that enlightened and liberating space in which the spirit—as the absolute—can most fully do its work.

It may be helpful here to frame Blake's project more precisely in terms of his predecessor Milton. Milton traced the error of institutionalized violence to a misapprehension of the founding story: for him, the most important element of that story is God's opposition by his antithesis, Satan, an opposition that must be resolved through Christ, with Adam as his dividend. Eve as the minus one completes the equation, for she is the remainder, the resistant, undigested kernel. If Christ is sublime (the plus one), Eve is the unabsorbable mundane; both Satan and Adam inhabit the interval between them. Blake understood this palpably, expressing it most clearly in *Milton, A Poem*. Milton's translation of Lucifer into Satan (a compeer into an opponent; an integer into an antiphon; civil war in heaven) is a kind of negation of the negation. It was meant to correct a world in critical error; God as the Infinite negated himself through his Son's finite being, and the resolution could only be the Son's self-sacrifice. This is what Schelling terms the nullification of the finite,[29] or what Shelley in "Ode to the West Wind" depicts as a dying-into. Christ negates error by absorbing it into the absolute, absolving humans of their abiding sin of self-division. For Blake, Satan as the self-centered deluder inhabits human being itself; therefore, the negation of the negation cannot be finalized as it is for Milton. Instead, the double negation must be repeatedly enacted as a sacrifice of the ego, giving up of the human delusion of control, possession, and knowing. This sacrifice is a capability the human can tap into because of the poetic faculty, a truth Blake announces in the final line of "All Religions Are One": "As all men are alike (tho' infinitely various) / So all Religions & as all similars have one source / The true Man is the source he being the Poetic Genius" (Copy A, pl. 10: 2–9). Dying-into as a poetic event is representatively enacted by Los in Blake's cosmic myth, but it is also demanded of whoever encounters the illuminated book. The ego's determined efforts to fend off alterity and to resist enlightenment—the human condition per se—must be negated or overthrown by the insight that turns the self inside out, rejoining it to what it had divided itself from. Imagine this as a reverse of Urizen's terrible self-making in the *Book of Urizen*:

> A vast Spine writh'd in torment
> Upon the winds; shooting pain'd
> Ribs, like a bending cavern
> And bones of solidness, froze
> Over all his nerves of joy. (Copy C, pl. 9: 41–45)

If illumination of immanent life reverses the ego's self-embodiment, closing down the senses and "nerves of joy" to just what the ego wants to perceive, as Urizen's self-making dramatizes, the poetic genius must struggle with the ego to gain insight. The poetic aspect is the opening outward that aligns with the positive potency of sympathetic compassion, or what Böhme calls "love." Los must struggle with Urizen, to whom he chains himself in the *Book of Urizen*, before he can learn to see his own egotism and its blinding effects. What characterizes Los's struggle with Urizen in the interval of his self-realization (an interval lasting through most of the illuminated books) is that the real threat is not the negative potency of resistant self-blinding that Urizen embodies but we all experience. The real threat is stasis, the refusal to struggle, to stay in the interval until insight occurs. As Hegel puts it, the struggle requires "the recognition of the logical principle that the negative is just as much positive, or that what is self-contradictory does not resolve itself into a nullity, into abstract nothingness, but essentially only into the negation of its *particular* content."[30] The struggle is necessary for understanding, for recognition of a larger truth.

This is an important point: the danger is not Urizen and his negative charge, for the negative is also positive, as when the Devil in *Marriage of Heaven and Hell* is the creative, positive force, whereas the angels are the dark agents of stasis and deathly inertia. For Blake, institutional power is motivated to maintain itself by reducing life to stasis and inertia, and Blake focuses particularly on religious institutional power in the *Marriage*. Death-bringing stasis, the condition of the state of Ulro, is what angels and clerics attempt to impose. This is not negativity as represented by Urizen, but the rejection of negation and of any attempt at struggle. Stasis is the antithesis of the interval as a *chora*-like space of immanent creation. For Blake, the mediating negative must be not only endured but also entertained as a processive factor that cannot be allowed to stall. Mediation in this moment is the becoming, or what Schelling calls the "informing," of the ideal into the real. It is the process of negating self-certainty, so that uncertainty takes its place. Uncertainty is the mental state that opens up to immanence. Therefore uncertainty is that crooked path to insight of the *Marriage*'s "Proverbs of Hell": "the crooked roads without Improvement, are roads of Genius" (Copy C, pl. 10: 10–11). The interval's restless deforming-informing diastolic rhythm of process is necessarily filled with revolutionary energy, negative drives, and compulsions that are also positive: Los chained to Urizen. Therefore, "The tygers of wrath are wiser than the horses of instruction" (*Marriage* pl. 10: 7). To bring these forces into fruitful relation means bearing with them, not chaining them down, as Urizen would have it. Bearing with the contradiction is the negative's fruitful process, and negative emotions like rage can break through delusive egotism just as well as poetic insight does.

In *Marriage of Heaven and Hell*, the Argument provides an Old Testament opening of prophetic rage, "Rintrah roars, and shakes his fires in the burden'd air" (Copy C, pl. 2: 2–3), verses that are followed by this elucidation: "As a new heaven is begun . . . the Eternal Hell revives. And lo! Swedenborg is the Angel sitting at the tomb" (pl. 3: 1–3). The tomb is not Christ's tomb, the sign of resurrection, and the angel is the false prophet Swedenborg: the tomb therefore figures only death and denial. The commentary on the prophetic verses is given in prose; if metrical poetry provides the space of writing that invokes the void with its positive and negative potencies, annotative prose steps out of the "violent opening up" of that space, as Blanchot puts it, to point to the death that waits those satisfied with nondialectical dogmatism. But it also points to the power of the dialectic, for if "the Eternal Hell revives," so too does the struggle: "Without Contraries there is no progression. Attraction and Repulsion, Reason and Energy, Love and Hate, are necessary to Human existence" (*Marriage*, Copy C, pl. 3: 7–9). Then Blake begins to unfold the reversals to which Swedenborg's angel should alert the reader: "From these contraries spring what the religious call Good & Evil. Good is the passive that obeys Reason[.] Evil is the active springing from Energy. Good is Heaven. Evil is Hell" (pl. 3: 10–13). Terms propagated by "the religious" are merely that: terms, not truths. This becomes clear when "evil" is anything that could be fruitful, imaginative, and energetic. Good would seem to define a death state; evil defines life itself. When we read that "Good is Heaven. Evil is Hell," we know that reversals springing from a contrarian perspective are already in play, their energy creating the dynamic of the plates that follow. This is removing the veil that keeps immanence, with its vibrant energy, undisclosed or rather, although always everywhere evident, unseen.

The powerful combination of visions, Memorable Fancies, and hellish proverbs that compose *The Marriage* constellate an anti-narrative designed to open the reader's eyes in order to see anew. The poem's I-speaker guides this process, himself undergoing such a revelation that in the end he discovers in his angel-guide a coward who has tried to ensure the speaker sees only the direst interpretation of his surroundings. In the Memorable Fancy that begins on plate 17, an angel appears to the speaker and deliberately distorts his vision: "O pitiable foolish young man! O horrible! O dreadful state! Consider the hot burning dungeon thou art preparing for thyself to all eternity, to which thou art going in such career" (Copy C, pl. 17: 11–14). And in the Fancy, they together descend into a church vault (the entrance to the Christian hell) and from there down into the depths until "a void boundless as a nether sky appeard beneath us & we held by the roots of trees and hung over this immensity; but I said, if you please we will commit ourselves to this void, and see whether providence is here also, if you will not[,] I will? But he answerd[,] do not presume O young-man . . ." (pl. 17: 22–28). Dangling over the void, the speaker-I proposes to commit to it, to tarry with the negative space of disaster and death-threat, whereas the angel sees only a dreadful abyss.

Indeed, the pair do behold "the infinite Abyss, fiery as the smoke of a burning city; beneath us at an immense distance was the sun, black but shining[;] round it were fiery tracks on which revolv'd vast spiders, crawling after their prey" (*Marriage,* Copy C, pl. 18: 3–7). Not so much a vision from Milton's *Paradise Lost* as a segment from Hieronymus Bosch's nightmarish depiction of hell in his *Garden of Earthly Delights* (c. 1490/1510), what the two see is a realization of the angel's prediction. When the speaker-I again encounters the angel on retracing his steps, the angel asks how he escaped the abyss, but the speaker has indeed grown in perspective. Turning guide, he forcibly takes the angel with him on a flight outward to a cosmic vantage point, available to him now in his newly awakened state. Nevertheless, even such logic can be misleading. When the angel complains at the end of the Fancy that "thy phantasy has imposed on me & thou oughtest to be ashamed," the speaker returns "we impose on one another, & it is but lost time to converse with you whose works are only Analytics" (pl. 20: 15–19). Whereas the angel's threatened hell was realized through sophistry, the speaker's visionary trip is decried as mere (imaginative) fantasy and imposition. As the speaker remarks in the next section, "I have always found that Angels have the vanity to speak of themselves as the only wise; this they do with a confident insolence sprouting from systematic reasoning."

For Blake, that first immediate opposition of self and object begins the road to immanent realization, but the mind must grasp its opposition to itself just as the speaker grabs the angel ("I by force suddenly caught him in my arms, & flew westerly" [pl. 19: 17–18]), and fly with that vision. "Opposition," as Blake intones after this Fancy, "is true friendship," which is the devil's truth and a visualization of both Spinoza's and Blake's highest state of becoming. Taken from the Hebrew, this word means "married" or "espoused," an ideal state of becoming-other. But to enter into the awakened state of Beulah, awakening has to occur, a gate has to be entered.[31] In non-Blakean terms, such a gate is the self-actualizing, potentiating interval that can lead to recognizing substance, and Beulah is the state of an infinitely stretched now, the timeless encounter with immanence.

That Blake's zoas each has its counterpart female emanation expresses a kind of thesis-antithesis dynamic in the human psyche's component parts. Moreover, because the emanations can alienate themselves or be alienated from their male counterpart, they demonstrate the inherent ability to house negativity, alienability, and otherness. The female is antagonist to the dominant idea (human = man); as such, she embodies the resistance always already at work in the gendered being, for boys learn to be men by alienating the feminine aspect of their self-nature. Although this dynamic should occupy the *Marriage*, it is more productively worked out in some of the other illuminated books, especially *America a Prophecy*. There, Orc and the shadowy female together constitute the antithetical element; they are supplements to each other, and their interaction is violent and effectual (the shadowy female becomes real, America becomes liberated). Once conjoined, in other words, they resolve the antagonism into a generative antithesis: they are negative energy with mediating, liberatory potential. Viewed in this way, the devils in *Marriage of Heaven and Hell* can be understood as literalizations of Orc and his mate's potentiating force, their mediating negativity. The devils are the agents of realization, and "hell" or negation is associated with the imaginative and liberatory potential of fire in *Marriage*: "As I was walking among the fires of hell, delighted with the enjoyments of Genius . . ." (Copy C, pl. 6: 16). Likewise, Blake associates his revelation of the "infernal" printing process—the artistically liberating form of printing that allowed him to conjoin word and image into a living poem-painting—with alterity's imaginative power. "I saw a mighty Devil folded in black clouds, hovering on the sides of the rock, with corroding fires he wrote the following sentence now percieved [sic] by the minds of men, & read by them on earth" (pl. 6–7: 24–25, 1–2).

But the devil's truth can only be seen and understood as artistic process after the speaker-I of *Marriage* "came home," that is, abided with the negative and its restless potential, understanding hell as the same as what is everyday, understanding revelation as taking place in the present moment of nonlinear time. "When I came home; on the abyss of the five senses, where a flat sided steep frowns over the present world . . ." (Copy C, pl. 6: 22–24). Just as in *Milton a Poem in 2 Books* (1804), when the deceased Milton, who is coming back to earth as a savior-poet, strikes Blake in his cottage garden on plate 15, so too does the devil of the corrosive fires belong to the home *and* the abyss, *heimlich* and *unheimlich*. It is in this differentiated perception that the illuminated plates demonstrate in a kind of multidimensionality. Reading becomes a process of recognizing the layers and feeling at home with their productive discomfort. The four worlds are located on the same spot; each pertains to a different mindset created by pre- or post-negation, pre- or post-encounter with alterity.[32] The "hell" of the Devil's corrosive truths enables one to find the purchase point, the way in to such variability of realizable reality.

In any case, the end goal of Blake's revolutionary art and "infernal" printing process is not to gain for himself entrance into the artistic city of London as "Golgonooza," but rather to paint both resistance and revelation as intertwining movement, always in dynamic relation as represented by the coiling serpent of his prophetic books. Revelation, like negation, might seem to force a standstill, but they are both productive, both an unveiling. Golgonooza is the city of manufacture created by Orc's father, Los (imaginative genius), and his mother, Enitharmon (spiritual beauty or inspiration). Together they are poetic imagination and inspiration creating revolutionary energy (their son Orc) and revolutionary art (a new Jerusalem). Located in the central part of London's actual manufacturing quarters in the late eighteenth century, Golgonooza was constructed by Enitharmon's loom to be a city of manufacture of the arts; it is a play on Josiah Wedgwood's utopian factory town Etruria, and references Wedgwood's political support for a Society for the Manufacture of Arts.[33] Such an institutionalization of "arts," which meant artisan's handicraft rather than the fine arts, would reduce Blake's art to reproductive printing. In

Wedgwood's factory, original artists' designs were reproduced by assembly-line specialists. But Enitharmon's loom weaves a matrix of necessity and freedom in which artists cohabit with their visions. Against Golgonooza, Blake envisions a new Jerusalem, which is the city of peace, the ideal society of the one-in-many, or fully articulated community of Eden. Spinoza calls this "intellectual intuition," the love that is fully integrated with Nature or/as God (VP33Dem). This essential concept in Blake's alterity of a fully articulated community is located exactly where Golgonooza, Ulro, Generation, Beulah, and Eden also belong—at home in London.

These worlds also map onto the human psyche. Beulah, between Generation and Eden, is aligned with the unconscious; it is the source of dreams and poetic inspiration, and poetic language. How one accesses and abides with Beulah determines what one makes of it: the unconscious is where contraries reside in dynamic relation without one dominating or suppressing the other, and it is therefore generative in its artistic potential but also in its cruel, victimizing tendencies that so infect the vegetal world. Blake's location of Beulah between torment and harmonic love reveals it to be the site of negativity, of mediation, and of access to inspired truth. To understand the nuances of this psychological insight, it is necessary to go further than abstract devils and Orc's revolutionary energy.

Milton's antagonist character Satan is a different kind of negative. Altizer argues that in Blake's *Milton* and *Jerusalem*, Blake reveals that God and Satan coincide (36–37). Therefore in the human, Satan—who is both *unheimlich* and *heimlich*—resides in the human heart and is "the Limit of Opacity"; his opposite is Adam, "the Limit of Contraction" (*Jerusalem*, Copy A, pl. 11: 21–22). As Milton imagines Satan, his shell-like body is an opaque carapace symbolizing the depths of true evil that no divine light can pierce. Adam, by contrast, is limited by his five bodily senses and therefore lives in a state of contraction, in which he is vulnerable to further contracting through self-imprisoning ideologies and power relations: "The Eye of Man, a little narrow orb, closd up & dark . . . The Ear, a little shell, in small volutions shutting out / True Harmonies" (*Jerusalem* pl. 49: 35–38). As a force of opacity, Satan deliberately closes the senses to further exploration and growth; his role is to inhibit progression, enlightenment, and access to Eden, for he is "Error." In this he is the exact opposite of the devils in *The Marriage of Heaven and Hell*. But unlike the zoas such as Los, Blake's Satan is a figuration for a state of being or, rather, of resisting being: "Satan is the State of Death & not a Human existence" (*Jerusalem* pl. 49: 68). People are not evil, but the potential for evil resides in them;

they are not themselves errors, but they can live in error by refusing their becoming, insisting on residing in Ulro.

In the case of the state of Satan—a state one can enter, as when "But Luvah is named Satan, because he has enterd that State" (*Jerusalem* pl. 49: 69)—there is no negativity that functions as the enlightening step forward of mediation and becoming. Just the opposite: Satan blocks both the light and Adam's potential by enhancing Adam's too-dulled eyesight, hearing, and other senses. Satan complicates Blake's world when a character enters into the state of "Satan." He then becomes a dissimulator, manipulator, and traitor who turns the community against the just man. When forced to confront Satan's confounding untruths, other characters are unable to adjust to their loss of status within the group; they lose selfhood. Satan's greatest evil, at least in *Milton a Prophecy*, is to create the conditions of this loss. His power is revealed when Milton recognizes Satan to be internalized: "Satan! My Spectre!" Thus the only solution to curing the world of Satan's tyranny is "know thou: I come to Self Annihilation / Such are the Laws of Eternity that each shall mutually / Annihilate himself for others good, as I for thee" (*Milton* pl. 39: 35–37). The only real solution to the problem of Satan lies in the hands of the true artist—Milton, Blake—who understands the effects of the negation of the negation. Only the artist can resolve the problem of the internalized Satan, the spectral presence that haunts the material world of Ulro. Forging his vision out of the warp and woof of necessity and freedom, the awakened artist envisions Eden from his standpoint in Beulah. And the only path to solving the problem of Satan is to offer up the self for the good of others, self-sacrifice for the good of the community.

There are two points to be made here. The first is that Satan resides within, but is different from the condition of negativity as the mediating agent; rather, he is opacity, blockage, an impasse in dynamic movement that stalls the interval. He represents what Spinoza calls "inadequate ideas," or "confused ideas" that block the reason and lead to a loss of conatus, an individual's power to thrive. The second and opposing point is that the willingness to sacrifice the self or/as the ego is central to Blake's vision of Eden. Again, Spinoza has something to say here: "A free man thinks of death least of all things; and his wisdom is a meditation not of death but of life" (IVP67). These two points coalesce when we understand that Los is the fallen version of the zoa Urthona, just as Satan is the fallen version of Lucifer, the Morning Star. Los the poetic genius comes back to himself when he realizes that he must give himself to that which he truly loves—the universe of beings—and so die to himself in order to become his true self, the reunited Adam. I return to the concept of dying-into shortly. The first point concerning Satan's internalization can be understood as the condition that is "Satan"—one of two limits that in Blake's creation myth Christ installed in the heart of the Ancient Man, Albion—and which therefore determines our own worldly existence and limitations, requires understanding that the state of being that is error or Satan leads to inertia. It is not mediatory, as are the devils in *Marriage*. It is a condition of subjectivity that affirms the ego's self-certainty and leads to self-division, even self-alienation. Negation is quite different: it is not a quality or condition of subjectivity but a movement in the dialectic of becoming that is resistance as the spur to reconsider what seems to be given. It is negation that enables the mundane to melt into the sacred, and everyday life to reveal itself as cosmic life. Although one can inhabit the state of Satan by entertaining the internalized quality, for Blake one can also leave it; to do so requires working through the process of negation, resistance, and remediation. It is in this way that Los, who enters error when he allows jealousy to cause him to imprison his son Orc, can later proceed through his own hellish journey until he can be acknowledged as the prophet of eternity (*Jerusalem* pl. 44). Los had to come to the realization of immanent life by dying into an ego-less state that allowed him to see the timelessness of the present moment as eternity itself. In his new insight, Los can also cast off delusion:

> Yet why despair! I saw the finger of God go forth
> Upon my Furnaces, from within the Wheels of Albion's Sons:
> Fixing their Systems, permanent: by mathematical power
> Giving a body to Falshood that it may be cast off for ever. . .
> God is within, & without! he is even in the depths of Hell!
> (*Jerusalem* pl. 12: 11–16)

God, too, is both internal and alterity, mundane and sacred. Los now sees that delusive untruths gain embodiment through systems, logic, arithmetic, and what Blake called in the *Marriage* "only Analytics." As such, they can be grappled with and "cast off for ever" in the enlightened seeing of immanence. This is the negation of the negation.

One of the main tenets of Blake's universe is that the four worlds or levels of existence—Ulro, Generation, Eden, and Beulah—can be traversed by virtue of negation. As only the negation of the negation will achieve any effect, each world is a mere transposition of the others, a turn of the lens, or a glance askew. Each time one abides in negation and commits to it, one is entering the space of the multiple. This is the process of calling the self into question, of revealing the self's certainty as an existential delusion, a crisis under wraps.[34] The existential subject who is actively engaged in the process of becoming is what the zoas' narratives demonstrate with their endless transpositions.

The problem of self-delusion versus existential crisis can be seen in the critical debate between whether Blake adheres to a theory of "being" or to a Hegelian theory of "becoming."[35] This debate often takes the view that Blake embraced the *either/or* dynamic in his early work but came to the *both-and* dynamic in his mature work. It is more helpful, however, to think about Blake's ontopolitics as the ethical understanding that the individual's self-conception is impermanent and in need of mediation. Its processing of the interval's negativity is a kind of color field or endless series of transpositions. Ethics puts this process under scrutiny: being-becoming dualisms are a futile way to approach Blake, who was allergic to dualistic thinking.[36] Engaging in revolutionary London during the period of George III's struggle to retain his American colonies, Blake knew well even in the early 1790s that "becoming" is a fraught concept.

For Blake, a revolution in understanding can only take place if a poetics and a formal apparatus are in place that promote the dynamic process of the reader as the subject under scrutiny.[37] This is the trial of human contraction; one must commit to the negative, opening oneself up to examination and therefore movement out of the stalled time of Ulro. From the sheer extent of plates Blake devotes to both Urizen's and Los's trials, it is possible to garner just how necessary this painful process is, and how necessary for the survival of the human psyche. If Los does succeed—and as the poetic, creative Imagination, he must or the world is doomed—Urizen as Reason will have less efficacy. The case is made in their comparative journeys for the destructive nature of those who insist on their individual subjectivity (Urizen), and of those who commit to the communal identity of the multiple (Los). Urizen's and Los's remedial trials are, then, of utmost importance.

The First Book of Urizen (1794) begins the cosmic myth that results in *Jerusalem*'s revelations; I return to it here to recapture some points made earlier in this chapter. The *Book of Urizen* is of signal importance because, as David Erdman points out, Blake's plates and notebooks indicate that all the books devoted to Urizen, his emanation Ahania, and his rival Los were originally to be sequential Books of Urizen (Erdman 804). But the illuminated books are not sequential; instead, they recursively retell the narrative from different perspectives, extending Urizen's story greatly and at the same time provoking the very differentiation within the one story that is the realization of One and All. By giving both Ahania and Los their own epic narratives, Blake recognizes their equal resistance to Urizen and his lack of control, despite his Zeus-like, thunderous attempts to control his manipulative emanation-spouse Ahania and his Prometheus-like opponent, Los.

Urizen begins his career as a force of darkness, resistant to light:

> what Demon
> Hath form'd this abominable void
> This soul-shudd'ring vacuum?—Some said
> "It is Urizen," But unknown, abstracted
> Brooding secret, the dark power hid.
> (*Urizen* pl. 3: 6–10)

Cosmic horror at Urizen's act of empire-making surrounds a creation that is not that of the prophetic artistic, but of a darker construction associated with "shadow," an unknown "Demon," "Brooding secret," and "dark power." The demon that may or may not be Urizen—"Some said," it is rumors and speculation even among the eternals—is surrounded by mystery, secrets, darkness, and self-closure. These are attributes of self-delusion, an "abstracted" state of self-centered experience. "Abstract" is one of the direst words in Blake's lexicon, associated with mystification and abstract reasoning that distorts evidential experience, manipulating people into accepting their victimization. The dark creation that ensues is "soul-shudd'ring," "all-repelling," and a vacuum—one of the most terrible conditions that can endure, causing cosmic distress.

Man's nature is thus made chaotic and disharmonious, and his vision is reduced to seeing only a projection of himself, unable to perceive beyond self-imposed limitations. In contrast to the dark and stony world Urizen forges, Los's creation is that of the natural or material world that he manufactures out of Urizen's terrible wilderness, demonstrating that Ulro is where Beulah also is. Los's and Urizen's worlds coexist beneath the Mundane Shell; for all those below this shell, sight is reflected back to the viewer so that another can only be the projection of one's own desires or fear. Los's mundane materials do not provide gates to perception, as Blake's variable palettes do, until he has gained access to perception beyond the limitations of the Mundane Shell. We can understand life under the Shell, before Los's awakening, as an inverted existence, walking the wrong way around with reason elevated far above imagination and sensuality. The way forward, therefore, is always crooked, off balance, and recursive. Urizen figures for Blake the human capacity to resist multiplicity, variability, and nondualism.[38] Urizen's is a determined closing down to anything but self-certainty as a negation of alterity. Nothing could be more disastrous, and for this reason Blake ceaselessly works to depict Urizen's failures of vision, of thought, and of becoming. It is Urizen who isolates himself, who alienates himself from community in "obscure separation alone" (*Urizen* pl. 5: 44).

The Eternals do not intervene, watching in dismay as Los struggles to oppose Urizen ("And his Feet stampd the nether Abyss" [*Urizen* pl. 13: 17]). But this conflict comes with a price to Los, who must perpetually grapple with Urizen so long as he remains bound to the vegetal world of the Mundane Shell; their grappling maintains a terrible equilibrium that resists the life-giving dialectic of the interval. Only after Los frees himself from Urizen and engages in the intense and absolute confrontation with the negative within himself (as Satan), putting the self in question, can he awaken from the interval through a sudden realization of immanence. Los is the exemplary figure for the recursive movement of restlessness in Blake's corpus who realizes himself finally by the end of the mythic cycle with *Jerusalem*.

Urizen's qualities, some self-appointed and some caused by Los's damning embodiment of Urizen (one that is closed in his ears, nostrils "bent down to the deep," brain, and eyes "fixed in two little caves" [*Urizen* pl. 11: 21,15]), continue to guide his journey as it evolves downward in a continual descent into the caves of Orc in *The Four Zoas* (1797), and so into his own hellish nightmare of self-absorption, nursed wrongs, and unexamined passions. The evidence of this poisonous descent into insistent self-delusion, un-allayed by any beneficial free fall in the void, is found when from under his heel the Tree of Mystery springs, an evil growth ultimately associated with the cross of the crucifixion (Night the Seventh, *Four Zoas*).[39] Unwilling to confront his own self-contradiction, Urizen chooses to remain in the hellish abyss of his own making and, like Milton's Satan, to proclaim it his kingdom. In Blake's vision throughout, Urizen names and figures the abyss as a hell; if Urizen sees this as his stomping ground, Los understands the abyss as a variation on the void-interval. It is here that Los tarries with the negative. It is a habitation he desperately does not want, one that divides his self from himself to such an extent that he chains his own son Orc down just as he had enchained Urizen. Bound to Urizen's self-inscribed negative, Los suffers with and through Urizen, who participates in his self-division:

> He saw Urizen deadly black,
> In his chains bound, & Pity began,
> In anguish dividing & dividing
> For pity divides the soul. (*Urizen* pl. 13: 54–57)

It is Los's true commitment to negation, not as a confrontation with Urizen but with his own otherness, that finally results in world-renewal through Los's dying into his poetic promise.

If Ulro feels virtual, Jerusalem, the city Los and Enitharmon begin to build together toward the end of Los's trials feels materially real. Blake depicts this by having Enitharmon weave the fabric of its reality. While "build[ing]," Jesus appears beside them and coaxes them from their bodily form, "Separating / Their Spirit from their body." Los is "Terrified at Non Existence," the most threatening state or non-state for subjectivity, but Jesus intends that he should understand such a state as redemptive because it is sacrificial. Los is indeed dematerialized; in response, Enitharmon's Spectre joins with that of Urthona, Los's original, unfallen form to which he is now restored. Their dematerialization is accompanied by the trumpets of apocalypse, the call to judgment, and the overthrow of monarchs so that "all Tyranny was cut off from the face of Earth" (Night the Ninth, *Four Zoas* 386–7, 388). But the more literal narrative of Los/Enitharmon's self-sacrifice occurs in *Jerusalem*:

> Fear not my Sons this Waking Death[,] he is become One with me
> Behold him here! We shall not Die! we shall be united in Jesus.
> Will you suffer this Satan this Body of Doubt that Seems but Is Not
> To occupy the very threshold of Eternal Life[?] if Bacon, Newton, Locke,
> Deny a Conscience in Man & the Communion of Saints & Angels . . .
> Is it not that Signal of the Morning which was told us in the Beginning[?]
> (*Jerusalem* pl. 93: 27–31, 35)

As Los dissolves into "this Waking Death," encouraging his sons to do likewise, he is yielding his subjectivity not to nonexistence but to a larger alterity that is Jesus. Jesus here stands not just for the savior but for the community of one-in-many, the concept of the people as participating in the One, as in the masses who populate *America a Prophecy*. This antinomian concept of the importance of the multiple over individual subjectivity is fully fleshed out in Los's sacrifice for the good of all. Part of Los's self-revelation, brought about through the rebirth of love, is that "Sexes must vanish & cease / To be," accompanied by the ending of all "Crimes . . . Punishments . . . Accusations of Sin . . . Jealousies Revenges[,] Murders[,] hidings of Cruelty in Deceit / Appear only in the Outward Spheres of Visionary Space and Time[,] / In the shadows of Possibility by Mutual Forgiveness forevermore" (*Jerusalem* pl. 92: 15–16, 17–19). To end sexuation and gendering is to end the othering of the female, with its accompanying jealousy, manipulative power relations, victimization, and disenfranchisement. What recognition of substance reveals is that gendered beings paradoxically produce the condition of unproductive antithesis, stalled time without redemption.

Los's exemplary self-sacrifice both enlightens himself and provides a hermeneutic praxis of active reading as imagining for the reader; this last is the end goal of the illuminated books. Blake's definition of sacrificial loss is a Shelleyan dying into alterity, but through the valuing of the one-in-many as community over the self's relative value. In this sense it is a repositioning of subjectivity rather than its complete loss, for "he [Christ] is become One with me." This communion transposes the me-ness of the subject so as to avoid the terrible fate of nonexistence, or the complete absorption into an otherness that cannot be known and has no substance. It is therefore not a giving of self over to the other, but a complete communing of self and whole, a rejoining of divided parts just as the male and female elements must conjoin for there to be harmony and the eternal circle. This resolution to the problem of being is a version of the Stoic and Spinozist pantheism of the One and All.

IV. Blake's Choric Void

In my reading, for Blake to imagine the One of immanent life is to start with the void. Lorraine Clark provides an approach to the generative void in terms of Kierkegaard's thinking about the negative. She argues that the philosopher of anxiety is the most apt analogue for Blake because of their radical Protestantisms. The "tension between religion and nihilism" and proto-poststructuralism in Kierkegaard's works, she suggests, best approximates Blake's proto-deconstructive moves. As she notes, Paul de Man has understood Blake to be "himself such a deconstructionist that 'there are no secrets or repressions to be exposed by deconstructive analysis'" in his works (Clark 2). Although Clark posits the negative as a clear opposition of good and evil and presents these as externalized, embodied concepts that can never be truly resolved as in a Manichean universe, her interpretation of Los's self-confrontation is helpful. The ultimate example of confrontation with the negative is that between Los and his Spectre, which is a "dialectic of . . . truth and error, life and death" that she reads as "a complex inversion of the Orc-Urizen dialectic—an inversion which mirrors and yet radically transvalues that earlier dialectic" (2).

Yet to put the Orc-Urizen dyad and the Los-Spectre relation (one external, the other interiorized) in an inverted relation that "mirrors" and yet "transvalues" conflates several steps in Blake's depiction of the Urizen-Los mytheme, itself a semi-unstable narrative. That evolving oppositional relation cannot be contained in the intense confrontation between Los and the Spectre, an internalized self-contradiction that actualizes the individual's split-consciousness. The internalized state of divided consciousness cannot be considered to "mirror"—either as a reflection of or in a left-to-right reorientation—an externalized dyad of opposed concepts. Rather, this is the moment of the restless interval, the generative struggle between self and Spectre that can bring on the sudden realization of self-contradiction and nondualistic becoming. Further, Orc complicates the Urizen/Spectre or outer/inner orientation by being both Los's progeny and the artist's revolutionary anger that Los in his fallen state lacks.

Nevertheless, Clark's reading of Blake within the context of Kierkegaard's revision of the Hegelian negative is helpful for understanding how Blake conceives the choric void in relation to the restless interval. The Kierkegaardian interval is the state of anxiety; it is an anxiety hovering between freedom and guilt that is an anxiety about nothing in particular but always anxiously with an eye to the future. Blake's particular vision—that the to-come brought on by Los's salvific self-sacrifice does not erase Generation or Ulro, nor is it the achievement of a historical *telos*—is aligned with Kierkegaard's version, in which the man of faith does not rectify the wrongs of rationalism or erase anxiety as the human condition per se. Indeed, Blake and Kierkegaard share an ironic perspective, visible particularly in *Marriage* and *Fear and Trembling* concerning totalizing systems that presuppose the possibility of a teleological end-goal in the world. Blake is not as reluctant to grant the movement of positing-negation a necessary role in the leap to freedom, but, like Kierkegaard, he too finds the leap out of the interval to be an irrational act. Indeed, it is an "absurd" act, for it is "on the strength of the absurd" that Abraham, in his anxiety over whether to sacrifice Isaac or not, puts him as a single individual "higher than the universal" (*Fear and Trembling* 85). Therefore, it cannot be a continuous movement from the possibility of freedom to actual freedom, because for Kierkegaard the self as itself only comes into being through the absurd leap out of despair into faith. Similarly, Blake's I-speaker in *Marriage* only truly knows or believes in himself when he clasps the angel and leaps out of the abyss-church-mill interval of oppositional energies into the void of space. The freedom of self-knowledge for both Blake and Kierkegaard can only be achieved in the vegetal, or natural, world, not through rational self-confrontation. Alterity cannot be entertained if fending it off, or what Kierkegaard calls "inclosing reserve" (akin to Urizen's self-closure) prevents the "qualitative leap" of Kierkegaardian self-actualization.

This becomes clearer in the concluding passage of *The Marriage*, in which the angel sententiously proclaims Christ's authority, and the Devil replies by condemning Jesus for sanctioning the ten commandments. The Devil may be read as a version of Milton's duplicitous Satan here, casting Christ out into an abyss familiar to readers of *Paradise Lost* as that terrible space through which Satan had to fly after exiting the gates of hell. But that abyss functions as the space of Satan's own leap out of hell into Eden, and in that interval he never (like Urizen) mentally leaves hell, for, as Kierkegaard remarks in *The Concept of Anxiety*, "In the demonic . . . Freedom is posited as unfreedom, because freedom is lost" (123). Blake's poetic demon is the double negative to the angel's complacencies. His revealed truth, freely disclosed, is the product of his negation of the deceiving angel (the No, as opposed to the not-neither); as such, it is an echo of Hegel's negation of the negation, which is the God-Christ-Spirit dialectic. As a double negative, the Devil's pronouncement is also a grammatical ploy that is the truth statement. Thus, "When he [the Devil] had so spoken, I beheld the Angel," who, negated, has just accepted the Devil's truth, effectuating his translation from interval to void-as-generative. The angel then "stretched out his arms, embracing the flame of fire, and he was consumed, and arose as Elijah" (pl. 24: 3–5).

Through Blake's "Bible of Hell, which the world shall have whether they will or no" (10–11), Elijah revealed in his *both/and* identity will be able to pronounce the coming of the Messiah, and therefore the completion of the New Jerusalem. He is also able to come home, for in his new identity, "This Angel, who is now become a Devil, is my particular friend. We often read the Bible together in its infernal or diabolical sense which the world shall have if they behave well" (pl. 24: 6–9). Thus, Elijah is both the universal and the antithetical, delighting in the revelation of "that One Man / We call Jesus the Christ: and he in us, and we in him, / Live in perfect harmony in Eden the land of life" (*Jerusalem* pl. 38/34: 20–22). He is alterity that is also the self-same, representing the nonduality that the encounter with otherness produces. Who "I" am in this particular encounter is more problematic. Is the poet-I speaking from the position of alterity here? Or is positionality interchangeable, with both the poet and the devil occupying each other's place as the same place? Together as nondual belonging they achieve ultimate truth; this can only be defined in Blakean terms as "read[ing] . . . together." And this revealed truth is accessible to all, "whether they will or no."

Both this chapter on Blake's treatment of the resistant ego and chapter 2 present representatively Romantic understandings of Spinozist immanence. However, chapter 2 does move in a different direction, exploring the darkest moments of the interval as a projection of the unconscious and its fears of self-loss. I explore Coleridge's "Rime of the Ancient Mariner" to understand how Coleridge's famously ambiguous poem achieves a recognition of substance as *the* ethical act, one that changes standard accounts of ontology. The hallucinatory stalled time in the Mariner's narrative of near-death experience produces its own self-contradiction, its own rejection of duality through an intense experience of immanence. This is nevertheless a story of ego and the way a self-enclosing ego meets immanence through its own shattering translation.

2

Coleridge's Wilding

The All is before the One. Necessity is before freedom. Nature is before what is external to and beyond all nature. And yet there is no time here because everything is in the process of this same, indivisible act. There is no life without the overcoming of death.[1]

—F. W. J. Schelling, *Ages of the World*

Lyrical Ballads is undeniably a landmark publication, a collaboration by two poet-philosophers struggling to put their own and others' theories of nature, the supernatural, and the supersensible into poetic forms that could gesture toward what exceeds representation in those three realms. William Wordsworth and Samuel Taylor Coleridge's poetic and intellectual experimentation prior to the 1798 publication was inspired by theories of how the imagination works, Spinoza's nature philosophy, and German Romantic poetry among much else. Coleridge's treatments of nature's wild force—its nonhuman-oriented dynamism—in his 1796–97 poems of the supernatural and supersensible find a high point in "The Rime of the Ancyent Marinere, in Seven Parts." This is a poem that subverts the transcendental model of the sublime so that embodiment is the only way to realize immanent life. If the sublime rips the awareness out of the body, immanence instead locates alterity in the horizontal: it is alterity located from the surface down. What Coleridge accomplishes with this Spinozist poem that differs from Blake's mythopoetical accomplishment is that his Mariner, however at sea mentally and egotistically, finds redemption through the body itself. It is not just the albatross's dead body hung from his neck, or the dead bodies of his nephew and mates that shift the Mariner's understanding, but his own body that, as I discuss later in this chapter, shares in the same substance and suchness as all things, sentient and insentient, being and object.

In the new nature philosophy, Nature's dynamism was the recognition of a life force beyond human control and its dualisms situated somewhere between and beyond Spinoza's rationalist philosophy of nature and the Enlightenment's scientized and objectified nature. If for Spinoza nature is one of the two perceivable forms of God's expression, he also posits an infinite number of other modes of divine expression that lie beyond human perception, thus providing a speculative space in which something else can be apperceived yet be inconceivable to the human mind. Coleridge imagines that something else to be a nature scandalized by the scientific distancing of the natural from the human will to know, control, and reify. Retitled "Rime of the Ancient Mariner," the poem depicts an encounter with nature's wild force, which had been suppressed under the schemas of science and aesthetics. The Mariner must translate himself from a solipsistic individual empowered by the self-interest and self-centeredness of Enlightenment science and capitalist economics that denies nature any embodied validity, motion, or conatus (the power to persist and thrive). The poem's project is to translate egocentrism into seeing clearly, solipsism into insight, with both never unbound from bodily felt sense. The Mariner must become the one whose vision is so different from other self-interested, deluded persons that he seems crazed. Yet his exhortations to the Wedding Guest are riveting; his is a poetic burden whose rhymes capture the universal rhythms of a living world. The Wedding Guest cannot help but be stunned by its telling force.

The Mariner accosts the Wedding Guest in the present now of the poem in order to recount his harrowing adventures during the last voyage at sea he ever took, one that changed his life so dramatically through encounters with supernatural and supersensible bodies: spirits, Death, Life-in-Death, sea serpents, even the albatross. Although the narrative proposes possible explanations for events up to a point—stilled winds, the Mariner's killing of the albatross, the other sailors' interpretations of this event—the crisis arrives during a period of blocked or stalled, hallucinatory time of nonmovement, and is broken by manifestation of the inexplicable itself. The crisis thrusts the Mariner into the immanent now, the interval in which conventional explanations and normative ways of seeing and thinking evaporate in the face of the what-is. It is this transformative moment that causes the Mariner to exchange his ego-centered perspective for an affirmation of all life, all sentient and insentient beings, all things. This embodied experience of deeply entangled interbeing, this insight into the true nature of things, is what becomes the Mariner's task to relate to anyone who resembles his earlier, deluded self, such as the Wedding Guest.

Poetic telling, then, is the Mariner's expression of self-translation, his ethical activity. It is an ethics that bespeaks an ontological truth that, however age-old, was entirely new to him; his realization is of a substance that bespeaks itself. As he learns, nature does not wait for humans to bestow grace upon it. The Mariner's blessing of the water serpents is a repetition only, as he sees beatifically that natural entities are already expressive of substance and already endowed with the universal rhythms of that substance. They self-bless, as it were. In "Rime of the Ancient Mariner," the interval is preceded by a period of hallucinatory time, its contra-dictions with the interval functioning to transform the Mariner's self-centered actions into virtuous activity expressive of ontoethical life. It is only through the challenge thrown at him by death that the Mariner can truly perceive, comprehending his prior behavior as death-in-life motion lacking the insight of felt sense. This type of motion in Spinoza's scheme leads to blocked or stalled bodies, the very fate of the sailors on the immobilized ship with their conatus all but disappeared during the hallucinatory period. What has led to this fateful scene appears to have been the Mariner's mechanistic practices. Movement without ethics affects bodies in denaturing ways: an albatross whose killing was mere play. The Mariner must learn a practice of tending-to, the attendance that leads to blessed activity.

A nature that is not composed of autonomous things but is instead interdependent with the human *and* the supersensible (as Spinoza's other modes of God's expression) is a nature wildly resistant to being categorized and repurposed to human ends. "Rime of the Ancient Mariner" can be read in a scientistic vein to find the thingness of nature: the voyage begins with the Mariner perceiving the albatross as a plaything while at the nadir of the narrative the Mariner finds that he himself has become a thing unable to speak or move. But the poem should rather be read as Coleridge's incipient version of speculative realism, animated by a Spinozist alterity as *Deus sive Natura*, God or Nature. What the poem expresses is a response to the science/nature and matter/thought bifurcations that culminate in "The Rime." The poem's nightmare teaches true vision, a living nature constantly in flux, and beautiful in its substantial being. The poem's redemptive understanding is of self-thinging, exemplified by the beauteous water-snakes, as participating in Spinoza's *natura naturans,* nature naturing.

The first half of this chapter asks the question of how "The Rime" imagines the human confrontation with nature's wild force so as to simultaneously stage the limitations of language to convey an apperception of the wild, and language's limitless capacity to render such apperception figuratively, rhythmically, prophetically. That is, how to translate the interval's restless movement between delusive diction and contra-diction into a narrative of endless transformation. How Coleridge represents this movement and how he reframes it in the *Biographia Literaria* nearly two decades later focuses the second half of the chapter, where I explore how the immanent nature that explodes forcefully onto the scene of the Mariner's hallucinogenic consciousness becomes what Jason Wirth terms "the practice of the wild" in Schelling's *Naturphilosophie,* and how Coleridge comes to terms with this wilding, seeking to rationalize it. Yet even in its later, 1817 instantiation, "Rime of the Ancient Mariner" refuses to give up its wild force; the poem's rhythms are too insistent, and the added, rationalizing, marginal narrative cannot cover it over. As I suggest in the chapter's second half, Wirth's is a valuable concept in providing a vision of Schellingian nature that Coleridge echoes and adumbrates. Inasmuch as the Ancient Mariner's task is to become receptive to immanent nature, Coleridge is depicting a universe immersed in wilding, bespeaking its immanent becoming as ideal and real intermeshed at the deepest, most intimate level of embodied interbeing. A speculative nature is not dependent on human surveillance or interventions, opening instead to all being including human being.[2] The poem inaugurates a doubled time of reading in its 1798 formulation of repetition and time shifts that is only exaggerated in the 1817 variation of a marginal commentary framing the Mariner's tale. This doubled or mirroring time enhances the hallucinatory effects of the interval of reading: the Mariner reads his voyage experience, the commentator reads the Mariner's tale, the reader encounters the enfolded tale as cosmic mystery much in the manner that the Wedding Guest experiences the Mariner's weird telling.

If scholars have been inclined to read both the 1798 and 1817 versions of the "Rime" as either Christian symbolism or as inhabiting the nightmarish psychoanalytic of the Gothic, the poem instead professes a practice of wilding that opens into an alterity of greater dimension than that of either Christian mysticism or Gothic haunting. Coleridge is reaching for something else here, even if he cannot readily accept its wild and destabilizing force. Something that is excessive, exceeding the bounds of a horizoned-off reality into the inhuman, the posthuman, and the suprasensible aspect of nature that doesn't distinguish real from ideal. Through Schelling's *Naturphilosophie* and the ideas expressed in his 1800 *System of Transcendental Philosophy*, to which Coleridge had mediated access by the time of the 1817 *Biographia Literaria*, the "Rime" can be seen as expressing nature's alterity in the sense that Schelling formulates it. Schelling's "wilding" as nature's capacity to open up otherness to us becomes a principal concept for understanding the experiences the Ancient Mariner undergoes that so drastically illuminate his understanding, fundamentally damaging his self-centered capacity to ignore the conditions and experience of suffering. His life after rescue is involuntarily devoted to impersonating the Real as a kind of life-in-death that parodies the terrible apparitions of the death ship (Death-in-Life and her mate, Death) so that others, like the Wedding Guest, can have the same transformative crisis that he did. He is a kind of walking Idea. It is a transformation that lifts the subject out of the radical/conservative binary that was dividing Coleridge's world as much as was the science/nature binary. In the revolutionary 1790s, Coleridge finds that "wilding" as poetic practice can redress such pacifying binarism by accessing alterity's energizing resistance to them. In this way, "the wild" functions as the paused clock time, or non-movement, of the interval that one must receive, open up to, if the initiating transfiguration is to take place.

Although Coleridge had not yet read Schelling's *System of Transcendental Idealism (1800)* because it had not yet been written, Schelling's ideas—which Coleridge absorbs and adapts along with Kant's critical philosophy and Fichte's neo-Kantian idealism as soon as he is exposed to these—reveal that Coleridge has taken from Spinoza something like what Schelling has understood from the emblematic motto of *Deus sive Natura*. Both Coleridge and Schelling responded to Enlightenment science with a recoil that acknowledges its scandalous division of the human from the natural world.[3] Both men had also absorbed elements of Eastern speculative thought inherent in Judeo-Christian mysticism. The combination includes structured-in Stoic speculative conceptions of immanence and Eastern overtones of nonduality and oneness.[4] These are the elements I want to discuss in Coleridge's famous poem, as well as his use of "rime" as rhythm and repetition to reveal immanent life. I see this metricity of poetic language—its insistent pulsations that regulate to some extent the wildness inherent in *poesis* while retaining the hidden depths of that wilding as a driving force—as being what drew Coleridge to poetry. Metricity captures the body's insistence; Spinozist poetry raises this truth to a higher level. Poetry offers a more vivid and transformative mode than philosophy while doing the same work as its sister; Schelling would not dispute this, as the final section on art, or more precisely, myth as thought's apotheosis in the 1800 *System* reveals. Where poetry has the undoubted edge over philosophy for Coleridge is its openness to alterity; not just to the supersensuous, but to Otherness in its immanent becoming. Only poetry opens a window in solipsism's prison house to something altogether larger than the human. But philosophy is the wellspring of poetry for Coleridge, and his poetry-making was ever infused with his philosophical investigations.

I. Spinoza's Infinite Perceptions as Absolute Unity

What Coleridge and Wordsworth were discussing of Spinoza's philosophy so intently during the "Spy Nozy" affair—which part of his analysis of nature's relation to the absolute, and of man's relation to both—might be gleaned from the *Lyrical Ballad*'s nature poetry, and allegories of it such as the "Rime."[5] After Coleridge's return from Germany, he confides in his notebook that Spinoza's monism has provided the conduit to the suggestive nonduality of the earlier supernatural poems such as "Kubla Khan." "If I begin a poem of Spinoza, thus it should begin: I would make a pilgrimage to the burning sands of Arabia, or etc etc to find the Man who could explain to me there can be *one*ness, there be infinite Perceptions—yet there must be a *one*ness, not an intense Union but an Absolute Unity"[6]—a thought that finds its echo in Wordsworth's allegorical dream of the Arab in *The Prelude* (V.56–140). Coleridge's own taste of Christian mysticism from thinkers such as Giordano Bruno, and the mystical thought inherent in Stoic philosophy, prepared him for what he was to encounter in Germany. There he discovered among the academic community an emphatic return to Christian mysticism (especially that of Jakob Böhme and Meister Eckhart) as well as an enthusiastic resurgence of Spinozism. Lessing's brand of both, and his spirited defense of Spinoza in the so-called "pantheism controversy"—Lessing said that Spinozism was the only true philosophy—provided a fostering environment for Coleridge's own thinking on the ineluctability of nature's productive force and its relation to the supersensible.[7] Richard Holmes describes the exciting spread of "Romantic reaction and mysticism that was then spreading throughout the universities of Germany—at Göttingen, at Jena, at Leipzig" in relation to Coleridge's "whole notion of 'criticism'—of the application of philosophical principles to imaginative literature," and ascribes this to Coleridge's new German orientation (*Early Visions* 221).[8] But the influence was more extensive than that; not just Coleridge's innovative literary criticism but his poetry making itself was touched and broadened. That Coleridge's reading had already inclined him toward what he would discover in Germany is revealed by Southey's anonymous criticism of the "Rime." Declaring the poem an ungainly attempt at German sublimity, Southey underscores the poem's aesthetic basis as much as its theo-philosophical one. What he does not appreciate fully is Coleridge's use of metaphor to bring those two elements together.

Goethe, Germany's foremost literary figure, actively sought to put philosophy (particularly Spinozist-inspired philosophy), aesthetics, and poetry in conversation, believing that metaphor captures the status of reality (the famous quote from *Faust*, Part II, Act V—"All that is transitory is but a metaphor"—summarizes Goethe's investment in the power of figuration).[9] Like Goethe, the Coleridge of 1798 had already recognized the extraordinary importance of the metaphoric figure for conveying philosophico-poetic conception, and especially for conveying nondualistic truths about the transitory, motile character of phenomenal reality—what he would soon call the "poem of Spinoza." Constrained by language, the human capacity to express what is beyond linguistic capture must find its outlet in figuration. The metaphor's capacity to act as the third term, the bridge or breath between two opposing states, has two heritages important to my argument. The first is its literary heritage, the recognition of the figurative vehicle's ability to convey an incorporeal truth. This is metaphor as the threshold between literal and ultimate meaning, with its ability to hold the first while presenting the second as its larger truth. The second is its Eastern heritage, the poetic capacity of metaphor to demonstrate the nonduality of two states as their at-onceness (the literal is never true, except that it is, whether or not the ultimate meaning that hovers behind is realized). Christian mysticism borrowed much from the ancient esoteric philosophies circulating the Mediterranean and communicated along trade routes, but at the very least it borrowed the concept of "Absolute Unity," as Coleridge puts it, and of the bridging middle term or "spark" in Böhme's schema. (Thomas McFarland notes that Coleridge "knew Boehme's thought from early adolescence on" through translations by William Law, and later thought him a genius on par with or excelling Plato.)[10]

Böhme's spark can be associated with the soul at question in vitalism, but it is better understood more radically. This middle, dynamic term—the chemical spark, as German Idealists would soon think of it—functions as a both/and. It is the mobile element, the spark that Böhme identifies as that which moves the divine primal opposition beyond the standoff between outward-directed love and inward-facing retreat to a new stage of expression. This new stage is not a resolution to the opposition but rather a realization of the life dynamic. The anonymous Christian mystic who authored the fourteenth-century manual *Cloud of Unknowing* wrote similarly that "this little word 'fire' stirs and pierces the Heavens more quickly . . . The depth is height, for spiritually all is one, height and depth, length and breadth."[11] In 1806, Coleridge will transcribe a line from Strabo that contains echoes here: "Though Genius, like the fire on the altar, can only be kindled from heaven, yet it will perish unless supplied with appropriate fuel to feed it . . ." to which he appends his commentary "Now the inspiration of genius seems to bear the stamp of Divine assent, and to attain to something of prophetic strain."[12] Both Strabo's and Coleridge's understanding of fire's relation to genius, and of the chemical spark necessary for both life and inspiration—of genius' spark piercing Heaven quickly—includes the fire's dependence on the world for its fuel. We might think of this middle, bridging term—that which sparks and partakes of both the "this" and "that" of the opposition, thereby producing the conditions for inspiration and revelation—in the way that Kant does with his faculty of judgment. Judgment partakes of both the understanding (how we make sense of empirical reality) and of synthetic reason (how we think). Judgment allows us to make determinations *and* to be reflective, both of which facilitate our ability to imagine and to appreciate, to speculate and to exercise the free rein of our intellect.

But this middle term is also at once corporeal and incorporeal when it is figured as breath and the Romantic breeze rather than light-producing fire. The breath bridges the inside and the outside of the body, creating a dynamic exchange between this and that, for the breath is both inner and outer. It exemplifies that which moves between two realms, as does the living present (hovering between past and future) and the surface (the active interface between depth and world). Importantly for the Romantics, wind resembles the breath as the middle term between earth and sky (recently scientists have discovered that the earth breathes, so perhaps the breath-wind association is more than fortuitous).[13] In Sanskrit the breath is "prana," life force, a not unreasonable conjunction here since Sir William Jones's famous lecture to the Royal Asiatic Society on Sanskrit's extraordinary philological importance was published in 1788, situating Sanskrit's potential as the ground of language.[14] The breath is, like the wind in both Romantic and Eastern literature, life force, the mobile intermediary between mind and world. It is the middle term that inclines toward aspiration, inspiration, and, to a very real extent, *ekstasis*. Without it, the Mariner's world dissolves into impasse.

II. Tarrying in the Middle Realm

The mistake is to think that the breath or wind is transitional between two opposing states or realms (stasis/movement, death/life, real/eternal) or that the spark is a mere chemical ignition causing transformation. The dynamic intermediate breath or wind is not simply a middle term. There are not two states and a third term, but a dynamic interchange or interpenetration that is constantly ongoing. One must tarry in the breath for that dynamism to be realized. And, like the river as a body of water, this middle state constantly renews itself: each breath is a new one, but it is still the breath, the inspiration that interfaces a being's inside and the outer world. The present moment renews itself in this way. The Mariner's spiritual translation consists in him self-locating perpetually in this present tense, metaphorically expressing the fact of interpenetration—which so few are blessed to realize—by repetition of his transformative moment. By renewing it as the present of tale-telling, he renews that moment as the present one and the one after, each an inspiration. The importance of "rime" as both rhythm and the instantiation of time lies in its repetitive force as *inspiratus*; its insistence is on the present and on movement, and its bewildering power stuns the Wedding Guest through the tale's insistence. The Wedding Guest's experience of the Mariner's experience thus extends the metaphorical and Spinozist expression of the interrelation of the three realms (life, breath, and death; sea depths, permeable surface, and heavens). So too does the reader's experience of the Mariner's presentness and the Wedding Guest's attestation of it.

In "The Rime of the Ancient Mariner," the wind as middle term suggests a breathing nature, at times an inspiration that pushes the mariners forward, and at others a suspiration and a critical withholding of breath or life force.[15] The mystical question—is it the wind that flaps the banner (or the ship's sails), the banner that flaps, or the mind that flaps?—is one of the problematics structuring the Mariner's voyage. The psychological question is another problematic that likewise structures the Mariner's experience: is the wind's participation in the eventful voyage part of a hallucination, and is this then an aspect of everyday hallucinatory experience or hallucination as transcendent epiphany? Both questions produce the philosophical encounter with a seemingly empirical nature resurgent with unaccountable phenomena, energies, and that which sparks combustion and genesis. The encounter turns from the explicable to realization: not this-and-that, but both-at-once, as when Blake's speaker-I in *Marriage of Heaven and Hell* understands, as the angel does not, that hell *is* heaven when viewed differently, the abyssal chasm transforming into the pastoral paradise with a shift in perspective. The Mariner, too, is tasked with coming to this realization, and for him too it is the work of the Devil, or at least of Life-in-Death and her companion, Death, to make the human see beyond delusive apparent reality to the truth of immanent reality.[16]

In 1804, after his return from Germany and several years after having written the first version, "Rime of the Ancyent Marinere," Coleridge is still thinking about the metaphor of the spark as breath/inspiration in relation to the transient and the permanent, or, as Goethe frames it, in terms of the temporal and everything it contains as but metaphor:

> Each man having a spark (to use the old metaphor) of the Divinity, yet a whole fire-grate of humanity—each therefore, will legislate for the whole, and . . . in this endless struggle of presumption, really occasioned by the every-working spark of the Universal, in the disappointments and baffled attempts of each, all are disposed to admit the *extrinsecum* of Spinoza, and recognize that reason as the highest which may not be understood as the best, but of which the concrete possession is felt to be the strongest. Then come society, habit, education, misery, intrigue, oppression, then revolution, and the circle begins anew. Each man will universalize his notions, and, yet, each is variously finite. To reconcile, therefore, is truly the work of the inspired! This is the true Atonement—that is, to reconcile the struggles of the infinitely various finite with the permanent.[17]

The Mariner's task, then, is to bear witness to that spark as both the wind and as that which loves (blesses; is compassionate) and is turned outward. He must recognize his own stalling or blocking or nonrecognition as the turn in, as facing that which withholds and kills. Confronted with the choice between life-giver and death-dealer, the everlasting yes and everlasting no as Thomas Carlyle puts it, the Mariner finally realizes there is no choice between the two because human will (a highly important concept in Böhme's thought for Coleridge[18]) and human freedom are not concerned with the work of such fine discrimination, such Kantian judgment. Rather, human will as human freedom, as Spinoza teaches, has everything to do with choosing atonement or love, which he connects to love for God as the highest form of knowledge in the last section of the *Ethics*, Part V.

How to articulate this moment of choosing, this revelatory exercise of free will, when the poet's medium is language, a tangled instrument at best? Blake used the combined arts of the visual and verbal to exploit such an entangled condition for revelatory purposes, whereas Coleridge doubles down on rhythm and rhyme, pulsations of the inspired breath, the wind combined with the fire's spark of visionary incandescence. It is to pit the "whole fire-grate of humanity" against "the every-working spark of the Universal" in order to realize "the true Atonement—that is, to reconcile the struggles of the infinitely various finite with the permanent" (*Anima Poetae* 81). To realize, then, Spinoza's "expression" as the two perceptible attributes of God, thought and things, as at once-ness and at(-)one(-)ment, is to comprehend immanent expression as the revelation of the deep relation of the myriad world of things. Deeply realized, the world of things—as tangled as language, and as entangled in the "infinitely various finite" as "with the permanent"—is finally boundless, unlimited, and unconditioned. But only if viewed correctly, or perhaps, heard correctly. For it is the Mariner's task to translate infinite diversity through narrative and repetition to those who, like himself at the start of the voyage, must be set free from their human bondage. (This is what in Book IV of the *Ethics* Spinoza calls mankind's bondage to the passions, which deter one from the divine love that is the revelatory expression of the life of things.) The auditor must, through hearing—truly hearing—turn from inward facing to outward facing and, in so doing, face love. This love is the inexpressible, the inconceivable, an intuition that is like a stunning blow: the Wedding Guest is stunned by the narrative's end, forgetting himself because no longer *in* himself through expiration.

In being tasked to convey the true reality behind the finite, the Mariner must undertake to parse metaphor. That metaphor, which I have thus far located in the poem as the wind, is more concretely embodied as the albatross. Who is this marvelous bird that the Spirit loved? It is not the great white seabird of later illustrators' imaginations, for it must hang from the Mariner's neck as punishment after the wind stalls, but it is nevertheless large.[19] Nor is it the omen of good or ill luck, since it seems to bring both or neither, a yes-no that says nothing. The Mariner is moved by the bird as chemical spark of Spinozist expression to a new stage of no-and-yes, like Böhme's primal element. Through the bird's appearing as part of his own appurtenances, the Mariner comes to realize and experience what Coleridge has discovered: how to put the mind-art of prophetic language together with the philosophical tradition that puts Kant's intellectual intuition (the intuition of the thing-in-itself) together with Spinoza's intellectual intuition as the highest form of knowledge prior to love of God. That is, Coleridge realizes how to square divine revelation with the writers that, just a few years later, he thought should belong in his library to make it properly valuable as his intellectual habiliment: "Plato, Aristotle ; Plotinus, Porphyry, Proclus : Schoolmen, Interscholastic ; Bacon, Hobbes ; Locke, Berkeley ; Leibnitz [sic], Spinoza ; Kant and the critical Fichte, and Wissenschaftslehre, Schelling, &c."[20] Eastern thought, by way of certain elements in Plotinus, Porphyry, and Leibniz, inheres in this collocation as well. By putting together philosophy as the long tradition of thought with poetry as vatic art, the Mariner realizes the past and future in the present of thusness. It is thusness that he is driven to impart to the Wedding Guest, who delusively believes that social festivity is far more important, far more compelling than the revelatory, and who is worried about time passing and the wasting of time. But it is the tale, or, rather, its telling—its orality and rhythm—that is the breath. The tale is the middle term between tradition and prophecy, between what happened to the Mariner in a strange sea and what the future does or does not hold for the Wedding Guest.

Time is, of course, one of the central metaphors of both poetry and philosophy. And time is what expressly stands still in the "Rime" once the winds have stalled. The phrase "for the time being" indicates how little tolerance the human mind has for temporal stalling, for non-movement. It is precisely because time stands still in the state of presentness that the present is realized as both infinitely here and infinitely extended. This is the condition of listening to the Mariner, of being stunned as is the Wedding Guest. Time stretches in the present moment, but if one is not attentively aware of it through constant activity, time is always already past. By wearing the albatross as his burden, and by watching his companions sicken and die as if by his own action of killing the bird (including his nephew, who in dying allegorically represents the Mariner's own death), the Mariner is positioned to attend to the present in an acute state of awareness, of time stilled: "The many men so beautiful, / And they all dead did lie! / And a million million slimy things / Liv'd on—and so did I" (IV. 238–41).

The vast sea, a time-being of enormous proportion, appears first in the nightmare vision of stalled time as a wasteland of contradiction, a non-moving ocean. What the Mariner must become attentive to is the deep relation of things in its depths and also at its surface. The sea serpents appear as the expressive force of sentient things, beautiful in their arising and breathing the world into being with him. He does not arise but remains upright; by not falling to the ground like the other sailors ("And the dead were at my feet," IV. 254), he has remained sentient and breathing. In this the bird around his neck has served him well; it is the sharp blow that wakes the vapid mind to the living spark. The bird itself, a body still resonant with life, intervenes in the oppositions of movement/stasis, life/death, and especially blindness/insight. But his awakening is simultaneously within poetic language *and* within Spinozist expression as the interrelation or geometry of things. The narratological logic is graced with Spinoza's geometrical method; the story must be retold, studied, and transmitted in its unfolding form for it to have its impact. Art and nature collude, the incorporeal and the corporeal producing revelation. The Wedding Guest takes the place of the Mariner, while the Mariner takes the place of the sea serpents: thus paired they become nondual, an intimate expression of substance. But clearly this occurrence demands the unruliness of nature to be present: this is not God's elegant plan, as in Leibniz's theory, but the interactivity of wild nature and mind in the cut that says everything.

To communicate his attestation, and the utter importance of its truth, the Mariner cannot do other than resort to narrative verse and its compelling rhythms, its breath. His force as he encounters strangers like the Wedding Guest is educative, but his agency is strange and estranged. He is much like the uninvited attendee Coleridge noticed at a German lecture: "At Göttingen, at Blumenbach's lectures on Psychology, when some anatomical preparations were being handed round, there came in and seated himself by us Englishmen a *Hospitator*, one, that is, who attends one or two lectures unbidden and unforbidden and gratis, as a stranger, and on a claim, as it were, of hospitality. This *Hospes* was the uncouthest, strangest fish, pretending to human which I ever beheld."[21] So, too, is the Mariner, uncouth and unbidden yet unforbidden, attendant on "a claim, as it were, of hospitality." Recognizably so at the kirk door, but also unbidden yet unforbidden and dependent on nature's hospitality in the vast sea of either scientized, objectified nature or resplendent, divine nature or both at once since these are perspectival versions of the same.

But how does metaphor convey what it is the Mariner experiences and what he has to relate? If metaphor is the breath, the bridging term that sparks realization between literal and ultimate reality, it helps to backtrack to what Coleridge was learning of Kant's system in Germany, but which he already knew something of in England where an article on Kant in the *Monthly Review* appeared as early as 1793, with an English translation following in 1797.[22] For Kant, reflective judgment—that bridging faculty between empirical understanding and logical reason—operates by way of an "as if" comprehension of nature's laws and reality ("as if an understanding contained the ground of the unity of the manifold of its empirical laws," *The Critique of Judgment*, 20). This is the reflective judgment at work, creating the assurance that nature is as we perceive it, and that this perception is real, even while the understanding perceives a contingency in natural phenomena. We see the river flowing, its currents ever changing the molecules making up the water and the microscopic life inhabiting it, but we judge it to be the same river day after day, the same body of water. Yet without this false reality, the truth of natural phenomena would never be known. We could never comprehend what we perceive as the "order of nature in accordance with empirical laws, and, consequently no guiding-thread for an experience that has to be brought to bear upon these in all their variety."[23] It is through the reflective judgment that what is beyond nature, the supersensible, can be intuited as beauty or as the sublime. It is the reflective judgment that is suspended in the Mariner until finally a different guiding thread—the dazzling tracks of the sea serpents—becomes apprehensible to him. And they are both beautiful *and* sublime, both natural and of the supersensible: that is, they are fully expressive. For Kant, beauty is intuited through subjective apprehension as "formal finality," whereas the sublime is intuited in the estimation of the objective "real finality" of nature (34). Both finalities are what Paul

Gordon terms "conceptless concepts" that bring together real and ideal, or particular reality and universal reality, the finite and the infinite. Spinoza provides the key for such conceptualization in Romantic thought because he links thought and thing so unequivocally as God's manifestation; each thing also exists as a thought, and both are gateways to absolute substance. For the Romantics, realizing this requires acknowledging the supreme importance of conceptless concepts.

Schelling came closer than any of the Romantics to grasping the full potential of such a principle and articulating it in a philosophically persuasive argument. And unlike Kant, Schelling locates beauty and sublimity not in an opposition but along a continuum or, like Coleridge's Mariner, in a simultaneity. Their apprehension occurs during "intellectual intuition," a term Kant borrows from Spinoza. If Spinoza defines intellectual intuition as the highest form of knowledge that leads to apprehending divinity in the deep interrelation of things, Kant changes this formulation to emphasize the objectivity of such things: it is the intuition of the thing-in-itself. Schelling takes both Spinoza and Kant further: for him, intellectual intuition is also aesthetic intuition and is the intense experience of the absolute in objective form. Later he will come to think that the absolute can only appear through a leap that breaks with absoluteness—that is, the continuity of real/ideal or finite/infinite must be broken for reality to be possible. But in his early philosophy, the real object simultaneously presents itself as materially real and (compared to ultimate reality) as therefore unreal; it is a gateway to the ultimate reality of the absolute. However, for the object to truly house both realities, it must be aesthetic, for only the artwork truly reveals ultimate truth. Moreover, the intellectual or aesthetic intuition occurs as an epiphany or *exstasis* that, in Gordon's paraphrase, "occurs in a state of union between the subject and object that is essential to art and creativity" (Gordon 93). If it is the artist's *exstasis* that allows the artwork to be envisioned and created, it is the artwork itself that is the revelation of absolute reality, absolute truth as the One. As this is a guiding principle of Romantic art, it might seem an unnecessary reminder to restate it here, except that when Wordsworth and Coleridge were hashing out the terms of their poetic endeavor in 1798, this principle was not yet available to them. Their conception of artistic inspiration would have more to do with Spinoza's intellectual intuition ("Nutting"'s spirit in the woods), since the trip to Germany was yet in the future, Schelling's *System* two years away from being published, Henry

Crabb Robinson's matriculation at the University of Jena four years away, and his essays on Kant and Schelling—and Coleridge's conversations with him about these philosophers—still further off.

What Schelling was to propound in his lectures on the philosophy of art soon after the publication of the 1800 *System* is what Coleridge seems to have already known or intuited in "The Rime": that metaphor—and more specifically, the metaphoric truth that is symbol, or the interplay of symbols that is myth—is how truth is realized and at the same time how truth co-arises with the natural world. Coleridge creates "The Rime" as both poetic art and as mythopoetry, the highest form of art for Schelling, and thus of absolute truth. It is also mind-art in the Spinozist sense of expression as revelation: reading the poem creates space for the reader to experience what the Wedding Guest does, opening up the possibility of those other divine attributes that Spinoza says are there though we can't perceive them. Surely that is what the supersensible is composed of, and what Blake says we could perceive if it weren't for the five gates of our senses that shut them off from us. It takes a mythopoetics to open up those gates, to go beyond human limitation in order to experience the infinite in the moment of recognition and present-ness. This is also the moment of freedom, or for Spinoza—and as the Mariner experiences it—the moment of abundant and generous love, the blessings on all things great and small, repellant and beautiful. Human freedom is, of course, constrained by human limitation, and is experienced as both a freedom from the passions and as a free willing to turn toward absolute freedom. Only the epiphany, the moment of awakening, can offer true access to this realm of seeming unreality that is the expression of the absolute, of substance and our substantial co-identification. Kant's "thing-in-itself," which can only be intuited but not phenomenally grasped, is what the epiphany reveals. Kant links his discovery of reflective judgment to the trifold of intellectual intuition (as the intuition of the thing-in-itself), artistic genius, and freedom (Gordon 92). In his early thought, Schelling discards this conception of the thing-in-itself, returning to Spinoza for a more expansive idea of the absolute in the relative. In the *System*, he defines the absolute as the "absolute identity" of the subjective and objective, the oneness of self and object, ideal and real. Schelling views the only fabricated object in which such an absolute identity can be revealed as the artwork. Through the artist's genius (his capacity for awakening and *ekstasis*, for being outside himself) and his creativity (which enacts freedom as the expression of the absolute), his artistic vision and prophetic sight (his intellectual intuition) can find its embodiment in the artwork. Coleridge arrives at the same conclusion in his mythic-like poem.

This absolute identity, which is the early Schelling's hallmark discovery, is what Coleridge intuits in "The Rime" through his mythopoetic use of metaphor to enunciate the time-pause of the interval, its opening into substance. But for Coleridge, the emphasis is on *natura naturans*, nature naturing in the sense of the absolute expressing itself in the relative. He would agree with Schelling, however, that art is the medium best able to gesture to the absolute through the music of poetic language and the tropes that suggest nonduality or, in Schelling's term, absolute identity. For instance, the albatross (often read as a Christ symbol) in my reading instead figures the manifestation of the breath/wind/spark. In killing the bird, the Mariner abuses his freedom, misguidedly confusing the freedom to love (to love God or Nature, it's the same thing for Romantics in the 1790s) with the freedom to act capriciously and at whim. In killing the bird, he also kills time as movement and breath, replacing the activity of the verbal breath/wind/spark with a stalling or deathlike stasis. With his death-shot, the Mariner symbolically kills the spark and thus kills the interface between the oppositional forces of yes/no, life/death, appearance/transcendence, subject/object. In this sense, the albatross's death is his own. Stalling the interplay between this and that means there is only dualism here, one in which the subject turns object. The Mariner understands himself only as object in this stalled time, this antithesis of the untimely interval but also its precipitator. In Spinozist terms, he is at the opposite affective pole from joy; drained of energizing affect, he is deadened to the immanence surrounding and involving him. The power of metaphor here, realizing the self as objective object, as thingness alone, precipitates a transformative moment of understanding, for just then the objectified becomes subjective and absolute identity is achieved; the spark occurs. The Mariner and the sea-serpents become each other, as it were, mutually blessed and blessing. The slimy things are revealed to be richly attired, "Blue, glossy green, and velvet black," and swimming in tracks that leave "a flash of golden fire," a spark of the life force (IV. 282, 283).

That metaphor is possible within the tangled condition of language, and not only possible but forceful with the force of expressive revelation, is made clear by the Wedding Guest's response at last to the Mariner's unbidden but also unforbidden narrative. He is drawn to the Mariner's strange glint that "doth make / My body and soul to be still" (V. 374–75). By the tale's end he is speechless, "like one that hath been stunn'd" (VII.

669). He must be speechless because the revelatory experience is beyond language, unutterable except by either figuration or expressive silence. What the Guest understands is that form and infinity are simultaneous, nature *and* God rather than Spinoza's "or." Figure's importance is not simply that of conveying image; it is the conveyance of the aesthetic intuition of the absolute. What Coleridge intuits is the inherent power of a poetry that tropes its own mythical status through intense rhythms, repetitions as mesmerizing effects. The Mariner's experience as a subject is transferred to the auditory reader, making us as much the object of those enchanting effects as is the Wedding Guest, and allowing us entrée to what the Mariner encounters in the dynamic spark. This is Coleridge's path to the absolute as the point of indifference between subject and object, the point at which the human ego falls away and the self-world identification can take place. The moment that the Mariner realizes that he is none other than the sea serpents is the moment that he blesses them unaware (IV. 289). Later, when the ship sinks just as the Pilot's Boat approaches, the Mariner floats on the ocean's surface (VII. 600). This is the membranous interface between depth and sky and the very surface in which the water-snakes were translated from slimy things to beauteous beings. What Coleridge articulates as a philosophical problem in the note appended to "Kubla Khan" concerning the ungraspability of the absolute (his inability to retain the dream vision after waking), and the inability to firmly locate it in poetic language other than by a series of metaphors and dream sequences finely worked out, becomes in the "Rime" a veritable grasping of the absolute as aesthetic intuition. It is rhythm and rhyme, with its terrible and translative repetitive force, and the mythic nature of a telling that must be endlessly repeated to be realized as true, that marks the major achievement of the "Rime." It is in this poem that Coleridge anticipates what he will soon value in the last section of Schelling's *System*: that it is only in art that the absolute can be made material, only in the artwork that "infinite thinking" is made visible: "It is the poetic gift, which in its primary potentiality constitutes the primordial intuition, and conversely" (*System* 230).

The artwork manifests the aesthetic absolute, beauty as truth. As Gordon notes, Schelling makes clear in the *System* that "art's relation to the absolute is not really a relation (art *and* the absolute) but, rather, its very essence (art *as* the absolute)" (116). Art expresses that terrible beauty as revealed. Philosophy fails to reveal substance as manifest expression, Schelling argues, because it is not invested in metaphor, image, rhythm, and sound; in the synergy between sound, color, and form as these create the sound-image of the absolute as the conceptless concept. If it is the task of philosophy to parse what art intuits for both Schelling and Coleridge, they both agree that it is the task of the artist to make this intuition manifest. Aesthetic intuition becomes, in this formulation, intellectual intuition in the senses meant by Spinoza and by Kant.

That is, the artwork is a profound expression of the deep interrelation of things, unknowable except through their self-expression. Conjoined, art and depicted things express the absolute identity of form and nothingness, appearance and disappearance.[24]

> I watch'd the water-snakes:
> They moved in tracks of shining white . . .
> They coil'd and swam; and every track
> Was a flash of golden fire.
> O happy living things! no tongue
> Their beauty might declare . . . . ("Rime" 274–75, 281–84)

Outward appearance of monstrosity is revealed to be its opposite, the unimaginably beautiful. The thing cannot be known as such, but it is realizable as participating in the unity of all things, its beauty manifest to those who witness. To reconcile the infinitely various, to paraphrase Coleridge's 1804 notebook entry of October 14 above, is not only "truly the work of the inspired," but is above all "the true Atonement": "that is, to reconcile the struggles of the infinitely various finite with the permanent." If the "Rime" began as a friend's nightmare combined with Wordsworth's idea of transforming that dream into a tale of crime, punishment, and atonement, it is Coleridge who saw a way to use these varied materials to create a mythic rendering of the human condition as a participatory one. It is the Mariner's atonement, his continual act of auto-narration to a participant other, that reconciles the finite with the infinite and that understands Spinoza's nature as *poeisis*: as that which unfolds as immanent bodies in full expression of their becoming. It is *natura naturans* (nature naturing) rather than *natura naturata* (nature as a done deal). As Schelling puts it: "it can be given to art alone to pacify our endless striving, and likewise to resolve the final and uttermost contradiction within us" (*System* 222), the contradiction of the negative that resists reconciliation, resists participation in the *naturans* or naturing.

But Schelling understands the identity of self and other as the indifference of the absolute in terms of self-consciousness, having inherited the model of the self as inhabited by a subjective self and an objective self (an "I" and a "me") from Fichte, whereas Coleridge is pondering a more Spinozist and Stoic conception of self-other identification. For the Mariner, the true moment in which the absolute presents itself is when he realizes his identity with the sea serpents. For Schelling, the artist is driven to creative activity because of contradiction: the urge to create must "proceed from such a feeling of inner contradiction" between conscious and unconscious activities, so that "free activity becomes involuntary" (*System* 222). The unconscious, of course, is also *natura naturans*, the becoming activity of our corporeal and incorporeal self-expression. It resists consciousness' attempts to transform *naturans* into *naturata* at every turn, but the break or cut in the "endless striving" is the artist's gift. In this way, the artwork—which expresses the identity of subject and object—combines freedom and necessity because artistic geniuses "are involuntarily driven to create their works" by "a dark unknown force which supplies the element of completeness or objectivity to the piecework of freedom." Therefore, the contradiction of conscious and involuntary but free activity "sets in motion the whole man with all his forces," which "is undoubtedly one which strikes at *the ultimate in him*, the root of his whole being" (222; emphasis his). Contradiction leads to identity through the expressive potential available to the artist. Although it is the artist who experiences this process, his is an artistic version of the Mariner's transformation from solipsism to co-identity. In this sense, Coleridge's poem is a presentiment of Schelling's aesthetic theory; as in the Mariner's vision, Schelling's footnote indicates that "the ultimate in him [the artist]" is synonymous with "the true in-itself."

However, the apparent resonance here with the initiatory scene of Coleridge's tale (the shooting of the albatross follows an unconscious urge) is skewed, for this is an act of destruction and separation, the very opposite result of the conflict between self and self-as-other Schelling envisages for the artist. What Coleridge portrays in that destructive act, instead, is the Spinozist crime of self-passion, of allowing desires and self to dictate life and death, value and worthlessness, importance and insignificance. By separating himself off from the bird's vibrancy, the Mariner separates himself from life itself, from participating actively in nature's self-realization. There is no freedom in the nightmare world that follows, signaled by the departure of the wind (the arch metaphor of both freedom and enlightened understanding); there is only dire necessity and finally death in all its hellish manifestations. Only by realizing himself as object, unable to speak or move freely, does the Mariner find himself again through the conflict of the conscious and unconscious, discovering his original, true self. That he has to suck some of his own blood to be able to cry "A sail!" (III. 153) on sighting the ghostly vessel indicates how divided from himself he had been prior to his realization. This is finally the "whole man" who, even without "all his forces," finds "the ultimate in him," the ability to recognize the absolute manifesting itself in another being: it is his moment of blessing that, in redounding back from the sea-serpent to himself, produces what Schelling calls "the feeling of an *infinite* harmony" (223; emphasis his).

This harmony is the product of the finished artwork; the Mariner experiences himself aesthetically as aesthetic intuition. It is this experience, this identity, he must—in order to atone—rehearse endlessly for each unenlightened person he encounters. It is not enough to claim that the Mariner is a figure for the artist and that his journey recounts the artistic process, as we are so tempted to do for "Kubla Khan." It is important to notice the absolute nature of the poem's truth concerning immanence and its identity of rhythmic expression with nature's expression; of the deep interrelation of things as it plays out both in the poetic stanzas and in the metaphors and images, which capture just how much the human is also the natural substance. This is no mere esoteric mystery, no simple ghost story. It is the poem's corporeal expression of "the dark unknown force" that Schelling claims "supplies the element of completeness . . . to the piece work of freedom" that is art (*System* 222).

III. Coleridge's Schelling's Spinoza and the *Biographia Literaria*

This half of the chapter focuses on Schelling's philosophy of what Wirth terms "the wild" and how it plays out in both Schelling's vision of nature and in his "speculative physics" as he conceived it. Current philosophical investigations have focused on concurrences between the speculative "nature" and "physics" of Schelling's thought and the recent directions in object-oriented ontology. Nature's "wilding" force as Schelling accounts for it in various ways provides a helpful lens for the uncontainable energy of Coleridge's supernatural as it arises in nature in "The Rime," even despite his later restraints on such wilding.

What happened between composing "The Rime" and writing his memoir/*apologia* during 1815–16? There is a clear return to politics as an element of brotherhood: the *Biographia Literaria* (c. 1815–16, pub.

1817) principally concerns Coleridge's collaboration and then rivalry with William Wordsworth. Fraternizing is accompanied by a clear turn away from a kind of gender politics in "The Rime" that casts nature as female and the human as male, a gendering so rigid that the wedding to which the Wedding Guest is being detained seems as devoid of the bride as it is devoted to the groom and his reveling friends. It is this brotherhood on land and that of the sailors aboard ship that nature's wild force calls into question. The *Biographia*'s masculinist agenda overturns this earlier gender politics, so much so that the wild force of the alterity in the "Rime" is effaced, along with the wild's deleterious effects on manly reason. Instead, the *Biographia* celebrates reason and ignores intervals of any kind, biographical or immanent. It does this even as it attempts to account for the force that compelled from Coleridge the astonishing poems of his earlier years, poems that seem to programmatically subvert the masculinist sublime as well as masculine reason: "Rime of the Ancyent Marinere," "Christabel," "Kubla Khan," "Dejection: An Ode." I would add to these Spinozist poems like "This Lime-Tree Bower My Prison," with its convoluted gender politics, and extend this grouping even to the more deliberative "France: An Ode" and "Fears in Solitude," which court the masculine sublime only to critique it. But to account for those compulsively produced poems as a response to the wild of nature, Coleridge undercuts his own re-manning by returning to Schelling, and thus to Spinoza. What begins as a rationalist project immerses him once again in his earlier engagements with alterity as immanence.

The question that inspired this self-revisitation can be posed as: what might be the force of the "anima poetæ," or soul of the poet, in a tumultuous world? The *Biographia Literaria* sets out to examine retrospectively, ruminatively, brilliantly, the seeds of this creative mind-soul in ways comparable with, and (Coleridge hopes) reparative of, Wordsworth's account in what we now know as the *Prelude*. To work out the full terms of his literary biography, Coleridge embarks on a rehearsal of the philosophical thinking that allows him to recast the poetic imagination as a powerful agent in a politically charged world. At the center of his early radical vision is an ecstatic version of the philosopher poet, the spiritualized being he had hoped Wordsworth would embody, and that the later *Biographia* still distinguishes as exemplary practice. In effect, it is Coleridge himself who best theorizes the creative imagination and best embodies it in its white-heat instantiation. Although he begins with theories of memory and associationism and moves on to post-Kantian philosophy, these are only a necessary prelude to working out his aesthetic thinking, much of which he consolidates around the contributions of Goethe, Lessing, Schiller's *Letters on Aesthetic Education*, and the Schelling of the 1800 *System of Transcendental Idealism*, thinkers who also influenced Hegel in the first course of his lectures on aesthetics in 1823.

Coleridge, like Blake, was interested in the primacy of genius and the artistic imagination for discovering the spirit at work in human creativity, and for giving much-needed weight to the power of art itself in the face of an increasingly scientifically driven society. But the Schelling of 1800, who espoused mind and nature as co-equal or as "identity," is useful to Coleridge here only in enhancing the arguments of Goethe and Schiller as Coleridge adumbrates, adapts, and transposes these into his own aesthetic theory of the secondary imagination. Indeed, he later discounts this Schelling, claiming to have been "taken in" by him in the early chapters of the *Biographia*.

At this point I'd like to introduce a risk, a "what if?" reading of the *Biographia Literaria*'s indebtedness to German Idealism. The relation is if anything a vexed one: depending on the critical lens Coleridge's treatment of these borrowed ideas is either an authentic merging of English and German Romanticisms, or out-and-out plagiarism.[25] It borders on the question of copy and imitation fundamental to discussions of artistic genius in both German and British Romanticism, a question both Schelling and Coleridge weigh in on. Let me flesh out the standard account of Coleridge's so-called loose paraphrases before posing my "what if." That account holds that Coleridge borrows, rewords, and even presents as his own Schelling's synthesis of Kant's and Fichte's thought—or rather Fichte's extension of the Kantian system. Schelling is in the position of translator, as it were, adumbrating rather than inventing his own system. Very young at this point, Schelling considers himself a follower of Fichte, completely embracing his ideas. Yet so much of Schelling's later thought is seeded here in the *System* that in no way should it be taken as merely parsing prior thought experiments. In truth, Fichte is not entirely convinced that Schelling is merely rearticulating his ideas, and feels there's some differentiation in the account, a revisionism that he's not happy about.[26] The difference here is that Schelling is clear about his translative Fichtean project, whereas Coleridge paraphrases where he should have reimagined, creating an alternative version of the Schelling-Fichte-Kant synthesis.

Like so many German intellectuals, Schelling had also been enraptured with Spinoza: indeed, the German academy was split between

Spinozists (the progressive position of Goethe, Lessing, Schelling, Hölderlin, and others) and anti-Spinozists (the reactionary and conservative elements of the academy, and Spinozist critics like Jacobi[27]) in what was known as "the pantheism controversy." For the Spinozists, what the earlier philosopher had to offer was a way out of the Kantian division of inner and outer, subject and object, a problem Fichte attempts to bridge but without success. Fichte posits the part of the self that can be scrutinized in the reflection of self-conscious thought, a "Not-I" that belongs to the "I." In recognizing the I as objectifiable, the self now has a way to comprehend other kinds of "not-I"s. But for Spinoza, asking how the self can truly know another object is the wrong question. Everything that exists is a mode of the one substance, "God" or "nature" as synonymous.

Perhaps Schelling is only putting a bit of Spinoza in his Fichtean *System* of 1800, but it seems to me that Coleridge is finding something more exciting there. My "what if?" has to do with that sense of excitement, that enlightening effect of Schelling's thought on Coleridge as he struggles to articulate the essence of his poetic creativity, its irruptive energy during his prolific early years, and his struggle to represent an alterity different from that of either the sublime or the Gothic in the "Rime." It appears that Coleridge has already sensed what Wirth has attributed to Schelling with his "practice of the wild."[28] The wild and "doing" it refers to Schelling's thought and philosophical practice after he departs from Fichte. It refers to the loss of self-consciousness when the I loses its sense of autonomy and recovers its original or vestigial self. That self resides below the level of awareness but comes into play during the flash of enlightenment that Schelling, following Spinoza, terms "joy."[29] Nature, instead of standing before us objectively (*natura naturata*), is the absolute in the midst of which we find ourselves plunged (*natura naturans*). Understanding being as dynamic for Schelling means understanding "the organic, non-mechanistic, genetic temporality of nature's coming to presence, that is, nature naturing (*natura naturans*)" (Wirth 6). In Coleridge's case, "wilding" refers to the strain of immanence that he never quite loses after the poems of *Lyrical Ballads*, created in the period of his most generative treatment of the synergy between the primary and secondary imaginations. For him, the most important point in this part of Schelling's *Naturphilosophie* is that to be thus plunged into the superabundance that is nature's becoming returns the human to its original, vestigial being. That human state of being is no different from nature's becoming, the same substance expressed differently but undifferentiated at its core. It is a state not so much of joy for Coleridge, as of mystery, the blessedness of the Mariner that might also drive one mad. It is this quality then, Coleridge's wilding, that formulates my what-if inquiry here. My project in this half of the chapter is to outline the steps that might reconstruct Coleridge's Spinozist Schelling as he makes Schelling's words his own, rather than to prove conclusively any claims about plagiarism or non-plagiarism. This will involve understanding how Schelling discovers that the original or vestigial self lies in doing-knowing as doing-art.

The texts Coleridge takes on are Schelling's *System of Transcendental Idealism (1800)* and his lectures on art given three years later. In the *System*, Schelling endeavors to turn Fichte's abstruse and constantly reworked ideas into a clearly articulated presentation: that is, Fichte's system if he had completely worked it out, a system that was to have been Kant's system if *he* had completely worked it out. Fichte and Schelling were constructing a way to bridge the subjective and objective so that Kant's transcendental synthesis was not merely the rational process of putting together concepts like quantity and space with experiential data. It was the putting together of subjective and objective from the perspective of idealism. More importantly, Schelling ends the *System* with a brief section on the aesthetic in which he revises the terms of Kant's *Critique of Judgment,* and in the process equates philosophical self-consciousness with artistic genius. Nothing could be more compelling to Coleridge than such a clear ground for thinking the philosopher-poet as realizable. The *Biographia Literaria* is a philosophical autobiography. Its very premise contains the synthesis of the rational and the experiential, but adds the very Kantian element of the aesthetic, although as poetic creativity rather than aesthetic judgment. This is an important divergence, but one already established by Schelling at the end of the *System* and in the lectures on art a few years later.

Rather than detailing how Coleridge engaged with Schelling's idealism at different points in his life and thought, and how his access to Schelling's early work and lectures through translations, interpretations, conversations and the resulting transformations formed the Coleridgean synthesis of the *Biographia Literaria*, I want to think through what Schelling's early "identity philosophy" or "ideal-realism" offers.[30] It was indubitably compelling for Dissidents such as Coleridge, and especially for Henry Crabb Robinson, who attended Schelling's lectures while a student at Jena and with whom (as well as with Ludwig Tieck) Coleridge discussed Schelling's philosophy.[31] Just as Schelling attempts to work through the contradictions in Kant and Fichte, Coleridge and Crabb Robinson along with a slew of others needed to resolve the conflict that for them similarly stopped Joseph Priestley's philosophy from being a true system. If Kant was unwilling and Fichte unable to resolve the subject-object gap, Priestley's philosophy was no stop-gap, because it also depended on an unresolved contradiction: one in which his insistence on a mechanistic universe (in which necessity meant a lack of freedom in human will) was coupled with an insistence on a miraculous God.[32] Kantianism seemed at first to offer a way out of the Priestley difficulty, but post-Kantian debates showed how unsatisfactory the refusal to account for the thing-in-itself was. Fichte's subjective idealism seemed an advance, but he too could not in the end produce a convincing model, and in any case his explanations were, like Kant's in the *Critique of Pure Reason*, notoriously difficult to make sense of. Schelling's overt appeal in the *System* of 1800 was to provide a lucid reformulation of what he conceived to be Fichte's version of a Kantian resolution of the problem in a clearly articulated and organized manner. But what was really compelling about his thought was his grappling with the question of freedom and necessity, and his theories of the status of the artwork at the end of the *System*, which anticipate his slightly later lectures on the philosophy of art at the University of Jena. On these two topics Schelling addressed issues of highest importance to Coleridge in his younger years, ones still resonant as he attempted to reconstruct his earlier thought for the *Biographia Literaria*. As he remarks, "I first found a genial coincidence with much that I had toiled out for myself, and a powerful assistance in what I had yet to do" (*Biographia* I. 160).

Therefore, my starting point for both human freedom and the aesthetic object in Schelling's early thought is not Kant; by necessity it is Spinoza, whose *Ethics* Coleridge knew, and which provided Schelling with a way to engage Fichte's thought in order to lay the ground for his own. Reduced to a mere "pantheism" (a term synonymous with atheism) in the Romantic period in both Germany and Britain, Spinoza's system as outlined in the *Ethics* is a highly developed theory of the possibility for human freedom and the role of intellectual intuition in realizing freedom of the will.[33] However mitigated Spinoza's account is by his dogmatic insistence on God as the origin of cause and effect, a chain of events whose inescapability means a universe as seemingly driven by necessity as that of Enlightenment mechanism, Spinoza was no atheist. And, despite the reductive way in which Romantics largely understood him as the philosopher of nature, Schelling's *System* reflects a deeper comprehension of the *Ethics*. Where Schelling uses a Spinozist approach to a philosophical concept (in sharp contrast to the overt attacks on Spinoza's dogmatism), we can begin to see the appeal of his accounting for the poetic imagination, and for the organic quality of the artwork.

The initial thing that stands out in the early chapters of the *System of Transcendental Idealism* is the recurring motif of a parts-to-whole that increasingly gains the character of an organic relation. This can be understood firstly in regard to Spinoza's account of the relation of bodies and the interdependence of this deep relation, and secondly to the intuitive grasp of the myriad world of things as a whole ("the wild" of Schelling's account of nature). For Spinoza, this world of things is God's "mind-world" as we are able to perceive it. Nature is God under the attribute of extension: every extended body and thing is in relation to every other thing as that which in its totality composes worldness. The human mind is able to grasp this relation insofar as thought parallels extension; therefore, everything in nature is perceivable and thinkable, or if unperceivable at least knowable because thinkable. This thinking is possible not because of the freedom of the imagination but because everything has as its corollary an idea of an extended body, an idea that other sentient beings can grasp. Higher cognitive beings such as animals grasp the idea of a thing more clearly than other beings, and humans grasp a thing's idea most clearly of all. All ideas of things are in the mind of God, including the idea of a human thought. Humans can recognize God's mind because it is perceivable through the expression of the mind-world that is nature.

The parallelism of thought and things is important not just to Coleridge's and Wordsworth's understanding of man's "second nature" but also to Schelling's identity philosophy.[34] It provides the clue to how to overcome the subject-object divide, for if an object is a finite or "fixed and static thing," the self is "*infinite activity*" (*System* 36; Schelling's emphasis). However, following Fichte, Schelling notes that the "self is intrinsically an object only *for itself*, and hence for nothing external." Moreover, "the self *becomes* an object; hence it *is* not originally an object"; becoming is an activity, so that making the subjective object propels the self into a higher mental state, that of self-consciousness in which the objective world can be grasped as part of mind-world. "If the self is originally infinite activity, it is therefore also the ground—and inner principle, of all reality" through "that action whereby the self becomes finite for itself" (36, 37). Here Schelling does not dismiss the Spinozist God so much as elide the question by promoting instead Spinoza's elliptical comments at the end of the *Ethics* concerning that part of the human mind that is infinite and thus continues when the finite parts of mind and body die.[35] Spinoza's parallelism between thought and thing becomes Schelling's idealist explanation (based on Fichte's "I" and "Not-I" account of self-consciousness) of how the human mind grounds the real world of things. It is an understanding that requires an accompanying grasp of parts-to-whole, or in Spinozist terms, the revelation of the relation of bodies and things that is the attainment of the deep interrelation of things.

For Schelling, the "I" and "Not-I" become "positing," or "self-positing," and "counterpositing," which is "the not-self" (37). Unlike Hegel's dialectic, Schelling explains that the "contradiction" of posit and counterposit produce that of infinite activity, an activity the self participates in through and as the finite "object of doing" (36). It is a contradiction in which the self "in this finitude [of the counterposit or self-as-object] *becomes* infinite to itself, *i.e* . . . it intuits itself as an *infinite becoming*" (38). Here the human mind moves into identity with the objective world, but on the condition of boundedness: "*Boundedness* (extended to infinity) *is thus the condition under which alone the self as self can be infinite*" (39). Here Schelling sounds particularly Spinozist: toward the end of the *Ethics*, Spinoza also establishes boundedness as the condition from which the highest form of human thought realizes its own freedom by recognizing God's infinitude. Form, as poets know, is the condition of true art; limitation propels the creative act. It is not hard to see the appeal of the limit-unlimited argument for the aesthetic thinker, and Schelling himself will connect the dots between boundedness and eternity with his discussion of the art object at the end of the *System*. There, in fact, he elevates the intuitive grasp of identity-difference to what only the philosophy of art (unlike rationalism, logic, or even idealism) can attain.

Coleridge's interpretation of such a transcendental conception leading into philosophy *as* art arises from Schelling's revision of his 1794 essay in which he grapples with Kant's philosophical system.[36] The problem is to adjudicate the multiplicity of the categories of the understanding with the one principle concept of relation, so that "the reduction of a multiplicity to a unity" reveals "a reciprocity of form and content."[37] One and All, multeity in unity. "A system is an organism, as it were," Michael Vater explains, "in which content and form, subject-matter and methodology . . . reflect into one another" in an "organic reciprocity." In such an organic system, a conceptual understanding Schelling continues to employ, multiple parts relate to a unifying whole not by virtue of some great chain of being but through their reflective relation (their mutual counterpositing). Most importantly, Schelling states quite early in the *System* that there is only one way in which the "simultaneously conscious and nonconscious activity" arising from the posit and counterposit tension can be exhibited in consciousness: this is "the *aesthetic*, and every work of art can be conceived only as a product of such activity.

The ideal world of art and the real world of object are therefore products of one and the same activity; "the concurrence of the two (the conscious and the nonconscious) *without* consciousness yields the real, and *with* consciousness the aesthetic world" (12). Art is produced when the original, vestigial self—the self forgetful of itself—is sourced and brought into the infinite activity of the self. When Coleridge speaks of the organic artwork and its harmonious relation of parts to the unifying whole, he is invoking not just the characterization of Kantian system in Schelling's account but also the "concurrence of the two (the conscious and the nonconscious) . . . *with* consciousness" that is productive of the aesthetic and yet parallel to the world of things. When Coleridge later refers to "multeity in unity" to explain aesthetic beauty (beauty as "the intuition of the one in the many"), he is referring to the Neoplatonism associated with Plotinus (Holmes 362), but the Schellingian, even Spinozist and Stoic undertones are there. And in the early chapters of the *Biographia*, Schelling's organicism as the reciprocal relation of part to whole holds sway. As Schelling puts it in his lectures on the philosophy of art, "The splendid German word 'imagination' [*Einbildunskraft*] actually means the power of *mutual informing into unity* [*Ineinsbildung*] upon which all creation really is based" (*The Philosophy of Art*, 32). The diverse world of things is both formed and imagined as a unity through the power of imagination (the artist's infinite activity of consciousness). For Coleridge, this is the principal achievement of the organic artwork.

In a correlative manner, we can understand Coleridge's account of the poetic imagination in relation to the artwork as drawing on Schelling's discussion of copy and imitation as generative (philosophy, he argues, is the "*free imitation*" of the original act of self-consciousness by which the I is "generated for myself at every instant") (*System* 48, 47). Both adaptations reveal how Coleridge's absorption of Schelling's work might be understood not as plagiarism but rather as the artist's use of real materials to produce something genetically through the originary self's infinite activity: that something is the philosophically transcendent aesthetic object. It is this object that the *Biographia Literaria*, despite its overt representation of Coleridge's later attitudes, still longs to recapture. In fact, it is legitimate to contextualize Coleridge's philosophical art, early and late, in terms of Schelling's philosophy of art. Much as the early Schelling understood *Naturphilosophie* as doing philosophy rather than as a "philosophy of nature" (a concept Coleridge felt he had worked through himself), he also understood artistic creation to be a form of philosophical performance in opposition to a "philosophy of art" that analyzes artistic traditions or aesthetic experience.

David Farrell Krell's investigation of Schelling's lecture "Deities of Samothrace," for instance, reveals how close Schelling came to inhabiting the art-as-philosophy paradigm. As Krell shows, this is a lecture in which mythology and revelation come together, allowing room for an interpretation of the lecture as performing that paradigm.[38] Intriguingly, it is Schelling who footnotes Coleridge in his *Historical-critical Introduction to the Philosophy of Mythology*, the late lectures delivered in 1841–54. There he gives a lengthy footnote to Lecture 8 in which he commends "the talented Brit" for having understood the "Deities of Samothrace" in an essay written for the Royal Society of Literature.[39] But Coleridge would have already seen the seeds for conceiving such a performance in the last sections of the 1800 *System*, which present art's ability to express the originary force of the poetic-creative act. It is worth commenting on it again: there, Schelling argues that the artist supersedes the philosopher in the realization of truth through the capacity to lose oneself—one's self-consciousness *and* one's conscious awareness—in artistic creation.

In his middle-period work of *Ages of the World* (c. 1809–27) and in the fictional dialogue *Clara* (c. 1810), Schelling captures the spirit of poetic artistry by way of philosophizing, though never so clearly or well as Coleridge is able to do in his meditative poems. In Coleridge's conversation poems and his rumination on the effects of analytic thought in the Dejection Ode (too much self-consciousness!), he is clearly not copying Schelling but rather realizing the idealist's paradigm. But in the supernatural poems—particularly "Rime of the Ancyent Marinere," "Christabel," and "Kubla Khan"—Coleridge puts into play the revelatory force of mythos, with its power of originary creativity, that Schelling points to at the end of the 1800 *System* and enacts in *Deities of Samothrace*. In the three poems mentioned above, Coleridge works hard to lose self-consciousness and consciousness, to allow the tension between posit and counterposit to hold sway over and against a dialectical resolution of the tension. His addendum remark that the fragment "Kubla Khan," written under the influence of laudanum, reveals a desire to lay claim to loss of self-consciousness as necessary to revelatory art. Immanence can only reveal itself in the return to unself-consciousness.

IV. Intuiting Alterity

Coleridge also wanted to lay claim to the enactment of human freedom in the production of the aesthetic object. Here too he finds sanction in Schelling, but in ways previously prepared by Spinoza in his last chapter of the *Ethics*. Human freedom for Spinoza is achievable and expressible as realization. It is not revelation so much as the highest level of mental clarity, intellectual intuition, that concerns him here. For Coleridge, perhaps the most useful concept the *Ethics* puts forward is intellectual intuition, which Spinoza calls the "third" kind of knowledge. More than the perceptive and cognitive mental activities that define the first two kinds of knowledge to lesser or greater degrees, and without being held hostage to passions that can muddy thought, intellectual intuition's primary role lies in understanding the nature of things to be interrelated and codependent. The freedom this kind of knowledge enacts is not God's freedom, or willing or willfulness, but a clarity in turning toward God and thus toward all things as these express nature and/as God.

Even in this highest kind of human knowledge, which Spinoza says arrives only with an effort of will and with a clear grasp of the first two kinds of knowledge (perception and logic) well in place, one is still engaged in a constant effort to turn aside human passions and greed to pursue a more aware inner life. What is this if not the Mariner's giving up of self, the self of his ungoverned passions responsible for his shooting of the albatross? Awareness here is reflection as it prepares one for the highest level of mental clarity that is intuitive, nonanalytic, rather than self-consciousness. Schelling, in articulating what he takes to be Fichte's main premise, comes extremely close to an idealist version of the *Ethics*' intellectual intuition. Schelling's subjective self-consciousness can attain to the level of Spinoza's rationalist self-awareness and intuition of cosmic understanding precisely because, as he explains, it combines both the conscious and unconscious minds in a dynamic process. This is a recognizable version of the Stoics' concept of immanence: the mind is both kinds of bodies, the thought-body and embodied thought, consciousness and unself-consciousness. And it is this highest intuitive understanding, this Spinozist revelation of immanence, that underlies Coleridge's poetic imagination, the very stuff of prophetic vision and artistic expression.

Coleridge, reading Schelling, re-creates the "primary Imagination" in the history of his own creative life as portrayed in the *Biographia Literaria*. The transcendental imagination is how both he and Schelling understand what is at play in Spinoza's *Natura* that intellectual intuition can grasp so clearly. In Coleridge's reading of Schelling, it is "esemplasy," the plastic imagination, or in Schelling, "Ineinsbildung."[40] All things yearn for the transcendental, procreative imagination, that which will bring them into Being through its own free choice and only after a thing's voluntary sacrifice of its selfish principle to a larger unity. The primary Imagination acts out of freedom or will, and it is for freedom that the thing willfully sacrifices itself to escape the rotary movement of necessity. Coleridge, however, grasped the plastic imagination and the primary Imagination principally as central concepts in the artist's affinity for the creative principle, whereas for Schelling, these are secondary concepts to that of eternal freedom, the pure essence of the Godhead. God creates voluntarily in an act of freedom as the will that does not will.[41] It is a creation that need not take place, and does so as an expression of joy, as "the lightening flash of freedom" (102). It is this joy at the level of the human that Spinoza intuits as ultimate knowing, resulting from the more limited human capacity for freedom.

However, the *Biographia* specifically associates human freedom with artistic generativity. Seen this way, the association of art's infinite generativity with that of nature, and art as the combined corporeal/incorporeal expression of that nature through its realizing activity, makes sense. Art is idea and intuition, material and form all directed toward expressing truth. And Schelling's nature philosophy holds a powerful key to that association: "The very idea of *Naturphilosophie* is not to define nature as a philosophical object," but rather to recover nature as "the *infinite* subject, i.e. the subject which can *never* stop being a subject, can never be lost in the object." This is not, as I've already noted, the philosophy *of* nature but "a gateway into the originating experience of philosophizing" (Wirth, *Practice* 17). As such, *Naturphilosophie* is also the gateway to the originating experience of myth-as-art, in the manner of Plato's mythmaking in the *Timaeus*, of co-creating the world by expressing infinite subjectivity *as* infinite activity and generativity. Coleridge's play with images such as the *ouroboros*, the self-consuming/self-completing snake whose conjoined mouth and tail represent both wholeness and infinity, illustrates his Schellingian understanding of both revelation and of doing. "The infinity of things," as Schelling later writes in *Ages of the World*, "is posited universally as eternity and present," as a simultaneity of being and doing that is the living universe.[42] For Schelling, this means that nature is alive; to engage philosophically with this reality is precisely what Wirth terms the "practice of the wild." Because Coleridge turns away from this practice after his radical years of prolific generativity, it is that period and his nostalgic yearning for them in the *Biographia* that best document Coleridge's experience of wilding.

For a radical poet-philosopher who wants both to practice wilding and to change the world, every activity or doing must be a form of expressing immanence. The endless notebooks Coleridge kept record this Spinozist revelation of the interrelatedness of things that is God's thought expressible in human insight. If language can't quite capture that insight, poetic language can capture or gesture toward expressive bodies.

> The western wave was all aflame,
> The day was wellnigh done!
> Almost upon the western wave
> Rested the broad, bright Sun . . . . ("Rime" 171–74)

For both Schelling and Coleridge, nature's vibrancy is its wildness; to engage that ceaseless energy of becoming as itself free is to entertain the wild, as Coleridge illustrates in the dark supernaturalism of his *Lyrical Ballad* poems, particularly the "Rime" and "Christabel." For Spinoza there is no wilding in that nature is God; however, there absolutely is *natura naturans*, or nature self-caused. And Schelling understands intellectual intuition in terms of the intuiting of *natura naturans* ("the autogenesis of being as a system of freedom," as Wirth puts it [*Practice* xiv]). For Spinoza, and Spinozists like Schelling and the radical Coleridge, nature naturing is opposed to *natura naturata*, or nature as passive object (nature natured, already created instead of endlessly becoming). The wild force of the first is opposed to how Romantics understood this second term to refer to human thought exerting control over nature, turning it into a disposable resource, something whose ruins early geologists showed was not only normative but already long underway.[43] Opposed to such ruinous rationalism is Spinoza's "intellectual intuition" as the highest form of human thought, not reason at all.

The question is, how far is intellectual intuition from artistic intuition? Or, how far is myth-as-revelation from poetic-expression-as-revelation? The distance between the two might be less than either Spinoza or Schelling thought. Coleridge seems willing—and both philosophically and artistically prepared—to unify the two ways of doing knowing that are, Schelling tells us, the highest forms of human activity: doing art and doing philosophy. The dynamic becoming of both activities is the expression that is revelation. This is the message of Coleridge's supernaturalism, but it is also the force behind "Dejection, An Ode," and other ruminations on nature-thought organicism as reciprocal interrelation. In these works of doing (productive rather than descriptive, becoming rather than passive), Coleridge is no mere parrot of Schellingian philosophy. Wherever critics come down on the question of Coleridge's borrowings as either licit or illicit, and however the question can be posed as rather one of copy and imitation, the more interesting idea lies in what it is Coleridge intuited in Schelling's early work.

More comparative then, both to Coleridge's radical period *and* to his conservative period, if more speculative, would be the Schelling Coleridge never read: that of the politically radical unpublished second version (1813) of the *Weltalter* (*The Ages of the World*), and of the subsequently conservative *Stuttgart Seminars*. Even the three available versions of the *Weltalter* taken together can be read in a light similar to Coleridge's working and reworking of the *Biographia* as first a preface to *Sibylline Leaves*, then as an expanded essay, and finally as a fully fleshed out work of autobiographical literary criticism that nevertheless, and like the *Weltalter*, is discomposed, nonlinear, organically construed. In Schelling's case, that discomposure arises not from discomfort with the material, but from the encounter with the wild as the *Weltalter* attempts to narrate and account for it. It is what Schelling calls in this text the barbaric principle, which arises from what is essentially the primordial unconscious (what Schelling terms the *Ungrund*, the unground that is prior to ground/*Grund*). The wild is, therefore, not from where joy arises as in Spinoza's intellectual intuition, but it is the source of an autogenic savage beauty, of the hidden logos or order of the Stoics. Unlike the *Logos*, the hidden logos (associated with Heraclitus's primordial fire) is the unruly.[44] It is what in nature can only be intuited aesthetically; Schelling tells us this directly, but Coleridge already knows this. In the 1800 *System*, Schelling states what is further clarified in the *Weltalter*: that nature is a poem, albeit an unself-conscious one. But it is the task of the artist and poet to re-present that logos-poem, which is why "artistic production, the creative life . . . is the zenith of human experience and the secret of all human disciplines and all human effort to master nature" (Burke 185–86).

In fact, Schelling's future direction was already a tension felt in the *System* of 1800 by a sensitive reader like Coleridge. Certainly he seems to have sensed a consanguinity, taking Schelling's lead of beginning his recapitulative project with what Schiller, according to Hegel, first articulated. Hegel explains, "It is *Schiller* who must be given great credit for breaking through the Kantian subjectivity and abstraction of thinking and for venturing on an attempt to get beyond this by intellectually grasping the unity and reconciliation as the truth and by actualizing them in artistic production" (*Aesthetics* I, 61). By combining philosophy and artistic beauty, Schiller made inroads into grasping the Concept, which is the spiritual that is "totality and reconciliation" in art (61). Schiller's subjective approach to the artistic concept, and Goethe's objective—and therefore naive and thus more successful grasp of the concept of the beautiful— are both "consideration[s] of the inner depths of the *spirit*" (61). The Schelling of the 1800 *System of Transcendental Idealism* brought this to a head. Coleridge, too, takes the lessons of Goethe, Schiller, Schelling, and Lessing to a consideration of the inner depths of the spirit as these grasp totality and reconciliation in art. Indeed, it is in the *Weltalter* versions of 1811–15 that Schelling best enacts what Coleridge finds so compelling in the *System*. In recounting the world's unaccountably ancient history as nature naturing, Schelling is concerned not with philosophizing art, but rather with putting it into practice through the form of a poetic, indeed, onto-mythical retelling of the divine spirit's prehistory. Thus, Schelling treats not of the spirit inherent in nature and art that finds its focal point in the concept, as Hegel and Coleridge understand the concept, but God's prehistory, and more specifically God's coming to *Logos*. A major difference is that Coleridge decides to work out his philosophical or critical system in the retelling of his own life, whereas Schelling tackles larger fare, working it through poetically as the prehistory of the world, as the biography of cosmic life.

As for Schelling, the *Logos* is also Coleridge's concern, although with a considerably more positive understanding of its force. Although his philosophical prehistory of the concept of the creative imagination concerns much of the *Biographia* (that agency which produces artistic beauty), it is the subjective *and* objective, self-conscious, *and* naive focus on the *Logos* and its politico-spiritual work that orients the epic of his critical life. Indeed, it is not for nothing that in 1889 the *Biographia* was published along with Coleridge's two finished Lay Sermons, both contemporary with it: *The Statesman's Manual*, the longer title of which explains that this is a manual of "the Bible the Best Guide to Political Skill and Foresight," and the second lay sermon, often titled *Blessed are ye that sow beside all waters*.[45] As these titles demonstrate, Coleridge's thinking in 1816–17 was very much concerned with the spiritual *and* political work of the creative imagination and its activation and dissemination through the word as ontoethics. Most specifically, this involves the philosophico-poetic imagination and the creating power of the logos, evinced in his projected title for another work, *Logosophia*, and in the entry in one of his notebooks: "*Logos*, the Creator! and the Evolver!"[46] By this point, Coleridge has reneged on the promise of the mythic imagination and the role of revelation suggested by the supernatural poems of his radical years, but he remains indelibly touched by his earlier practice of the wild and its ethical force.

Coleridge's embrace of the *Logos* contradicts the severity of Schelling's radical distrust of the *Logos* in the unpublished *Weltalter*, a distrust that transitions in his late period to a more conservative understanding of it as a necessary transformation of contraction into being, a kind of necessary evil as the only good possible. If the even more conservative Schelling of the *Stuttgart Seminars* coincides in certain respects with the conservative Coleridge of the *Biographia Literaria* and the lay sermons, the radical periods of both thinkers nevertheless deeply influenced their late thought. The second version of Schelling's *Weltalter*, and Coleridge's 1798 conversation poems are some of their most deeply philosophical works, continuing to haunt the later works of both thinkers, with Schelling offering a way out of this radical-conservative binary through the unpredictability of "wilding." For both thinkers, the wild generativity of their early, radical years continued to fund—perhaps in little-noticed ways—their later, more self-conscious pronouncements.

My what-if proposition frames seeing what Coleridge saw in Schelling's early writings: how to translate Spinoza's highest form of knowing—the intellectual intuition of God as/and nature—into artistic creation as the highest form of doing philosophy. This is doing-art as doing-knowing, a radical practice. If Coleridge throws off both Spinoza and Schelling after his radical period, in the *Biographia* he is still nostalgic for the state of total absorption into the vestigial, original self. It is the state so despaired of in the Dejection Ode, where an odious self-consciousness of analytic knowledge produces not-doing-art and thus not-doing-knowing. If that poem ends by recapturing the originary creative force of generative creation, nevertheless the sentiment that lingers longest is how enamored of and nostalgic for that force the despairing poet is. That the *Biographia* still longs for it is apparent in the chapters devoted to revoicing Schelling and Schelling's Spinoza, as if to re-create their original discoveries in an endless process of knowing-as-doing.

V. Gender in Effect

Knowing-as-doing might be the motto of William Wordsworth's walking tours, especially those taken with Coleridge. It is significant that the initiating spark for composing "The Rime" was a walking tour through the Quantock Hills in Somerset with both William and Dorothy Wordsworth. Ironically, their presence all but disappears as the poem takes shape. Dorothy Wordsworth's absence from so much of her brother's and Coleridge's poetry is remarkable, much more so than the few times each of them invokes her presence in their poems. Her curious position as objective-subject and subjective-object, to adapt Fichte's attempts to name agency despite the subject-object binary, is resonant in her own writing project in the Alfoxden and Grasmere journals. There, in her own version of immanence, bodies are not eclipsed or elided; instead, each one is witnessed and recorded as a participant in a community, a One. Her few poems, by contrast, illustrate her attempts to stuff herself into her brother's and Coleridge's poetics, which could not accommodate her extraordinary sensibility. "The Rime" bears witness to this incommodity by eviscerating her from the poem; like the bride of the wedding that inaugurates the poem's telling, Dorothy Wordsworth too is cut out of the picture.

It is therefore significant that the crucial figure of horror in the Mariner's nightmare experience of the void is the female Death-in-Life, while the water-snakes and other supersensible appearances are also feminized. The repressed femininity of the poem haunts its narrative in a manner familiar to readers of William Wordsworth's *The Prelude*, whereas the apotheosis of "The Rime" promises a healing of the rift between masculine and feminine life forces, as well as between the human and inhuman. This is a promise that William's masculinist project (devoted as it is to the brotherhood of poets) cannot tender.

Chapter 3 examines the way that four women writers, including Dorothy Wordsworth, represent their immanent encounters in language. Beginning with Anna Lætitia Barbauld's remarkable poems of immanence, I then examine Mary Wollstonecraft's lapses into immanent revery in her Scandinavian letters, Ann Radcliffe's immanent landscapes, and Dorothy Wordsworth's journals to argue for women writers' engagement with Stoic and Spinozist immanence. Because of the limits of educational exposure to these philosophies, only a very few women in either Britain or the continent were able to engage with ideas of immanent life. However, is it worth asking whether what these four writers reveal is a gender-influenced difference in their representations of immanent encounter. Each experiences the encounter as themselves a perceptual body; is there a real difference in their work from the great struggles of ego in Blake's mythopoetics and Coleridge's resistant mariner?

Section II

Corporeals: Embodied Difference

3

Barbauld's Sisters

Immanent Bodies

> It is true that being born requires one to breathe by oneself. Instead of teaching me how to cultivate my breathing, my culture had taught me how to suspend my breath in words, ideas, or ideals—something that led me to breathe in an artificial way and left me breathless.[1]
>
> —Luce Irigaray, *Through Vegetal Being*

George Eliot articulates a Spinozist position in *Middlemarch* when she writes that the awakened sensibility "would be like hearing the grass grow and the squirrel's heart beat, and we should die of that roar which lies on the other side of silence."[2] That roar is the equivalent of breathing fully, the kind of breathing with and into that Luce Irigaray suggests institutions teach us to forget how to do; breath and thought are separated, antagonized. Irigaray's conception of breath is extremely close to Spinoza's conception of joy: both describe that which gives life and motion; that which enjoins the all to attest to the one. Breath and hearing the intimate sounds of life are both metaphors for perceiving and expressing immanent life; receiving and yielding forth, the breath functions much as does joy. This chapter examines writers who, like Irigaray, worked with but also outside the prevailing attitudes toward nature, aesthetics, and enlightenment. They are also authors fully aware of their gendered reception by readers, and much of their clear acknowledgement of the perceptual body has to do with not needing to dramatize the defeat of the ego by immanent realization such as we saw in Blake's and Coleridge's poetry. It is not so much that because of their gender their understanding is body oriented whereas men's would not be, but that as women sensitive to nature naturing, embodied experience has fewer barriers for these four writers to break down.

Eliot is not one of the authors examined below, but her contributions offer insight into why the four authors I discuss were drawn to representing immanent life. Eliot produced the first major translation of Spinoza's works in English, and Clare Carlisle argues that Spinoza's works—especially his *Ethics*—were highly influential for Eliot's art. In particular, Carlisle suggests that for both writers, "form is essentially relational: neither Spinoza nor Eliot conceive of human beings as separate, autonomous selves."[3] This conception of form as integrated within a larger relational network means that corporeal bodies and texts, and incorporeal forms such as thoughts and emotions, interact in codependent ways. The difficulty is in opening our eyes and ears to envisioning and hearing that roar instead of whiting it out under an opaque silence of our inattentive, self-absorbed egos. Without perceptual insight, intrarelational interdependence goes unnoticed. But, Carlisle warns us, "relationality is also a matter of degree; considered in this way, it underpins an ethical principle of cognitive and affective 'enlargement of being' that is closely allied with freedom, power, and virtue—terms which are synonymous for Spinoza" (591).

During the Romantic period, one didn't have to have translated Spinoza to be affected by his philosophy, a point I discussed in chapter 1, nor did one need familiarity with Greek Stoic philosophy though the more famous names might be recognizable.[4] The well-read, the intellectually and the politically adventurous were primed for receiving millenarian and German Romantic ideas in circulation concerning Spinozist substance and Stoic embodiment. Anna Lætitia Barbauld, a highly educated Dissenter who studied the classics, and Mary Wollstonecraft, radical intellectual and Dissenting supporter, belonged to intellectual circles where these ideas were part of the larger debates on human freedom and political justice; Dorothy Wordsworth had direct access to her brother William's and Samuel T. Coleridge's discussions of Spinoza's philosophy; Ann Radcliffe was attracted to theories of alterity and was politically adventurous. While none of these women are known to have studied the Stoics or Spinoza extensively as Eliot did decades later, all of them had access to the political and ethical debates involving questions of equality based on deep interrelationality. Many of the ideas circulating in those debates directly called on Spinoza's philosophy, which itself was steeped in Stoic theories of embodied life, both corporeal and incorporeal entities, and how they affect each other.

One goal of this chapter is to push further the question of whether women writers of the period experienced or represented their experience of immanence differently from men writers, not so much in tune with Barbara Freeman's notion of a "feminine sublime," but to ask if immanent alterity might not be so traumatic an encounter for women as for men? Do women artists sensitive to the beingness of nature and natural objects relate to immanence differently, recognizing aspects of interrelationality that are analogous in some way to their domestic and familial networks of meaning? We saw that for Blake the realization that comes from immanence for male artists like Los is that the ego must give up the contest for dominance; sacrificing the ego is the only way into immanent life. For Coleridge's Mariner, immanent realization both shatters his ego and proves world-altering. Is the same ego trauma requisite for all artists? Might women experiencing immanent alterity find a different path from the ego's oppositions to enlightened nondualism? After examining four Romantic women writers' engagement with immanence, I return to this question of a gendered immanent encounter. One strong argument for finding a gendered difference in the experience is women's relation to their bodies as perceptual instruments, allowing them to overstep the initial resistance to bodily knowledge by ego projection that both Blake and Coleridge portray. Blake and Coleridge both appeared to view the body as embattled, and Blake's five sensory gates represent this: sensory gates that filter and block out "true" or illumined perception, with the nostrils—organs of breath and scent—particularly shut off. "The ever-varying spiral ascents to the Heavens of Heavens / Were bended downward, and the nostrils' golden gates shut, / Turn'd outward, barr'd, and petrify'd against the Infinite."[5] Immanent encounter reinvigorates the breath for those attuned to their bodies, opening the petrified senses to the infinite now; this is a realization Coleridge's Mariner is gladdened to have. My sense, which I explore in a later section, is that Dorothy Wordsworth in particular already has awareness of this attuned breath as part of the body's metrical alignment with immanent rhythms.

Bodies are integral to both Stoic and Spinozist thought and are what differentiate immanence from the sublime. If the sublime is transcendence of bodies and thought into the absolute, immanence is what integrates bodies and ideas at the deepest levels. How one perceives one's world either opens one up to immanent experience or closes that world down, as in Blake's mind-forged manacles and petrified senses. Importantly, it is the body that can truly perceive by going beyond the five senses through rhythm and breath, opening itself to immanent life. It is bodily felt sense and not Cartesian rationality with its preformed structures that leads to enlightenment; this is not to deny the illumination brought on by the sublime, in which the body is left behind, but to recognize the sublime's counterpart in immanence. The women writers I investigate in this chapter take the perceiving body as their poetic instrument for the enlargement of being: for realizing the interrelationality of all things including the perceiver. They do so in the project of bearing witness to and participating in an immanence that roars with life, that is gloriously there announcing itself. For writers such as Barbauld and Dorothy Wordsworth, this is both an ethical and ontoethical project: for writers such as Radcliffe and Wollstonecraft, immanence must contend with the more spectacular sublime that demands to be noticed. What begins with embodiment is dimmed, losing its force through a default aesthetic distancing for the two latter writers, and for Barbauld, immanence must give way to Christian divinity as a kind of necessitated pendulum swing between the two. For Dorothy Wordsworth, embodiment drowns out sublime ideology, and try as she might, immanence is the alterity she is attuned to and not her brother's sublime specialty. She perhaps had the most engaged exposure to Spinozist ideas along with the Stoic concepts Spinoza absorbed because of William's and Coleridge's intense discussions of Spinoza in their early years together. I therefore discuss Dorothy Wordsworth's works more extensively, as she is the woman artist best positioned to recognize and explore immanent life in her writing.

I. Barbauld's Expression

The earliest writer of the four women artists I explore in this chapter, Anna Barbauld provides my starting point for thinking about how women related to immanent alterity during the period. "A Summer Evening's Meditation" (1773) is an ode that intermingles allegory, meditation, immanence, and the divine to produce an early version of the Romantic ode that Coleridge and William Wordsworth would later make their own. The allegorical mix of Grecian, astronomical, and conceptual figures provide a backdrop or tapestry against which the speaker's mind and the night sky merge. This sets the conditions for an immanent space, an interval in which immanent expression can arise. Qualifying and disrupting this space is obligation, a fealty to patriarchal representation and to God. Allegory might give way to the space of immanence, as it does in Blake's mythopoetics, but for Barbauld the allegory has too many allegiances to neoclassical poetry and Baroque formulations. These are not her own but borrowed figurations (not zoas but "Contemplation," "Fancy," and "Time") and prosopopoeia, as when the sun is described as the "sultry tyrant of the south," who "Has spent his short-lived rage" (1–2). With these inherited guidewires to direct the speaker's thought, including frequent interruptive tributes to the divine, the interval movement of mind and sky toward an emergence of immanence is made restless, disruptive, and interruptive. Whenever mind and sky do begin to turn into each other, to merge into immanence, they are pulled apart again by a return to self-conscious elements such as prosopopoeia. Nevertheless, when a passage in the ode rises to immanent experience—even though it will be soon unsettled—the expression is that of immanent life.

Some of the most intense lines of "Summer Evening's Meditation" are those of immanence:

> one by one, the living eyes of heaven
> Awake, quick kindling o'er the face of ether
> One boundless blaze; ten thousand trembling fires,
> And dancing lustres, where the unsteady eye,
> Restless and dazzled, wanders unconfined
> O'er all this field of glories . . . (Barbauld 25–30)

Almost immediately this emergence of immanence is shut down by "And worthy of the Master: he, whose hand / With hieroglyphics elder than the Nile / Inscribed the mystic tablet, hung on high" (30–35), with a move both internal (praise of the divine) and backward (Egyptian antiquity), both moves related to the sublime. Nevertheless, there it is, immanent life replete with "dancing lustres" that turn the eye "Restless" as it follows the interval's dance between the turn away and the turn toward. What else is immanence but "living eyes," "trembling fires," a "boundless blaze" of life in the boundless field?

Further down in the poem the speaker again merges with the sky for a moment, witnessing its immanence as embodied, immediate, unfiltered:

> How deep the silence, yet how loud the praise!
> But are they silent all? or is there not
> A tongue in every star, that talks with man,
> And woos him to be wise? (47–50)

This revelatory audition is even more quickly clamped down by the "noon of thought" (51) and an allegorical "Wisdom." But within these four lines the "living eyes" are now tongues, the boundless blaze now a song—or is it the roar on the other side of silence? Its praise is ambiguous, leaving open the implication that it is a song of itself and not necessarily praise of a Christian deity. Although this song turns to human-centered speech, it also "woos" as its love reaches out to teach the wisdom of the absolute; it is a song of love that is the harmony of all things. At midnight it is hard to recall that it's not just the night sky but life itself that deafens with its roar lying just below silence, just beyond the gap between self-enclosing, but also self-limiting human, and an externalized world.

II. Radcliffe's Rapture, Wollstonecraft's Breath

Ann Radcliffe, best known for gothic novels that supplant the horror of gothics such as *The Monk* with sublime landscapes, also saturated her novels with verse, much of which she wrote herself. Immersed in poetry, her heroines use nature's sublimity to challenge the master narratives urged against them: that the forces of greed and lust each heroine struggles against are fated to win while she will be victim, not hero. The natural landscape plays out the affective fields of terror and love and the aesthetic fields of beauty and sublimity. The reader learns to trust the heroine's instincts as much through natural settings and her response to them as through clues about the villain's intentions. In the play between verse and prose, Radcliffe dallies with the immanent life of the forested land as it opposes the melodramatic and nightmare scenario the heroine is forced to navigate.

My key text here is *Romance of the Forest* (1791), written in the wake of the storming of the Bastille and the march on Versailles. As Jonathan Dent notes, "With the Revolution in its infancy in the early 1790s and its as yet unresolved 'plot' twisting and turning like that of a Gothic novel, it was proving difficult to historicise or contextualise this historical phenomenon."[6] Radcliffe's protagonist, Adeline, finds her story unfolding in trickster ways much like the revolution's plot: empty promises and hidden threats, tyrants and turncoats, with no end in sight. As Edmund Burke wrote of the Revolution, "Every thing seems out of nature in this strange chaos of levity and ferocity" (qtd. in Dent 156). As theorizer of both the French Revolution and the beautiful and sublime, Burke supplies the roadmap for thinking how the two fields of politics and aesthetics might fit together, but Radcliffe tracks a different path. Others might think the Revolution sublime, but she is more concerned about things seeming "out of nature."

Radcliffe allows politics to be the field of human greed and desire but keeps aesthetics for nature where things are steeped in their place. Even when human art seems most aesthetic, as when Adeline is abducted to the Marquis' pleasure villa and finds herself in a banquet hall that might be straight out of *The Faerie Queene* with its walls "painted in fresco, representing scenes from Ovid, and up above with silk drawn up in festoons and richly fringed" (156), it is deceitful, hiding danger. Silken sofas, pier glass mirrors, and flowers everywhere disguise the real threat of the Marquis' desire, his greed and hate wrapped into one soft package, and delivered with a carpe diem lyric. This is an aesthetic that Adeline finds suffocating, and when she escapes out her bedroom window it is as much that overpoweringly sensual room as the Marquis she is escaping. Even then, she finds herself in a garden "more resembling an English pleasure ground" than a French garden; that is, designed for allurement, not contemplation (164). The woods, too, are full of menace because they belong to the Marquis' estate, and even when they produce her rescuer, Theodore, it is by way of a nightmarish, unaesthetic scene of shadows and pursuit.

In contrast, once Adeline's story turns more positive, so too does the landscape. Now in Savoy at a small chateau, Adeline finds herself in the sublimity of the Alps, whose "deep solitude" and "solemn and tremendous scenery" evoke the sublime for readers (246). But the experience is descriptive rather than experiential; the adjective "sublime" is used multiple times without any evidence that Adeline is actually struck by it. Rather, she responds to it through the aesthetic distance that Kant's faculty of judgment requires instead of Burkean immediacy. But one night when she walks to a favorite spot overlooking the lake with the "stupendous mountains that environed it" (261), Adeline experiences immanence: "A few ragged thorns grew from the precipice beneath, which descended perpendicularly to the water's edge; and above rose a thick wood of larch, pine, and fir, intermingled with some chestnut and mountain ash. The evening was fine, and the air so still, that it scarcely waved the light leaves of the trees around, or rimpled [sic] the board expanse of the waters below. Adeline gazed on the scene with a kind of still rapture" (Radcliffe 261). Instead of the broad brushstroke used to represent sublime scenes, here each entity is named and placed within the web of relation. The trees are differentiated—thorn, larch, pine, fir, chestnut, ash—and placed: perpendicular or intermingled, singular or thickly settled. The air, water, and tree leaves merge and discriminate as all are "rimpled" or gently moved, ruffled. Adeline herself is pulled into this immanent life "with a kind of still rapture," the work of immanent engagement within this interval of stilled time and non-movement that evokes a verse concerning "the tranquil mind" (262). This is not the sublime strike, the transcendent experience of awe, but rather the realization of nature as *Deus sive Natura*, nature in its place with a human relationality fully implicated within. Immanent nature is a source of comfort and truth for Adeline, where human dissembling can't compete with the vibrant life at hand. By contrast, the sublime is either an invitation to self-centered thoughts ("But her chief amusement was to wander among the sublime scenery . . . whose grandeur assisted and soothed the melancholy of her heart," 260) or an aesthetic experience ("'The view of these objects . . . life the soul to their Great Author, and we contemplate with a feeling almost too vast for humanity,'" 265).

In Mary Wollstonecraft's *Letters Written in Sweden, Norway, and Denmark* (1796), the sublime is also a nearly textbook rendition of aesthetic distance, with a Burkean desire to catalog the scenery into picturesque, beautiful, or sublime. But like Radcliffe's heroine, Wollstonecraft, too, discovers in nature something more intimate and vibrant. For her, the breath is the link between her inner darkness and the landscape she encounters. It is what allows her to escape the logic of category and immerse herself in a landscape whose intimate elements reveal themselves to her. The distinction for Wollstonecraft can be found in whether she consciously draws on metaphoric description and prosopopoeia or loses herself in the attempt to re-create in language the immanent experience.

In Letter V, for instance, Wollstonecraft writes, "Approaching the frontiers, consequently the sea, nature resumed an aspect ruder and ruder, or rather seemed the bones of the world waiting to be clothed with every thing necessary to give life and beauty. Still it was sublime" (*Letters* 28). A bit further on, she writes, "The rocks which tossed their fantastic heads so high were often covered with pines and firs, varied in the most picturesque manner" (29). There are many passages like this in the *Letters* where she is showing her aptitude for travel writing and her familiarity with the aesthetic categories. But elsewhere Wollstonecraft allows herself a less mitigated, filtered encounter with the land and seascapes. "Sheltered from the north and eastern winds, nothing can exceed the salubrity, the soft freshness of the western gales. In the evening they also die away; the aspen leaves tremble into stillness, and reposing nature seems to be warmed by the moon, which here assumes a genial aspect; and if a light shower has chanced to fall with the sun, the juniper, the underwood of the forest, exhales a wild perfume" (*Letters* 39). Here the wind is like the breath as she breathes in what the forest exhales.[7] The elements of the scene are named and attended to, their dynamism and stillness two sides of the same coin, trembling into stillness. Gales have a fresh softness, so that again the polarity is felt and revealed as one thing only. This is the perceiving body at work, without the discriminating mind attempting to fit the scenery into prescribed slots of beauty and picture, aesthetic and religious. Yet, like Radcliffe, Wollstonecraft cannot rest with immanent life for long. She must show Imlay, her erstwhile lover and addressee, as well as the general reader, that she is versed in aesthetic theory. Just after the juniper "exhales a wild perfume" in the passage above, she writes, "Nature is the nurse of sentiment,—the true source of taste;—yet what misery, as well as rapture, is produced by a quick perception of the beautiful and sublime" (39). That she had not been describing either beautiful or sublime landscape does not impede her encomium of nature and the requisite nod to nature's impact on the affections.

So frequently does Wollstonecraft break the "rapture" of the immanent scene with metacommentary on morality, aesthetics, and her own melancholy that her letters provide an analog to Blake's narrative intervals. As for Blake, Wollstonecraft repeatedly depicts the struggle between ego-centered thoughts and opening up to immanence. The give and take of the interval maps onto her descriptive writing in a manner so clearly that of the interval that the scenic passages provide vivid examples of encountering Stoic and Spinozist substance. It is as if she knows this strand of philosophy as well as she knows her Burke and other contemporaries. Had Wollstonecraft allowed herself to stay immersed in the immanent encounter, she would have prescribed Dorothy Wordsworth's journal writing. As it is, she anticipates it, most particularly in her sensitivity to wind and breath, exhales and trembling stillness.

The arc of this chapter, from Barbauld's night sky in which immanence is located in the interval of intimate reflection, to Radcliffe's and Wollstonecraft's discovery of a nature more inclined to immanence than the distant sublime scenery would suggest, leads to Dorothy Wordsworth's journals, in which she tries hard to find sublimity but discovers immanence a more accessible, substantive, and intimate alterity. For all four writers, the sublime directs their gaze, but immanent life is what they find; and for all four, it is the perceiving body that allows immanence to arise as an Otherness that incorporates the body as one more relational and integrated component of the entirety. The perceiver realizes she is part of the All that makes up the One, and in that realization she is enlightened by what Radcliffe calls "a kind of still rapture" (261). This is an affective stance that for Dorothy Wordsworth isn't mobile enough to match the vibrant life she finds and enters into as a Spinozist realization of nature.

III. Dorothy Wordsworth's Immanence

Arguing for women's use of prose fiction to represent sublime experience, Freeman notes that "The sublime of Wordsworth, Coleridge, Keats, and Shelley finds its most typical formulation in epic or narrative, rather than lyric poetry, yet there is nothing inherent in the genre of poetry that makes it uniquely suited to or evocative of the sublime" (*Feminine Sublime* 8). I would go further: no ordinary prose can convey revelation because it is the word-image of poetic language, however it appears—in epic, lyric, or prose—that best captures nonlogical, epiphanic, nondualistic experiences. Nothing dictates that epic or narrative verse is alone the terrain of the sublime, particularly because the Romantic ode was the lyric form more typically associated with the sublime. But Freeman goes a step too far when she claims that "The genre of sublime poetry was effectively closed to women. Dorothy Wordsworth, or any woman of her period, could not have written a poem such as 'Tintern Abbey'" (8). Although Freeman's claims that Dorothy Wordsworth, unlike her brother, could not have written a poem such as "Tintern Abbey" rings true, I wonder if the reason is less the genre—an irregular ode such as Barbauld did undertake—and more because the speaker of William's ode addresses Dorothy in the poem, encoding her as a silent witness to his painful revelation. This insistence that the sublime moment capture everything *except* her may be the real reason she would not have written such a poem of sublime exclusivity, rather than immanent inclusivity. Perhaps because Freeman doesn't consider Dorothy Wordsworth's own poetic prose for evidence of whether this particular woman writer did attempt the sublime, she finds no evidence of a different kind of alterity represented there. The different alterity to be found in the journals is not the feminine sublime of Freeman's argument, although not so very different either, but the Spinozist and Stoic immanence of William's and Coleridge's nature philosophy.

The main difference between Romantic conceptions of the sublime and Romantic conceptions of immanence have to do with the former's emphasis on gaining or giving up mastery and the latter's having to do with the non-separation between self and other, thought and action, idea and being, art and nature. The sublime locates the terror of alterity; immanence locates its intimacy. In this sense, Keats's and Coleridge's different sense of the sublime as that which extinguishes self and identity rather than, as for Wordsworth, giving it mastery is still far different from Romantic immanence. Immanence incorporates the self and levels the ontological field. All things, all beings participate in immanence; all particles, all particulars are also the shared commonality of all being. This is the felt sense of Dorothy Wordsworth's best journal entries.

Dorothy Wordsworth's poetic sensibility merges with and emerges from her habitude, her inhabiting, her self-inclusion that escorts her through Alfoxden and then Grasmere and Lake District landscapes that permeate her sensibility as much as they permit her to seep into their sensuousness, but also their discreteness. In contrast to her journals covering the trip to Germany with William, especially the Hamberg journal where mostly towns and cities are her subject—and are found wanting—the Lake District is ever alive. If German cities they visited are all like Brunswick, "an old, silent and dull looking place," so too is the landscape. Even the roads were typically "miserably bad," while inns and palaces alike are alienating.[8] But in the Lakes, she is ever alert to the singularity of each thing, never lulled into seeing sameness or an overgeneralizing dullness. Even as she identifies something botanically or by its local name, in her attentive witnessing each entity resists becoming merely one of many, subsumed to anything larger than itself. That is, in this place where she finds belonging she understands category not as an issue of scale but merely as a way to greet other entities, to call them by name, to appreciate a particular greenness or silvery hue, and to merge with them sensually, perceptually, emotionally so that the lake "looked to me I knew not why dull and melancholy" in the first, and unhappy, entry of the *Journal* as an unpausing roll of expressible self-other feeling. Her writing, the journal writing much more than the few poems we know that she wrote, respects these forms of attention and develops thereby a poetic attitude and style that is appreciably materialist yet also sensitive to alterity as inhabiting vegetal being. "The Fern of the mountains now spreads yellow veins among the trees," she writes in a typical entry, "The coppice wood turns brown." By contrast, in the same entry she records some of William's observations made on the same walk, which are "affecting little things": "a decayed house with this inscription . . . in the church-yard, the tall silent rocks seen thro' the broken windows" (Friday, 12 Sep.). Whereas his attention is turned toward the human and the pathos this evokes in himself, I consider her nature writing to invoke both not-human and not-I at once, without the problem of ego intruding for either herself or what she witnesses. She locates herself and her perceiving eye in herself as subjective-object, a body-mind that recognizes agency all around itself, meeting it on equal ground as object to object.[9]

Immanent alterity is different from transcendent forms of alterity that resist language (the sublime's awe-filled silence, the speech-robbing terror of the Gothic, the illegibility of the Oriental) in that it makes sense through what human thoughts find expressed by encountered bodies. In the othered thing, object, or body, the aesthetic mediation necessary for the picturesque, beautiful, and sublime is missing here; immanent life requires recognizing one's own participation in it. And it requires finding a way to put into words what the encounter reveals—not to give it meaning but to recognize its expression of immanent substance. We might think of this as nature writing at its non–self-conscious best, where the distancing of aesthetic would miss the point. Bearing witness, giving homage: these are ways of engaging in immanent expression rather than giving voice *to*, speaking *for*. As a mode without aesthetic distance or judgment, immanent alterity is felt in the perceiving body as the other bodies joining in the intimacy express themselves as dynamically there. That vibrance has some relation to the theories of sympathy and vitalism of the day, but its difference lies in the *hen kai pan*. It is the activity of the molecules that the Greeks called atoms and Spinoza called bodies, ever moving, ever expressing their substance, ever affecting other atoms or bodies in the One and All.[10]

The "I knew not why" of the first Grasmere entry relates the unknowability of the immanent encounter while maintaining its expressiveness; the sentence is beautiful not because of poetic mastery but because it matches the idea embodied in the scene, its reflection of the whole. When one reads *The Grasmere Journal* as aestheticized nature writing, it becomes difficult to pinpoint what is going on. A comparison with William Wordsworth's *A Guide to the Lakes* seems to show the *Journal*'s accomplishment in a lesser light, as if its author had only partially mastered how to engage with the aesthetic. This section attends to how Dorothy Wordsworth as a perceptual body relates what natural bodies, nonhuman and human, express as their participation in immanence. Together, passages containing this kind of writing constitute a series of small revelations. What is different in her journal writing from the poetry and poetic prose of the women writers discussed above is that immanent life gains her full attention, unbroken by a need to prove familiarity with the aesthetic demands of the sublime or picturesque. Indeed, critical distance is the inverse of her intimate approach, her absorption into the landscape, and that landscape as inclusive and yet particular.

Dorothy Wordsworth's practice calls on a sensibility that, as much as it is informed by Coleridge's and William's intense debates about the primacy of the imagination over the fancy (the fancy, she believed, was where she could best contribute to the joint project of these poet-brothers[11]), was even more informed by her own experiments in participatory bodies. Without trying to prove what Dorothy Wordsworth did and did not absorb from her brother's discussions with Coleridge and others about Spinoza and Greek thought—discussions to which she was so frequently privy—I take the congruity between her writing practice and these earlier philosophers as her response to the concept of embodied perception. Life as an urgent matter of becoming, an ongoing dynamic existence, provides a unique opportunity for exploring nature's mobile beauty, and it was revelatory. What is missing from her nature writing is the spiritual element that so concerns William Wordsworth's own poetry. She does not attribute a vitalist spark or soul to the vegetal bodies she attends to in her writing because they need no translation into a human-centered ontology.[12] They are simply present in a particular moment and location. Moreover, awareness of her status as a woman creates a breathing space between William's concern with the expectations of high literary achievement and poetic authority. In this breathing space or interval, walking as an awakening to vegetal bodies provides dynamic movement and being entirely present, aware. This breathing space of awareness is purely local, found in small patches on her walks and unalloyed with meditations of past or future events. Instead, the intervals of nature-engagement nurse a communal poetic expression of the bodies involved. So many journal entries indicate walking, often as a back-and-forthing: "We walked into Easedale. . . Walked backwards and forwards between Goody Bridge and

Butterlip How" (2 Feb. 1801). As such, the interval is restless, expressing Spinoza's concept of cosmic rhythm in the attraction and resistance of bodies. The encounters are neither static nor aesthetically separated from the viewing self, and the breath involves a dilation and contraction that expresses how bodies affect and involve each other.

The breath as it relates to the conditions of embodiment is more than rhythm, however; for the Stoics, it is the local version of the divine breath, *pneuma*. Pneuma animates the living world, they held; it is "the active and rational principle of the universe . . . and enables the world to be regarded as a living thing" (Grosz 22–23). The breath is how the many becomes the All-in-One. It is apparent in the famous daffodil entry of April 15, 1802:

> Mrs. Clarkson went a short way with us, but turned back. The wind was furious, and we thought we must have returned. We first rested in the large boathouse, then under a furze bush opposite Mr. Clarkson's . . . I never saw daffodils so beautiful. They grew among the mossy stones about and above them; some rested their heads upon these stones, as on a pillow, for weariness; and the rest tossed and reeled and danced, and seemed as if they verily laughed with the wind, that blew upon them over the lake; they looked so gay, ever glancing, ever changing. This wind blew directly over the lake to them.

The breath is the wind, which exhilarates and exhausts: people walk and rest, flowers dance and rest. The breath is the daffodils in community, the humans in community with them, the lake participating in the breathing wind. The breath as dilating-contracting rhythms characterizes the restless interval and is more than a passage: it is that which passes through. Dorothy Wordsworth's nature walking is a practice of passing-through the categorical largeness of the One as Nature into the particularity of the All. Each particular body participates in the One but as an entity in the communal scene. So often this passing-through takes place in wind: "A whirlwind came that tossed about the leaves" (8 Nov. 1800), "The wind was up, the [lake] waters sounding" (26 Dec. 1801), "Rydale vale was full of life and motion. The wind blew briskly" (18 Mar. 1802). Passing-through occurs in the walked interval of breath even as it is the space of passage.

Although Julia Kristeva's theory of poetic language has helped me discover how the complexities of Dorothy Wordsworth's writing produce her unique subjectivity because it focuses on bodily rhythms and sound formations,[13] I want to turn here to the Greek Stoic understanding of the interval as the transition between habitable space and uninhabited void. This is how I understand scenic description in the *Journals* that captures a sense of communal being; various vegetal bodies are attested to but only as elements within the inclusivity of this or that patch of the locale. The interval is the place of becoming, of the All-One; as a concept it provides a way to understand those passages that incorporate poetic language as immanent expression. Here, the interval is not the stalled time of non-movement as for Coleridge's Mariner, but the dynamic pause between what-was and the to-come. This is movement as creation, the interval that is the *chora*. It is an extra-materialism, an immanence inherent in the material, as well as Spinoza's sense of immanence, so important to the Romantics, in which he raises immanence to "the orientation of substance itself" (Grosz 54). Spinoza's theory of substance as it is explicated in bodies involves the infinite in the finite. In his conception, the world is "immanent to itself" because ideality and materiality are involved, entered into and through each other. Thought *or* extension are both the same, each immanent in the other and both expressing the same thing. The substance of which all things are composed is "explicated" by God's attributes (thought and bodies, ideality and materiality).[14] For Spinoza, this is the Word and its adjectives realized. *The Grasmere Journal* treats the problem of substance as the communal "univocity" of thought and extension.[15] The journal is unconcerned with flights of the imagination, rending judgment, projecting meanings on things, or imposing the authorial self in terms of a "composition." Instead, natural bodies compose or constitute themselves as she encounters them by chance during local walks; these are bodies that share a univocity of corporeal being, of bodily expressibility.

Where Dorothy Wordsworth's aesthetics and natural philosophy align with composition is close to what Jane Bennett's speculative realism theorizes in its focus on the vibrant life of assemblages, uncomposed groupings, and heaped collectivities. I would add to these the mobile, living environment through which the subject itself moves and lives, an environment that comprised the signally impactful world of Dorothy Wordsworth's experiential ontoethics and the intervals of encounter. Her experiencing of the natural world can be described as an immersive practice, but one that never loses contact with the subjective center. It is not a self-loss but a participatory inclusion that opens itself up to a borderless state. On March 24, 1798, she writes that spring "advance[s] very slowly, no green trees, the hedges leafless; nothing green but the brambles that still retain their old leaves, the evergreens, and the palms." Yet suddenly, this: "The crooked arm of the old oak tree points upwards towards the moon." This sudden irruption of alterity into the assemblage of the not-quite-greenness of a tardy spring is not commented on or differentiated from the listing of the previous sentence. What allows for it to take place here is not hospitality but rather a wonderment, an *in-relation-with* that understands that more than one entity stands in relation, and that the co-presence is layered and deep in the most Spinozist sense of revelation as the deep interrelation of bodies and things.[16] The tree's crooked limb expresses the moon, expresses the tardy spring, expresses Nature's force. What can evoke nature's self-actualizing in this encounter is the stretched time of the passage, allowing the full sensing of what it is to be in among the other bodies also moving in this location. These discrete moments of witness within the larger environment in which a daily walk might participate undo the egocentric division of human concerns and "nature," allowing for a more intimate awareness of natural bodies within their communities. In order to represent this more ontoethical perception of vegetal bodies, I use the terms "the surrounds" and "environs" to more accurately describe Dorothy Wordsworth's encounters with immanent life.

One aspect of such a provisionary depiction of what "environment" can mean in Dorothy Wordsworth's opening up to the event of encounter is the expectation of biological homeostasis. Although we expect balance in nature, an immanent encounter can reveal something different: a deep interrelation of substance that nevertheless demonstrates a homeostatic imbalance. The human reaction is often shock at the intrusion of "reality" in nature's harmony. But in immanent life, disease and disharmony are also included, as much a part of nature as is beauty. The journal entries pay testament to nature's traumatic aspects, such as becoming fatally lost in a snowstorm, and immanence shares this with the sublime, but not as a transcendent awfulness.[17] This is simply what is; trauma and death are included in the One. Dorothy Wordsworth's environmental engagements are not produced by purposeful quests for homeostasis; nor does she represent human intrusions as unnatural. The human is as much a part of the chance encounter as the tree or lake; the stranger is strange in this immanent sense of alterity. However, the human almost always provokes dutiful description rather than a recording of immanent expression.

In this way the journals enact what Hegel theorizes when he describes the dialectical movement of thought from its initial stage to a clear idea with some truth value.[18] In Spinozist terms, its movement is away from the confused thoughts of human-centered activity toward the intellectual intuition of deep interrelation. Her passages of encounter evince *truth* in a manner unrelated to facts or veracity; they are passages of enlightened being. This is helpful for understanding how the ground and the grounded can veil, come to the fore, or merge with each other in an immanent encounter. What we see in the journal entries is that in normal experiences of nature, the tree or moss is present as immediately so, nothing veiled. But they participate in a larger whole, are not yet grasped minutely as particularities. As such, these natural bodies are recorded but not attentively so. In immanent encounters, however, the unity of form and matter as bodily object pulls apart to reveal an unconditioned and absolute truth lying behind the grounded thing: the truth of immanence as the ideal in the material body. Ground literally dissolves as Spinozist substance comes to the fore, the universal matter that connects and involves us all in each other as participants in the unconditioned whole. In the realization of this whole lies what Spinoza calls clear and adequate ideas.

How clear and adequate ideas of communities or assemblages of natural bodies conflict with received ideas of the self is something that the journals represent through an alternation between diligent fact recording and inspired writing. Neither type of writing in the journal entries represents the Lockean self-interested body or sovereign subject who walks alone, protected by his boundaries and balances, stabilized by his dominant position regarding otherness in all its human and material forms, and alterity in his spiritual relations.[19] What might it mean, then, to consider the perceiving body as that which makes room for less form and information by inhabiting a between-space or in-between that is not sovereign or self-interested?[20] Such a question opens up the boundaries between self and other to locate what exists: between those two entities; how they involve each other; and how each can reveal the other's entanglement in its immanence. The journal entries bear witness to what Donna Haraway terms a "sympoiesis" of bodies in moments of an assemblage-becoming.[21] Arguably Dorothy Wordsworth used nature to unbind herself from the constraints of a Lockean individuality based on self-possession and others' otherness, such as characterizes her brother's poetry. I want to suggest that the position of being in-relation-with was the most flexible counter to solipsistic sovereignty. This is the relational dynamic I read as allowing the harmonies of the encounters with nature she experienced outside the home and recorded in her Alfoxden and Grasmere journals.

The journal entries do not represent or reimagine the encounters with nature, or attempt to capture them, but act instead as field notes to the immediacy of the encounter, helping to remember or repiece the experiences in verbal terms. The entries are understood to be literarily unformed and often verbally contracted, whereas the poetic passages breathe and are verbally dilated. The between-space environmentally available in communal relations allows for a divesting of subjectivity that is truly liberating by providing alternative ways to understand one's place, one's body, and one's self. It is a different spatial relation to otherness and must represent itself as formally different as well; as anti-form. I read the journal entries as reflecting this resistance to form, as a refusal to treat the journal as diaristic, or as nature-writing per se, that is, as participating in a genre. They insist on "prosing," as the family called Dorothy Wordsworth's characteristic poetic style, and on a resistance to the rhapsodies associated with nature writing and its close relatives, travel writing and ethnographic writing.[22] Emmanuel Levinas considers the literary to be an evasion of responsibility to another. Dorothy Wordsworth, too, appears to eschew the imagined, fictitious encounter with others in favor of an ontoethical presentation of the encounter itself. The journal entries are idiosyncratic, insistently fragmentary, unconnected, and un-teleological. They neither record a life's journey nor re-create an interiority, and yet the formless prosing entries are uncontrovertibly poetic. That is, they are literary on their own terms, characteristically without figuration, nonalliterative, uninterested in wordplay, and nonfictional. If they are painterly, it is without a great concern for tonal differentiation; the concern remarkable in them is for variation of particulars as these affect the scene.

The task of the journals is ontoethical in this relation of alternative ways human and vegetal bodies relate to the collectivity as self-object and other-subject. For the Stoics, ethics focuses on "those impressions adequately derived from the ways the world is into ways of living that coordinate with, complement, and render comprehensible the divine breath that links everything to a common destiny" (Grosz 50). The shaping Dorothy Wordsworth gives her journal entries is one that pays attention to the breathing that infuses bodies and enlivens the world; the verbal rhythms match the bodily expression of those encountered through a variability. No genre or style formalities are imposed on the language that renders expressible bodies, bears them witness. I want to make the same case for how the "I" is treated in the journals as an anti-body or neutral self that not only refuses to impose form but also does not pass judgment. But this anti-body, which is neutral as is any other natural body inhabiting the environment, is only made possible by space as between-ness, as the pause of stretched time between what had been and what comes. In the journals it is associated with nontraditional diurnal rhythms such as walking at midnight when the moon is full, or late in the day—having stayed up much of the night and sleeping very late. The Wordsworths' unusual lifestyle was not therefore unnatural. Nature does not stop at nighttime and there is much to witness and encounter; all kinds of things sleep during the day, so that the diurnal rhythms she adopted were entirely in tune with her surroundings. The journals record a time that is less linear, despite the dates, than a pulsing rhythm of time. Even in format, the journal entries are kept sporadically, experiences and events sometimes recorded days later, or several days' events summed up briefly and without prosing. What the journal's field-note entries record is the sense of a time of presentness, of becoming and heightened awareness, of the moment itself without consciousness of what has been and what is to come. The connectedness of the moment extends outward into space rather than backward and forward into a limited and delimiting time span. For writers such as Blake, this extension into space is a connection to eternity and prophecy. For Dorothy Wordsworth, who refused the identity of artist, poet, or author,[23] the alternative connection of time and space in a manner that escapes the bounded body into the communal entity of the collectivity was wonder-ful.

This everyday sense of wonder in the natural sense of being enrapt avoids the dangers of Romantic transcendence and the sublime's awful morality, but it also avoids presenting William with a competing poetic imagination. Instead, wonder takes the place of poetic authority, wonder infused with the ontoethical that is what Levinas, in referring to the possibility of alternate status, calls epiphany (*Entre-Nous* 16). In its resistance to formalisms, the moment of the encounter with nature is politically and personally ethical in a manner that privileges bodies in-relation-with. Levinas, however, lades his in-between space of self and other with a moral responsibility to shoulder the burden of another, whereas Dorothy Wordsworth bears witness but without the face-to-face, and to both human and natural bodies alike. Her surrounding environment, which is not divided into separate ecosystems or divided from its surrounds, presents itself in entries that document passage and passing-through. Moreover, these surrounds are themselves momentary rather than momentous; they will change within the hour or when the moment of encounter is over. It is the ethical possibility of the in-between space with its connective lineation and spatial trespasses that allow for the encounter in nature to take place and for the spatial extension of the time frame to be recognized. Without the initiating ethos and its requirement for perceptive acuity—that quick eye for which Dorothy was noted—the ethical would not be directed toward natural objects.

As a writer, Dorothy Wordsworth had to absorb her brother's insistence on her own embodiment as female, as physically and ideologically defined, bounded, limited, compromised, and incapacitated by the historical exigencies of her culture, time, and place. But even if by virtue of her gender she had a sense of sight and its value different from Blake's prophetic vision and William's transcendent one, she had already created a way of seeing that is unique to her poetic sensibility. Coleridge and De Quincey noted her quick, absorptive eye that with its darting eagerness took in the details that together create the body of a natural scene. Because this visual activity and acuity were reserved for natural encounters rather than human activities, it is clear that the journal entries are where her ontoethics could be demonstrated. The entries can be read as themselves bodies that breathe, that have sense hovering over them in the capacity of expressing immanent meaning. For Spinoza, the affections are bodies' capacity to act and be acted on as corporeal forms. The degree to which bodies can act and be acted on (their affections) contributes to what they express as well as how they change through encounters with another. In the journals, affect is there, but the entries of nature writing refrain from dwelling self-absorptively on emotion; ego consistently withdraws in favor of the collectivity or the particular that reflects the whole.[24] Against the sublime experience as one of moral imperatives, the ethical imperative of the ecological moment takes on great integrity. One reads the journal entries and discovers a mental acuity that does not advance itself over the subject at hand but rather deftly integrates itself into nature's vibrant essence. "I walked as long as I could amongst the stones of the shore. The wood rich in flowers. A beautiful yellow, palish yellow flower, that looked thick round & double, & smelt very sweet—I supposed it was a ranunculus—Crowfoot, the grassy-leaved Rabbit-toothed white flower, strawberries, Geranium—scentless violet, anemones two kinds, orchises, primroses. The hackberry very beautiful as a low shrub. The crab coming out" (14 May 1800). Although the retrospect acquired in journaling at night after the walk imposes a botanical perspective—"I supposed" and "anemones two kinds"—the assemblage of forms comes through as the experiential event of bodies and sense coming together. "The wood rich in flowers" becomes each one for itself and yet in relation to the others, the wood, the day, herself, and all adjacent to and touching what then adds itself: "Met a blind man driving a very large beautiful Bull & a cow—he walked with two sticks." All of that is form, the human, the animal, and the vegetal merging with the shore, stones, wood, and herself: everything counts equally in this ecological encounter that is both presentful and substantial in the Spinozist sense. Form is itself part of the ethos, with the journal entries as remembering and attesting to the ethical moment. The ethical form of the journal entries is sketches without a narrative arc, and their sense of immediacy arises in the detailing of an equilibrium of parts contributing to the whole. This form moves the journals away from aesthetics into the visual realm; the entries emphasize what was seen rather than what could be made from sight. To intrude aesthetics in the entries would be to disfigure the immediacy of the ontoethical moment, to create a sense of a premediated "presence." It is not that the journals are devoid of poetic language, but that the poetic is part of the sight, incorporeal entangled with witnessed bodies. The ethical act is to record this entanglement.

The experience of encounter, unlike the domestic space or familial grouping, is constitutive—it is not a self-object encounter but an entering into, a participation that is not a becoming so much as a joining in. It is, at least for the moment, a self-becoming inasmuch as each body and thought that participates in the encounter is admixed, blended, and changed by it. Both Stoic and Spinozist philosophy insists on this blending of bodies, the affection of bodies and thoughts as they act on each other, irrevocably changing all involved. The encounter, whether immanent or simply immediate, creates eventful sense. Whatever meaning bodies had already generated, new sense is made with each new encounter and takes place whether or not these are known or unknown others. As the journal entries depict these encounters, they usually take place on solitary walks, as if talking with another human distorts the ecological experience or immediacy, the additional person preventing the present moment from being a sustained and flexible temporality, a moment at rest from interruptive or fragmenting activity. Moreover, the entries pay particular attention to environment as presentful rather than as background or aesthetic. Nature is not a compositional scene turning life itself into the picturesque object but a self-composing surround. The surround envelops the self in its materiality and enters into the self while pulling it into the larger whole. This is the communion of the One-and-All by which the self escapes its own solipsism as well as the double-bind of dualism. The journal entries typically avoid the self-other power dynamic, with its doubled binding/bondage that can explode into the sublime's terror. Even domestically, Dorothy Wordsworth prefers the friendship or familial group so that "I" and other takes the form of "we," a blending of bodies through the affections.

Embodiment, in terms of the journals, reworks "the object," whether human or nonhuman body, into a relational encounter of becoming and sense-making. The universe and the corporeal and incorporeal bodies in it are dynamic, always in a movement that even underlies the seemingly static, stable entities encountered. The journal entries attend to this movement frequently through the noticing of incorporeal breezes and how they transform the scene, changes in the incorporeals of light and dark on how natural entities appear and present themselves. How unusual this is can be gleaned from Levinas's comment early in *Entre Nous* that "We get caught up in things; things turn against us. That is to say that our consciousness, and our mastery of reality through consciousness, do not exhaust our relationship with reality, in which we are present with all the density of our being" (3–4). The ego has other options: our mastery of reality through self-consciousness is not the only reality available to us; alternative realities are accessible exactly by letting loose the constraints of selfhood. This requires attentive, open awareness, the very quality of the Alfoxden and Grasmere journal entries, because a differently experienced reality requires "the consciousness of miracle, or wonder." "The miracle ruptures biological consciousness; it possesses an intermediary ontological status between the lived and the thought" (*Entre Nous* 16). This intermediary ontological status is perhaps yet another incorporeal, one that enters into the immanent encounter as a condition for the human perception of immanent forms.

IV. Perceptual Bodies

Even the lines that begin the Alfoxden Journal, copied over by William, who clearly valued them, depict a self "merged with what we think," to quote Levinas, "launched" into the world (*Entre Nous* 3): "The green paths down the hillsides are channels for streams. The young wheat is streaked by silver lines of water running between the ridges, the sheep are gathered together on the slopes" (20 Jan. 1798). Here is a community of vibrant things, of thing-body assemblages that together exist as an assemblage to be encountered whole. And that whole is absorbed as an entity of participatory parts as is reflected in the imagery intended to capture that absorption without hermeneutic intervention. The green paths are streamlet basins for the silver lines that streak the wheat; green becomes silver, both rich colors that image a rich earth, a fecund nature. But there is no indication that the observer is in the scene. Rather, she bears witness to, and involves herself in, this scene of natural self-absorption in which human intention has been erased and nature is bountiful in and for itself. The scene does not exist *for* her, just as it is not beauteous for the farmer's or shepherd's sake. Here we might perceive a subject discovering, or on the threshold of discovering, that *she* exists to encounter the interval, the entre nous. It is she who must on the one hand recognize thing-power and material agency, and on the other hand be ready to be launched into the interval space that allows access to the scene of assemblage and reassemblage: paths that turn to streams, greens that turn to silvers and then to woolly white. Here is a hint of the ontoethical subject to come as the journal continues, who will launch herself into the moment, choosing that mode over the prophetic one of interpreting allegorical or exegetic messages provided by a God or a spirit in the woods.

That first move, of bearing witness to bodies both corporeal and incorporeal, is her version, I believe, of Levinas's "infinition," the ever-recommencing of the instant in what we term "the present." This is the interval, the space of stretched time in which ego forgets itself and immanence presents. In the instant of the interval, reality unfolds. As she passes through the vegetal, *being with it* as the absorption of self into another kind of being, as the being-with that defines her walks, we find the passage of the journal and the passage of the vegetal experience coming together as one. Infinition as the interval infers the sense that each moment offers the chance to be differently, to begin again on other terms. However, Dorothy Wordsworth forebears to assert the instant's definitive quality as a mark of or remark upon consciousness' renewal as Levinas does. That would insist too much on a self-probing interiority, and instead of focusing on self as a move forward, her writing suggests that in encounters with nature's infinition, the potential for the recommencing moment surrounds her and rebirths her as not-quite-herself because changed by the movement into and merging with that moment as a becoming part of that whole.

Mobility creates the conditions for the recommencing moment, for passing-through. In her journal writing, Dorothy Wordsworth often records only an activity such as walking, baking, or who drank tea, or the weather: "A very fine morning, warm weather all the week" is an entry for April 1798 that could belong to either the Alfoxden or Grasmere journals. But when she writes on 1 March 1798, that "The shapes of the mist, slowly moving along, exquisitely beautiful; passing over the sheep they almost seemed to have more of life than those quiet creatures," she acknowledges the mist shapes as actants and perceives that the sheep are as much inanimate matter as they are living beings. And she acknowledges the resistant force of things, the thing's intrinsic quality that is a constitution, a source of its vibrancy or vibration, and that which makes the thing a potential or consistent actant. When she writes about follies built to beautify the landscape, she determines the aesthetic problem to be one of blindness to the vibrancy already present, a misperception or a misrecognition. On 15 April 1798, she writes: "Walked about the squire's grounds. Quaint waterfalls about, about which Nature was very successfully striving to make beautiful what art had deformed—ruins, hermitages, etc. etc. In spite of all these things, the dell romantic and beautiful, though everywhere planted with unnaturalised trees. Happily we cannot shape the huge hills, or carve out the valleys according to our fancy." This determination is apparent in the word "things" to name deformations: ruins, hermitages. And the unnaturalized trees, although not included in the category of things, are associated with it through the digressive backstep of the "though": "though everywhere planted with unnaturalised trees." A plantation, then, and not a woods or natural grove; yet the dell had resistant force enough to overcome the artifice so that the "though" is both a return to the category of thingness and a step forward into the dell's romantic beauty, its very life. Happily, nature is itself resistant to human shaping and carving; it is not a sculpture but an active agency, "very successfully striving to make beautiful what art had deformed," as she so perceptively writes. The conjoining made possible by the subordinating conjunction "though" is a stylistic choice, but it also indicates a threshold for Dorothy Wordsworth the ethical subject. In this passage she asserts a morality on the observation—the trees are unnatural, "happily" the valleys are not. The Grasmere journal entries repeatedly associate morality with man's destructive force, with the ethos of the encounter providing a resuscitative breath. She will bear herself as witness *in*, rather than *of*, the experience; she will become an actant in the entre nous and seek out infinition for itself such as she is not yet able to do in the Alfoxden Journal, or rather, has not yet discovered the possibility of doing.

Begun in late January 1798, the Alfoxden Journal would have covered the period of the Wye tours in July and August, but Dorothy Wordsworth makes her last entry on 22 or 24 April 1798, when she and William walked to Cheddar and William continued on to Bristol to see Joseph Cottle. She wrote a long letter in July to her cousin Elizabeth Rawson as well as other shorter missives, but it seems likely that for the most part she was spending most of that month and the walking tours engaged in other kinds of discourses from that of written observation or communication by letter: conversation, internal thought, launching herself into nature. From William's ode on Tintern Abbey and his comment on the "gleams" from her "wild eyes" (l. 148), it also seems likely that these walking tours were as productive for Dorothy's poetic imagination as for her brother's, and that the enormous gains in poetic insight and prosody that make their appearance in the Grasmere Journals were not merely the product of a miserably cold and isolating winter in Germany but reflect instead an intense immersion in the poetic project of her perceptual ontology.

Yet even at the start of the Grasmere Journals, Dorothy Wordsworth is still struggling with the problem of proper perception. "The valley very green, many sweet views up to Rydale head when I could juggle away the fine houses," she wrote on 14 May 1800. Here the uncomfortable morality is swallowed up in her own depression at being left alone by William and John on their visit to Mary Hutchinson. "[B]ut they [the fine houses] disturbed me even more than when I have been happier." A moral-imbued landscape perspective appears to have obscured her Alfoxden ethical commitment to the scene.[25] It is not the folly of man that she despairs here but that she cannot fully engage the moment: the fine houses disturb what might have been an entre nous moment. She is too much in herself here: "The lake looked to me I knew not why dull and melancholy, and the weltering on the shores seemed a heavy sound." To be launched in the moment, to be alive to the life in other things and to the thingness in oneself, requires a co-vibrancy, an alertness to the vibration of alternative being, space, and time. This is not to be confused with a vitalist nature or with transcendence, which are William's province. Rather, Dorothy is learning to recognize her own responsiveness, her "quickness," as Coleridge and De Quincy termed it, to the vibrations of matter and to the collective identities of natural assemblages. She is understanding what compels her about local or mundane alterity, and what small revelations can offer.

That the Grasmere Journal entries of encounter reveal her achievement of perceptual ontology is as much apparent in the well-remarked prosing passages as in less prosody-enriched entries that also reveal the identification of an entre nous moment. "We walked before tea by Bainriggs to observe the many coloured foliage the oaks dark green with yellow leaves, the birches generally still green, some near the water yellowish. The sycamore crimson and crimson-tufted, the mountain ash a deep orange, the common ash Lemon colour but many ashes still fresh in their summer green. Those that were discoloured chiefly near the water" (Sunday, 12 Oct. 1800). The headiness of this passage, its omission of any punctuation to slow down the pell-mell of thoughts between "many coloured foliage" and the green-yellow meld of the oak leaves, and the present-ness of the entry despite its past tense, finds its resolution three days later in the morning: "After Wm had composed a little, I persuaded him to go into the orchard. We walked backwards and forwards. The prospect most divinely beautiful from the seat—all colours, all melting into each other" (Wednesday, 15 Oct.). Again walking, the back-and-forth movement creates a launching effect of immersion even though the prospect is distant: the colors are "all melting into each other." The agency of this movement, this vibrancy, belongs to the scene and its accumulated assemblage.

It is a scene, however, and not a surround; they are on a prospect, and an aesthetic sensibility has transformed encounter into appreciation. On Sunday each kind of tree and leaf color had its presence remarked, but here the effect is of having been already immersed, of remembering what had been and attempting to resurrect it, as in a poem on the subject. Nevertheless, she retains an effect of coloredness as opposed to colors, and of thingness and belonging to that thingness, as opposed to individual objects that must be objectified. It is this immersion that is "divine" in its prospect and not the prospect itself that is transformative. Unlike William's "eye made quiet by the power / Of harmony" ("Tintern Abbey" l. 47–8), here the eye is not separate from the body, and although the prospect is "most divinely beautiful from the seat—all colours, all melting into each other," she continues the entry with "I went in to put bread in the oven and we both walked within view of Rydale." The prospect and the bread are of a piece, with the activity of walking providing the combinatory agent; at the same moment, William intersperses the prospect with composing a poem. For Dorothy Wordsworth, the prospect is not an inspiration transcendently divine, but "divinely beautiful," a momentary aspect of immanent beauty coherent in itself if viewed from the seat, and one that it owes only to itself and that exists only in a combined but not homogenized state of assemblage. Here she has managed to salvage an encounter in nature from the distortions of aestheticization and figuration, indicating the transitoriness, the moment-ness of as a resistance to reification, creating for herself a space for the anti-body.

For Dorothy Wordsworth, the pausing that occurs in the interval of encounter is a participating in the multitude, a taking in of the assemblage in the instant of the pause. The momentary encounter heightens the awareness of existence as a mutual endeavor—neither a striving nor a stasis, but as the infinitely expansive moment of beginning, of renewal. Dorothy Wordsworth's present moment carries no awareness of pastness with it—that is William's burden. Her renewal and recommencing of the moment focuses outward rather than within. It is not an experience of Levinas's "face of the other" or of singularity, but a recognition of the whole in its particularity of bodies together, the entre nous as a self-becoming that is only possible because it is forgotten in the vivid awareness of and integration with immanent life.

I read Dorothy Wordsworth's journals of field notes recounting her passings-through to be a troubling of time with an eye toward memory and justice, and a differential version of causality and politics, and thus history.[26] Turning time and being away from being and nothingness—an emptying out of self, something that might be easier for a woman without means—and toward time-being as ontoethical practice is what the journals document. By contrast, domesticity implies constant activity for her, chores that ensure the home space continues as such, even when such chores also include journal or letter writing, or fair-hand copying for William. The home cannot be a place or space of rest; that must be sought out-of-doors. For William, the home space is one of restorative respite, or of a reading and writing that feed his translations of the often violently conditioned Otherness he encounters within his memory and imagination.

However, here in the passage discussed above, which occurs near the end of the Grasmere entries, awareness struggles with resistance to self-conscious aestheticizing, intruding on the descriptions of the scene-setting and the scene. Setting the scene, unusual for her, frames the entry and its vision both in terms of William's poetic labor and, at Dorothy's invitation, his presence in reflective walking, an activity that combines both mental and physical faculties. She ameliorates the scene through insistence on an immanent beauty, the result of collective rather than transfigured scenic presence. At the same time, in its recollection of the prospect in "Tintern Abbey," the entry emphasizes the distance involved in the scene that neither surrounds her nor awakens her enthusiasm, the "wild eye" as William figures her perceptive glance. Carefully negotiating here the difference between the enthusiastic vision with its political potential—a potential for insubordination she has mediated throughout the journals by deferred entries, the deferrals mitigating emotions and wildness but not transposing or disciplining them—and the pacified vision of "emotions recollected in tranquility," she responds to the "wild eyes" of "Tintern Abbey" that there had been reified and her viewing stilled into part of the picture plane. Here she actively constructs the framing of the picture, including both herself and William in it as in "Tintern," but actively engaged on a reflection that cannot be made transcendent. And then, to assure there will be no resulting metaphysical leap, she turns from the prospect to that most mundane, repetitious, and unpoetic of activities, baking bread for the meal to come. Through the journals, Dorothy Wordsworth has unobtrusively responded to and intervened in her brother's poetic vision. If he did not hear the difference in what was immanently present in the journals, this did not prevent her construction of an ecoliterary anti-body, and an anti-form by which to express it, that discovers in the moment's infinition experienced with the local other a response to the metaphysical void that haunts her brother's nature poetry.

V. Entre Nous?

The survey above of Barbauld's, Wollstonecraft's, Radcliffe's, and Dorothy Wordsworth's various representations of immanent experience has certain elements of similarity, such as the careful delineation of the various entities, their locatability in the here-now, and their interrelationality in the immanent encounter. Another similarity is that each of these writers bear witness to what is on the other side of silence—the mundane, the uncultivated wild thing—as a perceiving body in relation with other bodies. As such, their sense of shared substance or oneness is either intimated or clearly felt. But is this truly a gendered difference in the encounter with alterity? Are there perhaps other ways to explain what is going on in these texts? To answer this last question, I draw on related theories of relationality between self and other/Other to see if there are explanations other than gender difference for what occurs in these texts. Emmanuel Levinas's conception of the "entre nous"; Jane Bennett's understanding of the assemblage; Jean-Luc Nancy's notion of the "singular plural"; Nietzsche's idea of the eternal return; Luce Irigaray's understanding of vegetal being and the breath are all suggestively explanatory. Drawing on them allows me to position my interpretation of Romantic women's texts alongside these alternative philosophies of subjective or object-oriented relationality to see whether or not gender is a determinate factor.

I begin with Levinas and Bennett. Levinas's construct of the "entre nous" situates the self and other in the simplest formation of binary opposition, but his theory is important because the focus is on the ethical subject. The "entre nous" of the binary opposition occurs in the time-space of the interval; and that binary relation is ontological, having to do with life or death of the Other. In addition, the self and Other in the "entre nous" have the potential to become a "we" or interrelational community, although only after the entre nous encounter. By contrast, Bennett's conception of "vibrant matter" in the assemblage announces community immediately, one constituted by the human viewer's attention. Furthermore, her analysis of the interrelation of bodies and things, corporeal entities and incorporeals like electricity and magnetism, extends the idea of what constitutes immanent life.

Although Romantic writers like William Wordsworth and Coleridge considered the breeze, air at high atmosphere, rivers, and other effluents entities analogous to an incorporeal like the soul, such poetic references typically occur in lyrics focused on the poetic ego, such as Coleridge's "This Lime-tree Bower my prison" (1797). Bennett's representation of community as integrated at the deepest level of substance, by contrast, relies on a nondualistic encounter that diffuses the self-enclosing ego, and on the human viewer's sudden awareness of the vibrant matter before her. Bennett's theory of relationality comes very close, especially to Dorothy Wordsworth's journal entries of immanent life; but it is also strongly correlated to object-oriented ontology (OOO), a philosophy to which she has strong leanings.[27] Because OOO determines corporeals, including humans, as objects, and nonhuman objects as being beyond human experiential knowledge and as resistant to association or intercourse, I have decided to leave it aside. Timothy Morton, for instance, defines an object as a "weird entity withdrawn from access, yet somehow manifest" (qtd. in Bennett "Systems and Things" 225). An important aspect of immanence is the experiential insight gained from encounter in which there is no withdrawal or veiling. Furthermore, OOO is a philosophy that rejects enlightenment out of hand. As Bennett makes clear, to define objects as withdrawn but manifest, apart but "always leaving hints of a secret other world," is to mystify objects so as to evade the ethical imperative that immanence teaches ("Systems and Things" 225–26).

Levinas, by contrast, only treats the ethical imperative of the "face of the Other," leaving all insentient bodies and incorporeals aside. In his introduction to *Entre Nous*, Levinas explains that his philosophy is predicated on the intersubjective formation of the reason and "the transcendence of the '*for-the-other*' initiating the 'ethical subject,' which initiates the *entre-nous*" (xi). Levinas's radical subjectivizing of the Other uses the interdynamic space between subjects that we can extend to natural entities as well.[28] In an intermediate space that has the possibilities of Plato's creative *chora*, the dynamism between, and in excess of, subjects becomes a space of affection, of the feelings that arise in tandem with the expressive contact between bodies and between thoughts. Jane Bennett explains why things might turn against us if we insist on a self-consciousness that objectifies its species-awareness over an openness to subject-objects, or existents with affective capabilities. Conceiving of "the other" disguises the fact that "things" are undergoing movement and change, affecting and being affected by other thing-bodies. This is far from the fuller objectification of human subjects in the internalized objects theorized by Freud that form much of the hauntings of Romantic poetry's engagement with transcendence and the uncanny.

As Bennett notes, an alternative model for understanding encounters between the self and the material world emphasizes the capacity to act as a body's self-expressibility. Action or movement between bodies participates in immanent expression by understanding such encounters as occurring "between ontologically diverse actants" (*Vibrant Matter* xiv). The body is itself matter, and for the Stoics and Spinoza, the body is composed of other bodies, from organs and muscles to the ideas and dreams that are also bodies. Corporeality requires not just material existence but organization and the capacity to express the universe's order. The material encompasses the range of human, animate, and inanimate beings, and incorporeals that compose our social and natural worlds. In their interstices are the sites that give rise to sensibility and imagination, the sites that are affecting. For Dorothy Wordsworth, to witness the living fabric of intricately relating things is revelatory, the alterity of small matters. This is itself immanence.

It is the interface between both Levinas's and Bennett's versions of the ontoethical encounter in which I believe Dorothy Wordsworth's peculiar and radical understanding of the gaze in particular can be found. The gaze as she employs it—not the Freudian gaze of lack and desire, but the "wild eyes" for which the men of her acquaintance commended her—is the vivid element of full awareness, full openness to the present possibility. It is how she encounters "the wild" as I investigated it with Coleridge and Schelling. It is an openness that enables the present moment in nature to become available to her, providing a medium of between-ness or immediacy and of assemblage-awareness, collective spirit as well as the collective or assembled body. This is the one-in-many of a natural encounter, the witnessing of the essential commonality of these particular bodies in the universal patterns of movement and change. And rather than view these encounters as traumatic, like William's spots of time, or as disruptive, as in De Quincey's hallucinatory experiences of thing-power, Dorothy Wordsworth clearly views these encounters as requisite for the ethical subject.

Dorothy Wordsworth's familial situation during the short period of her artistry was tempered by the communal home that she, William, and often friends such as Coleridge inhabited, and that created an experimental social environment. The lack of regulation in their daily life, of daily rhythms, may have made it easier to not overlook the mundane. It was here that she developed her perceptual ontology made active by the constant affecting of her thought and body. At the same time that William was evolving his Romantic understanding of the self-other relation through seeing into the "life of things" ("Tintern Abbey" l. 49), Dorothy was creating her own more nuanced understanding of what perception can allow one to know, where the self belongs in an arena of multiple and various kinds of selves, and how far the limits of the entre nous, the affective field of the assemblage, and being in-relation-with might extend.

It is only by escaping domestic drudgery through the freer sociability and domestic practices of her brother's cottage, making long walks alone possible, that Dorothy discovers her path to spirit and alternate reality. Even so, one's condition is at once social and natural; the natural world through which she walked as actant in order to bear it witness shared a commonality with her social world of domestic things. Just as her garden of peas or of transplanted mosses just as much as a swallow's nest extended her domestic space into the natural world, so did she find communities of wildflowers and birch trees, social aggregates of animate life to be inhabited by no mystical spirit or imaginative life but rather, like life with William, by their own small vibrancies and ontological force. "To think," Levinas notes, echoing Heidegger, "is no longer to contemplate, but to be engaged, *merged with what we think*, launched—the dramatic event of being-in-the-world" (*Entre Nous* 3; my emphasis). This too accurately describes Dorothy Wordsworth's thought; her precipitation into the moment, noted by Coleridge as accompanied by the quick eye, is what distinguishes her expression both as embodied and literary activity from that of William, who used the moment to distill it into art.

William's sense of accomplishment in his poem of the leech-gatherer, not at the time and not even in the moment of composition, but only finally in the organization of poems into a large enough collection to comprise the poet's interpretation of the world, is a recognition that he now truly sees and knows. This is a seeing and knowing that his sister never lays claim to, even in seeing her description of meeting the local leech-gatherer several times rendered as a publishable poem. Her journals and poems are not continuously rewritten in fair-hand, not rearranged and re-collected. Rather, they are not even recollected, but remain parts of the intangible memories of past days, a few dried leaves and flowers and insights of what was but is not now. That sense of the past is far different from William's spots of time. It depends on the condition of being launched, of understanding that the moment itself is the thing, and that all that participate in that moment—whether or not perception is activated—belong to the entre nous. This is what the prosing passages reinstate as the now of the event, in contrast to the past of the day's memories.

Acute perception, then, is the activating element in Dorothy Wordsworth's ontology, and indeed, in the other women writers discussed in this chapter. It is not only the precipitating element; it functions almost as yet another incorporeal that enables a body's capacity to act, to affect and be affected. There is not the sense in her letters, journals, and poems that an ethical practice is foremost in her mind, or that thinking oversteps activity as movement. There are parts of a woman's day when housekeeping is best accomplished by the mind not perceiving too keenly, and there are many moments of family interaction when engagement with each other subsumes an active intellection. Yet she is able to find even in those moments the opportunity for recognizing her being-in-the-world, finding in a half-eaten apple the sign of departure and temporary loss, and discovering in the planting of peas not so much the joy of seasonal renewal as of a renewal of the self's appetite for the keen moment. If an ontoethics of perception was striking enough for Coleridge and others to remark upon, and to enable William's selection of a compelling line or scene when it inspired him to his own version, it was also not a signal enough departure or innovation for them to adopt as their own. Nevertheless, I want to suggest that a feminine ontology of perception belongs to the larger Romantic project of reclaiming a philosophy of immanent alterity.

Acute perception—or wild seeing—as an ethical practice involves being completely in the body, paying attention energetically, putting it at the forefront of experience. It is clear from the Alfoxden and Grasmere journals that, as for Spinoza, bodies and thoughts are not correlated but are rather expressions of the same thing. As such, perception and ideation are part of the density of being a female object, while recognizing one's participation in a collectivity of objects is an ethical practice. Dorothy Wordsworth's walks through nature, as early as the Wye Valley meanderings, were a project of precipitation into the moment rather than of engaging with the past as William's famous ode to Tintern does, where in a singular moment he embalms her in an endless cycle of remembrance in order to himself remember and to be remembered.[29] Instead, for her such purposeful walks were a launching, an eager entrance into the ambient space between self and all else materially embodied that is itself alive with vibrant possibility. It is a space in which bodies come into contact through perception and movement, expressing themselves in their vivid commonality. That entrance is marked not by detachment or slow perception but by an intentional openness that enables engagement with the panoply of Otherness perceived as vibrantly alive rather than spiritually quieted. This is a version of the interval in that time is stretched; however, movement isn't paused or restless but is slowed, attentive, open to whatever comes. It is the revelation of all being, attained through a mobile being-with whether slow perception takes place seated or walking.

In the revelation of being and being-with there is a singularity that is also multiplicity, and an indication of infinity or the One that does not cancel the All, or particularity. This is not an elevation of the object to the level of the subject, as in OOO, but rather an instance of what in German thought such as Fichte's was being conceived as a merging of subject and object. It is a combination of the individual tree leaves *and* the banks of trees in their particularity, in their namedness, and their gentle presence that the perceiver not only witnesses, but witnesses as a by-product of the density of their surround. The All as the One, the particular as the surround. The natural density feels at home with the density of being she embodies and carries into nature. Her description of them is not performed with an alert accuracy that forgets the self, that enters into the surround without selfness. The immanent reality thus encountered is itself transformative and vivifying. For her, descriptive writing is both the record of the encounter and the opportunity to piece together an experienced density in an articulated visual field, to do it justice.[30] Indeed, there is something compelling in Dorothy Wordsworth's prose writing to which Bennett's ecophilosophy and Levinas's "idea of a truth that manifests itself in its humility" open up for us (*Totality and Infinity* 55). Coleridge alludes to the same compelling quality in Dorothy's "eye watchful in minutest observation of nature" and her taste—that is, herself—as a "perfect electrometer," a comment that gets at the mind/thing embodiment of which Dorothy herself seems aware.[31]

If Levinas's entre nous and Bennett's assemblage are both helpful in understanding how Dorothy Wordsworth's immanent encounters partake of each yet are not quite either one, two other philosophers have proposed concepts of encounter and interrelationality that may help make the case stronger for a gendered distinction in the experience, or at least the recognizability, of immanence. Nietzsche's proposition of the eternal return offers another way to understand what Levinas termed infinition, which Luce Irigaray's philosophy of the breath conceptualizes even more helpfully for my purposes. I want to suggest here that Dorothy Wordsworth carved out not just a poetics different from that her brother was creating, but also one that created a version of the self as perceptual body that goes beyond what Barbauld and Wollstonecraft in particular had accomplished. In part, this being-with is her praxis in natural encounters, but it is more. "Occasionally the truth will finally triumph, there is no doubt: some kind of error was fighting on its behalf," a Nietzschean aphorism involving the incorporeal of fate that describes Dorothy Wordsworth's new way forward.[32] But Nietzsche's concept of fate, "amor fati," and the eternal return beg the question of woman, as Luce Irigaray points out in her critique *Marine Lover*.[33] As both a Romantic and a Stoically informed philosopher, Nietzsche believed that the affirmation of life in the eternal return involves *all* beings, as he has his prophet Zarathustra say. The error is that, as Irigaray points out, Nietzsche cannot see that this has to include the sexed other as well, even though his worldview is androcentric, binary and oppositional; not at all congruent with the immanent philosophy he proposed. The fateful error of sexism is fighting on Dorothy Wordsworth's behalf in that her immanent practice is a creative response to that opposition; neither silenced nor imitative, she carves out her own uniquely attuned practice.

The eternal return as Nietzsche conceives it provides a different way to understand the interval of present time. The eternal return needs to break out of a repetition of every instant through art and self-fashioning, so that self-transformations change mundane life into something new. This is a more pressing version of infinition that merely opens up the instant to change. Nietzsche's view of time could be adapted to Dorothy Wordsworth's transformative praxis that incorporates her seeing into the interval of natural encounter, although it lacks the breath that transforms mere nature into vibrant life.

By contrast, William Wordsworth's determination to pursue poetic art as his transcendent project creates a temporal distance from the instant—forcing it into the past so that it can be remembered—and a spatial separation from the encounter that translates immanence into aesthetic judgment and transcendence. But the necessary error that undergirds his project—women are men's helpmates, household laborers who also help as amanuenses, as field note takers, as walking companions, as philosophical conversationalists—allowed for and encouraged his sister's independent adventuring, and experiencing what is immanently there. It is in this sense that Irigaray's intervention in Nietzsche's sexism is important for realizing that Dorothy Wordsworth has embraced "amor fati," love of fate, taking her life-conditions to the furthest intensity possible, becoming herself most when she incorporates selflessly into the natural encounter. This embrace of fate opens up the possibility of revelatory immanence. Her practice puts into play what Irigaray asks of Nietzsche, which could be asked of William Wordsworth: "And everything you conceive, you believe can be brought into being. But if the bottom that underlies appearing escapes you, how can it be given existence?" (*Marine Lover* 60). The answer is: through his sister's poetic prose treatment of immanent becoming—both nature's and her own—that escapes him, so that he takes her journals to support his poetry. She is the bottom, the helpmate who escapes him. For he is writing at secondhand when he adopts her firsthand accounts; she has seen immanence, but he sees only matter for transcendent verse.

I propose that William's nature walks take part in the bifurcating movement of constant differentiation, one that directs him toward a dualism between ego and world he struggles with in his poetry, whereas

Dorothy Wordsworth uses infinition—the constant rebirthing or breathing of the instant as the present moment—to track how she is experiencing a more capacious being-with as she moves through a landscape and its surrounds. This tracking proves a strategy for warding off the binarism that also differentiates sexuate beings; moreover, it pushes infinition into the eternal return. Being-with allows her to embody her bodily status relationally to other objects that are also agential (subject-objects). Like her own, the vegetal body breathes, moves, communicates, interacts, and functions in community. Being-with thus opens the subjective-object to the experience of alterity,[34] for that is exactly how alterity functions: otherness explodes subjective identity and the ego's fragile control over that identity. Having momentarily given up subject status in order to be her own "wild" eyes, Dorothy Wordsworth enters into attentive infinition, which achieves what Irigaray terms "an intimacy that tries to express without completely revealing, for such revealing would destroy it," that is, destroy the plurality of meaning (*Vegetal Being* 7). Moreover, moving through a vegetal surround for Dorothy Wordsworth is neither an encounter in Levinas's sense, nor a sudden thrust into the Open that Heidegger proposes and that William's "spots of time" document. It is an awareness of the deep relation of bodies and things that characterizes Spinozist revelation. A pantheism, that is, in many ways *more* in touch with the pantheist controversy in Germany arising from the resuscitation of Spinoza's doctrine of *Deus sive Natura* or nature/reality actualizing itself, than the men who are theorizing it in her own environs.

Perhaps the philosophical conceit that is most apropos for understanding a feminine recognition of immanent life is Nancy's "being singular plural." This notion opens up Levinas's "infinition" and "entre nous" to "being-with." In *Being Singular Plural*, Nancy finds the concept of being-with to encompass "an ontology of bodies," whether these bodies are "inanimate, animate, sentient, speaking, thinking, having weight, and so on" (84). Here Nancy is being specifically Spinozist in articulating thought and extension as bodies that affect each other rather than being positioned against each other: "'body' really means . . . from body to body, in the dis-position." Like the Stoics, however, the being-with of bodies is shaped by language as well as the corporeal: "Not only does a body go from one 'self' to an 'other,' it is as itself from the very first; it goes from itself to itself; whether made of stone, wood, plastic, flesh, a body is the sharing of and the departure from self, the departure toward self, the nearby-to-itself without which the 'self' would not even be 'on its own.'" Nancy's account of the way in which bodies of all kinds retain their this-ness while also changing moment by moment helps clarify Dorothy Wordsworth's field activity, movement as affection.

Nancy proposes that the human is inhabited by its plural singularity, which "exposes the world and its proper being-with-all-beings in the world," disclosing that "as the world" (*Being Singular* 85). That unveiling requires the thinking-through and the speaking part of sentience that calls on language, whose relation to bodies is through their self-expression. Language is "the exposition of the world-of-bodies as such, that is, as originarily singular plural. The incorporeal exposes bodies according to their being-with-one-another . . . They are amongst themselves [entre eux], as origins" (84). This revision of Levinas's entre nous describes the vegetal environs of Dorothy Wordsworth's journaling and the assemblages she encounters and participates in. Her need to write of her field experience, then, is more than record keeping for William to feed his poetry; it is the very necessity of the incorporeal to do its work, to express itself. "Language," Nancy writes, "is the exposing of plural singularity."

This is, then, the ground of art for Dorothy Wordsworth, with extension to varying degrees to Barbauld, Wollstonecraft, and Radcliffe. F. W. J. Schelling writes that reality when viewed properly is that in which "eternal ideas as such can become truly objective [e.g., nature or art] by becoming their own symbol . . . as particular forms. That which appears through them is merely the absolute unity, the idea in and for itself." The absolute unity, the truth of the encounter as exposition and expression. These particular forms are either nature or art, for "nature and art are one": "art does not strive to compete with similar products of nature as regards actual concrete elements. It seeks rather the pure form, the ideal, of which the thing itself . . . is simply the other perspective."[35] We might say, it is the other expression. That pure form is what Dorothy Wordsworth strives to capture in poetic prose, language so natural it falls away from itself, refusing formalism in order to pay attention to forms themselves as the bodies that matter as trees, wildflowers, mosses, rocks, and light. Light is not irrelevant, whether moonlight or glancing beams of the sun, for light is "ideal unity within the real unity," as Schelling puts it (119). That is, light is the ideal concept that reality actualizes in our visual field: the incorporeal that is also corporeal. Such light is not unidirectional, but rather a participant in the assemblage as is the breeze: more, light *becomes* the viewer's gaze that penetrates the mundanity of the surrounds in order to fully see its form as bodies touched by light, touching each other, becoming through and in each other, interpenetrating as assemblage but also participating in the dynamic interval of the instant as an untimely experience. Language, then, becomes the way to attend to Coleridge's "multeity in unity," the way to bear witness to eternal nature in its self-formations.

Light as the incorporeal corporeal, and poetic language as what bodily expression gives rise to, coalesce in women artists whose perceptual bodies are attuned to both; how much more so for those who are themselves attuned to wild seeing? Schelling notes that color is how the ideal concept of light becomes real: by coupling with non-light (corporeals), light is realized as color or "obscured light" (*Philosophy of Art* 120–21). Thus, the incorporeal entity of coloredness is the recognition of the ideal unity expressing itself within the multiplicity of colors all working together; it is the transformation of the incorporeal into the corporeal. Singularity within the plural, and the truth of that plural as singular. For this kind of artful indiscrimination, the immanent surrounds through which perceptual bodies move involve the natural or informal interactivity of bodies in motion (trees don't only bend with the wind or turn to the sun's rays; they communicate and move in ways the Romantics intuited).[36] But surrounding the surrounds, as it were, or underwriting them, is the gendered difference by which Gilbert Imlay can expect Wollstonecraft to document her travels for him in her Scandinavian *Letters*, and William can urge his sister to keep a journal because of her remarkable eye—which is neither the organ of specularization[37] nor the organ of surveillance, and especially not the organ of scientific observation—for him.

Canvassing these philosophical propositions concerning the interrelationality of being has enabled a broader consideration of how being and writing changes when the person experiencing immanence is a woman. Although Nancy's idea of being singular and plural comes closest to articulating what enables a feminine immanence, certainly Bennett's assemblage and Irigaray's breath are critical for understanding why these writers were attracted to mundane scenes of natural bodies in association with each other, and how encountering such scenes could lie on the other side of silence. The notion of community exceeds the weight of self-explanation, the Romantic breeze is reconfigured as breath itself, the face of the Other becomes all the entities immanently encountered. Embodied being is recognized and witnessed as immanent life.

In chapter 4, language as the medium of the poetic art is itself at stake, and found wanting. Human language and the expressibility of corporeal and incorporeal bodies, we will see, are less compatible than poets would wish. Moreover, the next two chapters move in a different direction from the first three chapters by examining how Romantic writers engaged with specifically incorporeal bodies as sites of immanent encounter: Percy Bysshe Shelley with the dream vision and Thomas De Quincy with hallucination. One is prophetic, one is nightmarish. What each foresees has to do with the immanent encounters that inform them. Chapter 4 focuses specifically on Shelley's *Triumph of Life* as incorporeal dream vision, and the dead bodies it reinvigorates. Finally, the question is, when language fails to express immanence or its truth as a living practice, what follows? Shelley's poem suggestively falters at the point where an answer might be formulating, but the *Triumph* gives hints concerning that landing place.

Section III

Incorporeals: Dream Visions and Nightmares

4

Percy Shelley's Immanent Language

> And now I see how fleeting is my life?
> Nay more, the life of all—and in the flight
> Of the Sun the manifest ruins of the world.
>
> —Petrarch, *Triumphus Temporis*, from *I Trionfi* (I. 67–69)

Romanticism is itself an event, one that questions itself and challenges us to question it. As Ron Broglio and Robert Mitchell define it, "Romanticism generally has been understood in terms of immanence and transformation."[1] Immanence here refers not to Stoic and Spinozist philosophies but to Gilles Deleuze's treatment of immanence and revolution or change, though the two meanings are not entirely at odds. Deleuze is important later in the chapter for analyzing the final portion of Shelley's *Triumph of Life* where the problem is one of immanent transformation. More immediately, the challenge Shelley's poem poses is its self-questioning in a manner closer to deconstruction, whereas the poem's structural failure at completion reflects the antagonism between deconstructive ploys and the immanent event.

Shelley's unfinished poem, composed between May and June 1822, both questions the event of Romanticism and announces it through its inexpressibility—that is, through the word fragments and ellipses of the poem's final lines. These lines, I argue, indicate that imaging a future of immanent awareness—one that like Blake's Jerusalem involves enlightened seeing, enlightened recognition of substance all the way down—is so difficult that it may require a new language, one suited to the mythopoetic project of Romantic immanence and an incompletely expressible future. Critics have generally understood the poem based on the weighty and overwhelming first part of the poem, which depicts the despair of the ironically termed "triumph" itself, the parade of self-enslaved captives. But the force of the poem may well rest on the last lines Shelley worked on, with their incomplete, fragmentary vision of a futurity beyond a language that had ensnared philosophers and sages as much as the non-contemplative and unthinking crowd. Shelley's *Triumph* presents itself as an allegorical history of distorted and blindfolded thought, self-enclosed ego driving the way forward to an equally blinded future. An alternative, immanent future begins to be foretold but is in fragments, inexpressible or not yet expressible. The incipient question toward the end of the poem, at the horizonal wall with its mysterious rhymes, is: what does it take to get over that wall, to move and see differently? Another question suggests itself in terms of Romantic immanence: how can Spinoza's geometry of movement, its lines and planes in which bodies move, mobilize an immanently embodied future? How might the *Triumph*'s Dantesque *terza rima* indicate a rhythmic movement that can propel us past the broken-off last lines, propel us into a beatific vision such as ends the *Divine Comedy*?

Whether we examine the mainstay of the poem or the last lines, we are in the time-space of an incorporeal body, a dreamworld that is plausible enough to *feel* like substance has been granted it, to feel tangible in the way that actual dreams do. Shelley has given his poem a materiality and a space that feels both embodied and inhabited. What does it mean to locate poetic language in the absence of substance, in the hallucinatory space of the time-paused interval? In such a dream space, the expression of substance and the potentiality of bodies appear distorted, disfigured, and uncanny. In the *Triumph of Life*, their appearances arise for the speaker with the urgency of quest as he literally questions them; the force of this quest is concentrated on the figuration that is revolutionary philosophy itself. If the *Triumph*'s dreamworld is a dark and threatening one, its vision also holds out the promise of no distinction between subjects and objects; immanent life as expressive plenitude.

Dark Interpreter, Tilottama Rajan's 1980 book on Romantic discourse, draws its title from De Quincey's name for a haunting figure in his opium dreams as a figuration of his unconscious self. This is his other-self, the Not-I of his ego, which speaks a deeper truth than his wakeful self can do. In Shelley's dream allegory, the figure we might call the dreaming speaker's "dark interpreter" is the revolutionary philosopher Rousseau, a ghostly Virgil who acts much as De Quincey's haunter does although less threateningly. Shelley's use of the dream vision offers, like De Quincey's hallucinations, an interval space as vantage point from which to investigate what the self-conscious, solipsistic mind cannot fully contemplate. The figure of the dark interpreter points to seeing the potential energy for the hallucinatory interval's self-actualizing work, as well as a way to understand the tragic nature of the triumph's staging and what I read as the hope of its sudden breaking off. This breaking of language concerns the majority of the chapter, but the interval and staging are issues that allow me to rethink the poem's last lines. I propose that they point to the possibility of multiple worlds, coexisting co-arising expressions of the universe in which one of the worlds might permit expressing immanence through what Shelley calls "rhymes of wonder."

Rajan interprets the weight of *The Triumph* as resting on the dream vision's necessary doubleness. The dreaming Poet recounts the allegorical vision he sees while remaining firmly on the sidelines, both in the margin of the dream and yet not grounded in it (unlike Rousseau). Doubly situated as both stilled spectator and active dreamer, the speaker is also encouraged by his guide-interpreter Rousseau to both passively watch the allegorical procession before his eyes *and* to participate in that procession, however disillusioning that experience will prove to be. Both states are necessary for the enlightenment inaugurated in Rousseau by what he calls "the shape all light," an incorporeal that provides an intervention quite different from De Quincey's dark interpreter. Like Coleridge's Wedding Guest, Shelley's speaker realizes immanence secondhand through Rousseau's remembrance of the "shape all light." And like the Wedding Guest, that mediation enables the speaker's transformation, the vivifying light affecting his own sight. Seeing becomes seeing truly, alterity rending thought into sudden realization.

I begin with the ending and the last four lines, a fragment with the occurrence of two ellipses, until the final "Of" that begins the fifth uncompleted line midway through the final stanza Shelley wrote, leaving the poem unfinished at his death. The *Triumph* asks us to extend, extemporize, dwell in the dizzying rapidity of movement of life's march of time.[2] As Joel Faflak has noted, "the poem's indeterminate ending answers its own final question by opening the poem ceaselessly to the radically uncertain future of life itself."[3] Rather than imagining this "triumph" as a slowed version of suffering and humiliation, enslavement to the imperial corporate body, Shelley imagines a vertigo of motion, a sweeping up of humanity into the vortex of a fateful present. This sense of intense movement begins with the first lines: "Swift as a spirit hastening to his task / . . . the Sun sprang forth" (1–2). Even though the imagery is apparently bright, it is blighted by the "mask / Of darkness," which, though falling with the Sun's speedy approach, also prevaricates. For far from a mere masking of what is essentially bright with the dark, this mask is both the masque of darkness that will be the triumphal march of the speaker's dream as a hideous parody of life controlled by ideological oppressions, and a prelude to the dark imagery of the poem throughout. It is not long before the speaker's vision, "that trance of wondrous thought" (41), which is a blind seeing rather than insight (for the Poet is confused by the spectacle until his guide, Rousseau, provides an interpretive key), beholds "a great stream / Of people . . . hurrying to and fro,"

> All hastening onward, yet none seemed to know
> Whither he went, or whence he came, or why
> He made one of the multitude, yet so
> Was borne amide the crowd as through the sky
> One of the million leaves of summer's bier. (44–45, 47–51)

This is the temporality that characterizes self-blinded movement, a "hastening onward" that wards off the possibility of a different future through infinite recursion to the past.

Later I discuss how metalepsis functions in the poem as a kind of interval to break from this blind faithfulness to history and its repetition so that nothing is learned because immanence—what the figure of Rousseau calls the "shape all light"—is closed off, unseeable. What the triumph represents is refusal or negating in advance of a different future; as Shelley's Rousseau explains, encountering immanence means forgetting history's bondage. The problem the poem poses and begins to attempt to resolve is that of breaking the frame created by such a distorted space, one envisioned as an insane flight hemmed in by chaos and fear. Blindfolded and dizzy, both charioteer-leader and dancing followers need to see without distortion, to see the common substance of their world that binds them through their common life force rather than through ideological bondage.[4] History, Shelley suggests, tells us nothing about the forces that corral us along this flight path that turns back on itself in a temporality that goes nowhere—and history certainly tells us nothing about the nature of horizons, because we do not learn its lessons.

But it is this horizon determined by the past that Shelley puts in doubt by way of the poem's dream state interval. Such doubt widens the Enlightenment frame, with its insistently finite horizon developed from Western epistemologies, to other possibilities including a posthuman world. Interestingly, contemporary thinkers have found Spinoza to be a philosopher of the posthuman world. This aspect of Shelley's inhuman dreamworld helps open the vista of a possible future beyond the horizon of institutional violence, war, and the abuse of nature. The poem's project becomes, in the end, to discover a way out of the traps of either Humean skepticism or a Kantian walling off of being—two philosophical attitudes against which the *Triumph* finally crashes in its last stanzas. It is in the poem's provisional ending that an overleaping of the two positions begins to manifest.

Shelley's visionary poem, in the moment of its apparent crashing against the walls of skepticism and reason, wants and desires to locate just such an epochal terminus where Otherness designates neither loss of the self nor the in-itself, and that can prevent another incarnation of Napoleon's bloody triumphs across Europe. The terminating question Shelley asks in the *Triumph of Life*, which the poem itself has asked throughout—"Then, what is Life?"—suggests the possibility that Otherness lies not on the other side of subjective, anthropocentric limitation and finitude, but right here right now. As Alan Rawes notes, even the last time this question is posed in the final lines, "the poem has not arrived at an ontological blank."[5] The poem entertains a free-range understanding of Life that absorbs the human into it, as well as human perversions of the Good and truth, or what Rawes discusses as equivocality. "Life" is both the distorted dance that follows the charioteer and a figuring of the One and All, both delusion and enlightenment equivocally held. Such equivocality would eschew the need to stage the contest between idea and substance, in order to imagine what it might mean to inscribe anew, without distortion, blindness, automaticity, or finitude. Or it might imagine this if the poem could be finished, could be differently written, if its terms could be thought.

I. Life Writ Large

My interpretation of the question provisionally prompting the poem's ending—a poem foreshadowed by the Poet asking "And what is this? / Whose shape is that within the car?" and Rousseau's answer, "Life" (*Triumph* 177–8, 180)—rests on a reading of the ghostly presence of its guide. But is this life as perceived reality or life itself? My own reading is influenced by Ian Balfour's study of singularity in Derrida's Rousseau and in Rousseau's *Confessions*: singularity is always crossed by the generic.[6] In thinking about the singular and the generic as distortions of the "One" and the "All," the problem of singularity arises. It is immediately evident that Shelley's description of Rousseau as marked by his "disguise" of "an old root" of "strange distortion" works within this crossing, which is not a defacing of the body but a forcible re-seeing of the body's expressibility. It recalls the "mask of darkness" that hides another version of what is there at the poem's beginning (*Triumph* 204, 182–83), and also indicates the refigured Rousseau as having been marked by the trace, the embodied writing that for Shelley reinscribed Rousseau as a misguided corpus.

In revisiting Derrida's reading of Rousseau, I hope to illuminate why it is this philosopher Shelley finally singles out from those he had considered equally as important in earlier drafts.[7] Although Rousseau had indeed been part "of that deluded crew" following the triumphal car, he asks the speaker to "forbear / To join the dance, which I had well forborne" through a "deep scorn" (the scars of which he bears on his corpse-corpus), which "Led me and my companions" to resist the mad dance of Life (*Triumph* 188–89, 191). Or rather, Rousseau and his few companions have scorned the machinations of the arche-trace, the insistent rewriting of which the poem accuses "those spoilers spoiled, Voltaire, / Frederic, and Kant, Catherine, and Leopold, / Chained hoary anarchs, demagogue and sage" (235–37). In *Of Grammatology*, Derrida is less kind to Rousseau, seeing him as being one of the spoilers, but he nevertheless grants the philosopher pride of place as the middle term between Plato and Hegel for his prescient analysis of writing's role in both the centering of presence and its deferral. Because we have learned to be contained by writing's horizons, we—like Shelley's crowd—are aligned with the four-faced, eye-banded charioteer of Shelley's triumphal car.

Derrida's reading of Rousseau's importance rests on his recognition of the limits of language. But the *Triumph of Life* asks Rousseau to help move the dream vision beyond such perimeters into a different plane with a different horizonal potential. In the *Triumph*, Rousseau acts as the poet-speaker's Virgil, interpreting the pageant, discovering its trace, and spectrally pointing a finger to a different horizon unconditioned by scientism's rejection of passion or embodiedness as way of knowing. For

Derrida, Rousseau is always unsettled by passion's unsettling priority over need. Despite his attempts to settle passion into its place, passion's prewriting in the business of survival and articulation becomes, in Rousseau's anthropological scheme, inverted (as subdivision of sound and meaning, understanding and reason, which is "the opening and closure of a cleft," according to Derrida, or the making of a judgment[8]). The *Essay on the Origin of Languages* (1743) asserts love's role in the immediacy of touch (versus the mediacy of gesture), and love's role in inventing drawing as well as, plausibly, language ("Love might also have invented speech")—but if it is need that in general motivates language, "Dissatisfied with speech, love disdains it."[9] However, pity is the passion more befitting Shelley's Rousseau; pity is the moderation of amour propre—self-love, which is a corruption of *amour de soi*, love of self—into compassion. If the *Essay* places judgment before pity, the Second Discourse (1754) makes pity anterior to reflection. Thus need (in which reflection prompts the preservation of the species) follows passion (love of self, self-love, and pity); communication displaces sympathetic communion. Shelley's spectral vision shows the detrimental effects of not following this scheme—of species preservation distorted by language's death-grip, of self-love's violence absorbed into linguistic warping. "What the ancients said most forcefully they expressed not in words, but in signs; they did not say it, they showed it" ("Second Discourse" 241). Language as the first social institution, according to Rousseau, is founded as a distancing trope, as not just sign but metaphoricity (here figuration is a lack rather than Coleridge's plenitude), with the need to communicate by gesture logically displacing the passion of an immediate touch and voice, following after it. He notes, "the needs dictated the first gestures, and the passions wrung the first utterings [*voix*]" (245). This unsettling, in which need overrides passion only to install death into language as distance and metaphor rather than touching intimacy, disturbs the provenance and authority of signs (articulation and writing are the malady of language, its "fatal advantage,"[10] and if "the most vigorous speech is that in which the Sign has said everything before a single word is spoken," too often symbols lose their meaning and power to the condemning inefficacy of "circumlocutions," 241). Rousseau therefore distrusts words, as he does not the accentuation of music, and the musical intonation of poetic speech, both of which are more originary and less dangerous than writing because they are less destructive of presence (the very thing "Life" robs from human being in the *Triumph*). "The speech of the first men," he notes, "were Poet's languages" (245). But for

Shelley, if poetics is grounded in musical intonation, *poesis* is grounded in the affiliation of sound with figuration, in the sound's affinity in relation to the sign's differential potency, its gesticulatory capacity—indeed, in its imaginative intimacy. *Poesis* as allegory—as resounding figure—provides the only recuperation of a full meaning possible in the face of language's ontotheological death grip (a fate Shelley sees as written on Rousseau's body/corpus before his conversion by confession[11]).

That Shelley would choose Rousseau to interpret life's pageant puts into question not only Rousseau's idealization of love's power in his biographical writings, but also the capacity for philosophy to reveal life's perverting delusions. What is less doubtful than Rousseau's idealizations is his facility with the legible, with reading as interpreting rather than decipherment. This is the site for Rousseau, Derrida argues, of unease, suture, inversion, and perversion.[12] But Shelley's Rousseau offers a different instruction. Rather than point back to origins, his ghostly finger pointing gestures not *toward* so much as *beyond* current epistemic limits; predictive, pre-vocative, provoking an elsewhere as a way out of the metaphysical trap of signs and beyond the Anthropocene. If Rousseau himself saw gesture as less meaningful than either touching voice or metaphor, it is because it is also less immediate. But Shelley's Rousseau points intimately and tellingly otherwise—at once confessional and prophetic. The lines "Before the chariot had begun to climb / The opposing steep of that mysterious dell, / Behold a wonder worthy of the rhyme" (*Triumph* 469–71) indicate the nature of this beyondness, which is not the supplement but rather its abolishment. The wonderment of rhyme is exactly its inscription of accentuation, music, and most importantly passion—"the wondrous story / How all things are transfigured, except Love" (476). Shelley asks us to follow the index of this passionate trace as it avoids inversion, perversion, transfiguration, and supplementation, since it names the absorptive beyondness that the poem's breaking off cannot or does not yet know how to inscribe, but toward which, with Rousseau's help, it gestures.

Such a gesticulation is necessary to ward off the blindness, the necessary not-seeing, that Derrida takes as the essence of philosophical discourse without which the aporias of the metaphysical tradition cannot be overcome. Shelley depicts this in the *Triumph* as the fourfold blindness: "The *Triumph of Life* is actually two antimasques presenting four visions of man's 'blindness,' perhaps representing the four faces of the charioteer with their banded eyes," as Barbara Estermann points out.[13]

Shelley has already understood such blinding in making Rousseau not blind but hollow-eyed, "And that the holes it [he] vainly sought to hide / Were or had been eyes" (187–88). The philosopher-seer's eyeless state is precisely what allows him to guide the poet-dreamer in "forbear[ing] / To join the dance" of "this sad pageantry" (188, 176), and in forbearing the Poet might then refuse the automatism of language, of a discourse that closes down on itself. Derrida's designation of what he calls the animal-machine of reading and rewriting that reacts with automaticity is essential to his concept of the trace as the infrastructural articulation of the arche-trace, or interdependence of self and Other without which presence itself cannot be conceived. It is the interplay between the self and its objects presumed essential to human self-consciousness, but in Romantic immanence this is the very block to a presence that is always already there. As an auto-machine (according to Derrida, but also Rousseau), writing accords better with self-consciousness and ego; it stumbles and misses when it attempts to capture the experience of alterity. An immanent presence revealing itself to those whose egos have dropped away, and the vision of an immanent future of unconditional hospitality, are both beyond language's capacity. Language, and writing in particular, have a slippery grasp on the signified; how can either represent what does not await its own expression?

But immanence is never only the absolute or unconditioned; it is always also and simultaneously bodies and form, both of which express themselves. The visionary state, which elevates the poet-speaker into what Kant considers the highest stage of beautiful art, enables a poetry in which the sublime framing of the frenzied crowd and the charioteer's mad course finds its limits at the horizonal wall with its mysterious writing, its rhymes of wonder. What Kant views as the unlawful freedom of the imagination, which must be adjudicated by the lawful restraint of the understanding, may very well be preparing for free flight as Shelley breaks off writing in those last lines. As Kant also notes, poetry is more moral than the other arts; in Shelley's case it is also more ontoethical.[14]

Shelley's most moral poem—a quality noted even by Mary Shelley, who appeared not to like the poem (perhaps for its relation to his infatuation with Jane Williams recorded in the interceding poem "Written in the Bay of Lerici")—pushes beyond a mere liminality ordained by the sublime register. Its transgressiveness, verified by a simultaneous unreasonable and unlawful desire for Jane and erasure of Mary as abiding presence, suggests the violence inherent in a sacrificial structure. The structural ploy I have in mind is Derrida's concept of autoimmunity as the function that derails unconditional hospitality—the very feature of immanent life. Shelley holds on for dear life to Jane and the body-spirit she represents, his latest "epipsychidion," because of the threat to life his vision represents. His inability to finish the poem may well be his doubt that immanent life is accessible, that unconditional hospitality as the "shape all light" or enlightenment can be achieved. What gets sacrificed in the poem is not just the endless stream of suffering humanity hurried on by a frenzied self-blinding; populations are sacrificed so that the state can keep the door to a different future firmly closed.

Shelley's response to the machinations of sovereignty dramatized in the "triumph" inheres in the hints of a future-to-come in his poem's terminating points. It is an immanent future, one unconditioned by the demands of state for exclusion, privilege, and punishment. His imagining cannot be of an ideal republication state, as is Rousseau's in *The Social Contract* (1762), because Rousseau's political state still excludes, still creates hierarchies and therefore deluded thinking. Instead, Shelley's poem prepares for the possibility of an unforeseeable future beyond the horizon of statism. To imagine a horizonal "beyond" is not to envision a distinct event such as revolution, but to imagine an alternative, composible world where immanent life is fully expressible. This conception must go beyond the truth-idea of *Prometheus Unbound*, that love is a revolutionary force, since the *Triumph* seems to anticipate necessary action after Rousseau has imparted his revelation to the speaker, unlike Prometheus's patient endurance. But how must the speaker respond to the revelatory? This is one of many questions that arise in those final lines where language is too fallible and given to disintegration.

In the ideological machine epitomized in the Car of Life, suffering is the predominant human experience. Christianity tells us it cannot be otherwise. Rousseau, hovering in the ectoplasm of *The Triumph* and bearing the marks of that suffering on his body, represents by his oeuvre the rational ways that suffering has become "natural," and that deluded seeing results from the lawfulness of the understanding interceding in a Kantian imaginative freedom that is illicit. Such remediation is of course problematized by Rousseau's own biography: "real life" as it is experienced under the delusions created by a self-affirming ego. Moreover, his corpus of published works had come to stand in for what Cary Wolfe calls an "auto-immune auto-indemnification" that authorizes sovereignty at every level.[15] But in his ghastly condition, Rousseau's role in sacrificial indemnification is revised by way of his own dead body marginalized from the multitudes in Shelley's dream-vision. This vision produces an altered state, a poetic possibility in which sovereignty is unveiled as a mad careen destined to slam up against the walls of its own horizon. The alteration makes possible a different plane in which doors might open, in which an unconditional hospitality does not usher others into the spaces of the proper, but rather welcomes the ground of a futurity not yet imagined. The unlawfulness of the imagination is not, as Kant believed, an ugliness not subject to the dictates of taste, but rather the dismissal of a necessary adjudication of justice by law. For Shelley, law can only be evil because it refers justice to the dictates of pragmatism, the proper of the subject self, and sovereignty. How might what can only be called an immunitary rationale for limiting the application of justice ever ground a futurity at all? We might view this as the difference between a marriage that necessarily mediates love by way of pragmatism and a free love that opens the door to an unimagined relation, to a commingling without adjudication, to a truth without a past. Such an analogy might indeed sit behind the inexplicable poor taste of the poem to Jane, probably written before two-thirds of the *Triumph* had been completed.[16]

To draw out the implications of the argument briefly sketched here, I focus on how the *Triumph of Life* points toward freedom, democracy, and immanence. It is an idea that opens up to the possibilities for a posthuman turn in such a plane, the prospect at which language falters and poetic sound and metaphor can only carry partially inscribed meanings. However, in these falterings I believe Shelley is struggling to sound out his vision for a more humane, enlightened, and immanent futurity. This is the implication of the *Triumph*'s maddened and dizzying progress. That speed is essential to a new plane of immanence developing. One of the ways to speed up while still inhabiting the structures of the past is metalepsis, the two-at-once of metaphoric achievement. If, as Donald Reiman suggests, metaphor provides an analogous relation, a side-by-side correspondence of idea and impression, metalepsis imposes an inverted correspondence, in which logic skews otherwise.[17] The possibility opened up by the dizzying movement of the triumph, by way of its reversion to the past, begins to dissolve not into a metonymy but into a metalepsis, in which two tropes at once—a doubled metaphoricity (the fading coal *and* the mind's inconstant wind of the poetic imagination of Shelley's "Defence of Poetry"[18])—opposes the double finitude of writing by "reconfiguring the relationship between a 'before' and an 'after,' an anteriority and what this anteriority makes possible or forecloses," as Kir Kuiken explains, allowing the imagination, or we might say the poetic dream state, to be the site-source of "ever-changing future alterations."[19]

Metalepsis as the poetic device by which the future can open up by way of the past—rather than via metonymy's side-by-side logic—becomes in *The Triumph* the condition of the possibility of a new plane with a new horizonal opening to a compossible future. I am imagining Shelley imagining Deleuze and Guattari's plane of immanence, wherein the speed of thought is made possible by the constellation of the event to come configured in the evental concept.[20] It is this concept, this eventful thought, that opens the poem's horizon to a positive infinite, to a futurity that can be thought without resort to history, albeit not without a repurposing of the past and its necessary conceptual contributions. The dizzying vision of the pageant is accessible to the speaker-poet as insight, so that "speed in the van and blindness in the rear," which brings the suffering multitudes so "little profit," offers the speaker a path toward an undistorted and thus possible futurity (*Triumph* 101, 100). Schelling defines freedom as the infinite appearing as the finite, which might be parsed as the infinite appearing of the infinite. Either way, futurity in the *Triumph* can only be thought as something beyond representation but which the present event can open itself up to.

Access to this futurity requires a variant eye, one open to immanent realization; self-enclosing blindedness, as in the charioteer's, is the cancellation of what makes representation possible. By contrast, the canceling of sight in Rousseau's hollowed eyes is the condition of seeing out of this world, for insight, or for seeing immanently. Although Rousseau gestures toward the past, he is the guiding hand in the poem toward an as-yet to be represented future. Derrida remarks that portraits of the blind are "prey to *allegory*," their depictions perceived as a "specular folding" or "withdrawal [*retrait*] in meaning of itself." By contrast, language "always speaks to us *from/of the blindness* that constitutes it."[21] Shelley makes clear that such blindness—specular folding or blindfoldedness—is the condition of this ego-driven, self-referential world as well as of language. The possibility of a future as something we are not blindly acquiescent to, but an unconditional welcoming of the yet-to-come, releases allegory or folding into the replete what-is. Shelley does not allegorize Rousseau so much as allow him to tell his story of becoming-immanent. In this recursive tale of conversion, however, Shelley does allow Rousseau the specular folding of seeing otherwise. Yes, meaning is presented allegorically, but the light-filled Shape of his vision is his: the speaker and reader must experience their own revelations. He does so because the problem for Shelley is how to welcome such a future without deferral or blindfolding—or at least, with a different relation to the externality of self. For this, the Rousseau whom Shelley depicts is helpful. What Derrida calls spacing, or the endless deferral of meaning, blinds us to just how non-meaningful a life lived can be. Its enabling slipperiness can result in the headlong careen of Shelley's allegory of unmeaning life. Language can only under extraordinary circumstances leverage the scuttling of meaning into the dizzy rapidity of thought that energizes a new plan of thought, a plane of immanence that yields expression. The plane of immanence is "the horizon of events," or evental concepts: "The plane of immanence is not a concept that is or can be thought but rather the image of thought, the image thought gives itself of what it means to think," which stands in contrast to "the slow brain" (Deleuze and Guattari, *What Is Philosophy?* 36–37). This immanent plane figures what happens when the self-actualizing alterity encountered in the time-paused interval produces an aftereffect by which reason (in witnessing immanent life expressing world-spirit) can grasp and transform itself. Moreover, only philosophical "friends," such as Rousseau is for Shelley, "can set out a plane of immanence as a ground from which idols have been cleared" (43). It is such a plane, such an immanence, that Shelley's poem calls for, invokes, but cannot see in its last elliptical lines. But it is what Rousseau, by gesturing toward the past, helps Shelley's speaker metaleptically envision, if only in its barest contours, as the cliff walls of wondrous rhyme: "Before the chariot had begun to climb / The opposing steep of that mysterious dell, / Behold a wonder worthy of the rhyme" (*Triumph* 469–71).

"What is Life?" Shelley's speaker asks, struggling blindly with the *repli* of death into Life, the supplemental sacrifice that protects and indemnifies life.[22] Reiman notes that the "Essay on Life" was "perhaps the most important single document of Shelley's intellectual development" (*Shelley's "The Triumph"* 12). The essay divides the immutable celestial realm from the terrestrial, necessity-driven world. It provides a cosmology to house Shelley's purposefully chosen array of symbols, but the *Triumph* asks about a different conception of life: what is *Life*? This is the question the posthuman turn posits, since there is no longer a possible illusory tying of origin and life to certain biological forms, while sentience itself has become less definable. Shelley's potentiated future, predicated on opening the door to a new plane of immanence, holds open the possibility that a just world without suffering might be possible. Shelley the vegetarian might have embodied such a world with non-objectified subjects that, regardless of their species, would not be required to supplement the idea of justice with their suffering. Such a world, however, would have to be free of the deferral or the endless play of differentiation that inscribes the world we know. To depict a different world, one not yet visible, would require a new writing without deferral, hierarchy, origin fables, distinctions that wound. For Shelley, such a world could not yet be written—but the ellipses that punctuate the last portion of the poem he *did* write, mark where the leaping off into a new writing might occur, where a new concept might gather itself for an event to come of wondrous rhyme and immanence as what is without distortion. Rawes discusses Shelley's "compelling rhyme schemes" in deconstructive terms to demonstrate how the *Triumph*'s rhymes allow Shelley to ponder equivocality and contradiction as themes (Rawes 78). But contradiction—to speak against—might be exactly what is called for in changing the course of the blindfolded charioteer, that is, the track lines that seem to determine human "Life." Contradiction in the wondrous rhyme, the poem's broken last lines indicate, requires a new plane of thought, one in which immanent life is not contested by ego, reason, self-interest, and exclusion of others. This is the unpredictable and thus unspeakable event of overleaping the horizon. The difficulty for Shelley is, how to face into what even poetic language stumbles over, how to voice the wondrous.

Rousseau's blind seeing and the blind faith he gestures toward recalls the Mariner's endless recitals of the moment of insight, of the wondrous. The repetitive nature of both their recountings suggests that a new plane of immanence resists voicing; immanent life is replete with expressive corporeal and incorporeal bodies. In its resistance to human language, there is a resonance with apophasis, or the voiceless voice. What speaks without language is what can give voice to expressive bodies and immanent life. There is almost the sense at the broken-off ending of the *Triumph* that the wondrous rhyme, the *terza rima*, can itself carry the vision forward into the future-to-come. Shelley's perspicacious weaving of blindness, unvoicedness, limits, futurity, and freedom creates a poem that awaits the phenomenal day, the world-to-come that we must anticipate yet cannot possibly foresee. Derrida posits the *chora* in the anticipatory function: it is "before everything," yet "would give rise or allow to take place," opening up to "the unforeseeability of an event that is necessarily without horizon."[23] Because the *chora* is fully Other in its nonbeing and anticipation, it offers a place in which futurity can begin to be thought. It is only at the limits that futurity can even be gestured toward. The choric interval contains both the space of the dream vision and the possible future that lies beyond the horizon.

The problem in the *Triumph* that is "before everything," against which the choric interval is staged, is the multitude following the arrogantly blind-ful charioteer. Suffering as they are in their maddened dance, they represent self-delusion itself:

> They, tortured by the agonizing pleasure,
> Convulsed and on the rapid whirlwinds spun
> Of that fierce spirit, whose unholy leisure
> Was soothed by mischief since the world begun . . . (*Triumph* 143–46)

They present a parody of the One and All, instead of what should be "the truth of the other, heterogeneity, . . . disseminal multiplicity, the anonymous 'anyone,' the 'no matter who,' the indeterminate 'each one'" that is the other truth of democracy (or liberality, or freedom) that opposes the autonomy and ipseity that we hold dear to democracy (*Rogues* 14). To see these whirling and convulsed dancers differently, as suffering but also heteronomic rather than intimately enjoined, is to begin to differentiate egotistical self-blindness from the no-matter-who of a democracy-to-come. This is the gesture already in place, moving readers from the dissolving of particularity into a mob scene to the dissolving of delusion by the time Rousseau appears pronouncing "Life." This gesture forces the speaker-poet to begin again, "But first, who art thou?" (*Triumph* 180, 199). Rousseau's explanations cause the speaker to understand that "God made irreconcilable / Good and the means of good" (230–31). We now have a safe vantage from which to discern the difference between the conditioned and the unconditioned, between history and futurity. "Life" has been this deluded dance, but it is indeed blindfolded. Futurity has the potential to open up to insight, enlightened life.

It is not enough to be a brilliant philosopher to achieve enlightened life. Kant is included in "those spoilers spoiled," which also include Voltaire (235), those reasoners and mechanists who have brought on the "Sorrow, terror, anguish, despair . . . [that] are often the chosen expressions of an approximation to the highest good" ("Defense" 529). A future-to-come must, by the evocative stopping point of *The Triumph*, open up to the whoever-comes and not just the select few and self-chosen. The universal subject must be understood to be the One and All. The ellipses materialize the untimely interval just as the preceding portions of the poem have figured it. "The most unfailing herald," for Shelley, which is also the "companion, and follower of the awakening of a great people to work a beneficial change in opinion or institution, is Poetry." And it is the task of poets to be "the hierophants of an unapprehended inspiration" that might motivate such an awakening and such a change, for poets are "the mirrors of the gigantic shadows which futurity casts upon the present" ("Defence" 535). The courage required to welcome such a future is wrenching; its unvoicedness both compels, in the sense of the apophatic call, and stops short, in the sense of an illegible moment. In both cases language fails, as it does the multitude whose frenzy is all that can be represented. The future must be wrenched from the past at such a point; it must exceed the promise held by all pastness and go beyond the breaking point.

Frenzied activity, then, must be part of the breaking of the limit, the push beyond the grounds of the triumphal careen. That the speaker stands apart from both the multitude and the frenzy does not preclude his taking part in futurity, a partaking that may already be beginning with the fragmentation of words into ellipses. As Derrida notes, "*ellipsis* names not only lack but a curved figure with more than one focus. We are thus already tween the 'minus one' and the 'more than one'" (*Rogues* 1). Ellipses as the incapacity of language to represent, and yet also suggest what cannot be said, what is visionary: ellipses also intimate a rhythm, a fidelity to the beat of the line. The heartbeat or breath of life itself.

II. Disfiguration or Distortion?

The Poet's encounter with Rousseau, and Rousseau's narrative, take up the majority of the poem. As the speaker and reader learn about Rousseau's encounters with the "shape all light" (*Triumph* 308–433), we also learn that he has been translated by that shape, becoming increasingly hollowed out. He is metamorphosed, in de Man's words, to a state "in which his brain, the center of his consciousness, is transformed" ("Shelley Disfigured" 99). Whereas Rousseau's recurring focus is on the "shape all light," de Man reads the speaker as avoiding the shape-light through his narrative fragmentation at the unsubstantial end or leaving off of the poem. Such a reading suggests the ending might be unsubstantial in the sense of a dissolving substance (something impossible in a Spinozist universe), or it might be insubstantial, an unmeaningful fragmentation. While both are plausibly true, the notion of the incorporeal as figured first by Rousseau and then by the poem's dream vision is also plausibly a problem of the specular fold that enables rather than prohibits insight: "Happy those for whom the fold / Of" are the last words of the poem.[24]

The ending also contains the kernel of the whole poem—not as fragment but as ellipses, as points of departure for curves that move elsewhere as a leaping out of the spatiotemporal horizon of the poem. Rousseau himself points out in his essays on language that time is the essential medium of language creation (or, as Levi-Strauss puts it, "the infinite space of time that the first invention of languages must have cost" [qtd. in Derrida, *Of Grammatology* (1997), 121]). There are indeed violent linguistic acts that occur in the poem, each more damaging than the violence depicted in the triumphal parade itself. The poem is eventually revealed to be a "mutilated textual model [that] exposes the wound of a fracture" (de Man 120). But the violence is itself a disease, a genetic self-destruct mechanism, and it is this disease that Shelley's poem narrates. Neither Rousseau's writings nor the voiced narrative embedded in the poem remain by the *Triumph*'s end. This fragmentary ending records language's demise in ordinary terms as it makes way for a new expressive mode. Its self-violence is played out neither as the figure of a hollowed-out (diseased) Rousseau nor as his "recapitulative" narrative in which logic dissipates,[25] but as language's final failure to capture through anything but its own erasure—its ellipses—what might speak itself beyond blindfolded Life's horizon.

This ellipsis is related to Rousseau's hollowing out: diseased by the light's erasure of his self-consciousness, of his presence as writing and as predecessor figure, Rousseau himself is reduced to a periodic gesture, like beats in a measure rather than Cartesian stopping points (for Descartes, points stop things dead; Shelley's Rousseau continues to move after death). Translated by the light into an ellipsis of himself, Rousseau's hollowing is of his self-presence, his consciousness as center of self; he thus sets the stage in the poem for the transfiguration of the narrative at the end into ellipses. This follows how Shelley would have understood the Platonic formulation of light's essence. Schelling is helpful in laying out the idealist terms of this essence: "*The infinite concept of all finite things, insofar as it is contained in the real unity, is light* . . . Light = concept, *ideal* unity" (*Philosophy of Art* 119; emphasis his). The "shape all light," then, is the concept of the All and One because it is at once the concept as ideal unity, "but [also] ideal unity within the real unity"—that is, it gives shape to both the absolute and the particular. ("In the opposing unity," Schelling notes about the real unity that is "the development of objectivity into itself," "identity can be comprehended only as unity within *multiplicity*"—which for Shelley is the parade of writhing figures in thrall to the charioteer.) Rousseau's vision of light as the All and One erases his identity as it absorbs him into the absolute. The dissolution of his ego requires an accompanying dissolution of language, which is distinguished by its relation to the ego, that human component that must make sense of the world through semiotic codes and symbolic concepts. If language will then be recuperated, there is still something of the erasure of ego-identity in this experience that remains, that transforms ego relations such that, like the Ancient Mariner, one simply can't go on in the same way as before the encounter. The light's interpenetration functions something like transduction: the introduction of foreign DNA into a cell for curative purposes. The dissolution of ego for Rousseau is related to the dissolution of language at the end of *Triumph*: things simply can't go on in the same manner after the speaker encounters Rousseau's encounter of the "shape all light."

Derrida writes that the "other ellipsis of the metaphysics or onto-theology of the logos" is the "effort to master absence by reducing metaphor" (*Of Grammatology* [1997], 106). "Onto-theology," however, is the very beast Shelley is trying to eradicate in *The Triumph*; for Shelley, this is the real disease of language, subjectivity, self-consciousness, and knowledge that creates the horizonal parameters of a "Life" that enslaves us. Transduction becomes a necessity, and Rousseau is the viral agent who introduces the foreign DNA into the poem. But the "shape all light" is no mere metaphor; it condenses philosophical speculation since Plato concerning the essence of light as the most absolute of all concepts that can find form in the real realm. To imagine the "shape" as mere metaphor reduces, indeed, dissolves it into sensory presence. Metaphor has its relation to "truth";[26] but for Spinoza there is no truth other than substance all the way down and deep interconnection. Rousseau's translation from egotistic self-consciousness into a forgotten selfhood is accompanied by metaphors for light that offer little narrative reason except for losing self-blindedness. That is another version of Spinoza's "truth."

To interpret Rousseau's history of illuminating confessions by way of metalepsis—as a metaleptic recursiveness—allows for the movement that will transform or curve itself into a possible future, one replete with immanence that is without logocentric, androcentric, and anthropocentric distortion, and thus a new paradigm. This movement is the leap to a new plane of immanence at the poem's ending, a potentiating move toward the All and One as a sustained experience of becoming. Only such sublation of human egotism into the higher concept of absolute community could condition such a possible future. If Schelling views light as "the element of the ideal that is manifested in nature, the first breakthrough of idealism" (*Philosophy of Art* 120), Rousseau's response to that breakthrough of idealism is to lose the capacity for symbolic representation as it encodes self-identity. De Man notes that the question and answer enacted by the figures of Rousseau and the speaker (the question of "'whence I came, and where I am, and why—;'" *Triumph* 398) is that of "a question whose meaning, as question, is effaced from the moment it is asked," in the structure of a forgetting (*Rhetoric of Romanticism* 98). For de Man, this repeating pattern of question, effacement, and forgetting (rather than question and answer) functions like a knot that "arrests the process of understanding." Or, perhaps, lifts understanding into realization. For Shelley, Rousseau the writer has, "in a sense . . . overcome the discrepancy of action and intention that tears apart the historical world, and he has done so because his words have acquired the power of actions as well as of the will." His words "literally, are actions" (*Rhetoric of Romanticism* 103). Language, that is, becomes a component of idealism's breakthrough into the real insofar as it is potentiated. But the *Triumph* undermines this understanding of historical intervention, change, and dialectical movement. Rousseau is himself faulted for not valuing history's truths, but not because history must be taken as dialectically progressive—rather, because of its evidentiary and repeating truths. If Rousseau's arrestingly ineffective language in the poem is read metaleptically, in which the cause substitutes for the effect, truth may still be achievable, for in this way history and the future are exchangeable. The question cannot have an answer, because the answer can go both forward and backward in contradictory style. More importantly, in classical rhetoric, metalepsis creates a passage from one context to another, effecting a change in terms that opens up a third way. We might say, it is the movement of the energy from one plane of immanence to another, that which enables the event that announces change. In *The Triumph*, that event is the chariot careening toward the chasm wall of wondrous rhyme. It is announced, but not comprehensibly articulated as an evental idea, for the rhyme is not legible in the terms that hold sway before the leap it announces. Promising everything, like the "shape all light," the wondrous rhyme signifies potentiality, both as the power of creative language and as the power of significant movement that opposes the recursive forgetting of Rousseau's and the speaker's "why?" as well as the enslaving movement of the chariot's triumph.

Without making a connection between the effacement of history, of self-consciousness, and language without figuration (language that baldly proclaims truth and therefore blinds), the "shape all light" is exactly enlightenment. Only this metaphorical presentation can give a sense of the life-changing immanent encounter Rousseau had. The experience also gave him an alternative future. Is this, perhaps, the sense of the ending? That veering off course is how each individual body in Spinoza's schema can come to enlightened understanding, which he calls "intellectual intuition"? That is the intuitive love of God, that is therefore the love of Nature.

In the poem yet one more thing that comes into question is what counts: natural rhythm or energy, and movement as periodic units as representative of life beyond self-blinded activity. Counting is a way of signifying without the representational limits of signs or a blindness to metaphor. Shelley goes further, with measure in the *Triumph* obliterating thought. For Rousseau in the Second *Discourse*, measure or counting functions in both dance and music as a more primary and primitive medium than the sight/light medium of the image and sign, which comes later as touching is replaced by the distance of gesture and then drawing.[27] Counting comes down to points of measure, of comprehension, of community. In the *Triumph*, Shelley shows light as the scene of what de Man calls "optical confusion" (106), which we might call image confusion, in echo of the vision that is delusory for its participants, diffusive for community, and difficult for the spectator Poet to interpret. "The thematization of language in *The Triumph of Life* occurs," de Man notes, "when 'measure' separates from the phenomenal aspects of signification as a specular *representation*, and stresses instead the literal and material aspects of language," adding that "it is precisely these 'feet' [of the *terza rima*] which extinguish and bury the poetic and philosophical light" (113). This literalization of language that ignores metaphor, this death of poetic capacity and of an originary communication, is precisely what Rousseau finds to be the history of language as a whole. For Shelley it is the history of Western political ideology as well.

In Rousseau's highly political theory of language's origins as developed in *The Essay on the Origins of Language*, metaphor and music were early on prone to instability. He posits a geographical development of language, such that in northern regions the passions and desire are substituted and repressed by work and the need that provokes it. Passion there takes the form of violent emotions, of fury, and speech turns toward articulation and away from tonality and musical speech. Writing is therefore "at the north" where articulation is heightened; writing allows for history, which "hollows out" both vowel accent and articulation, "extending the power of writing (226). "Our tongues," Rousseau notes in the *Essay*, "are better suiting to writing than speaking," an observation noteworthy for the *Triumph* in which Rousseau's writings are metaleptically hollowed out in favor of his spoken recitative, which nevertheless has no historical compass. Moreover, the "oriental corpse is in the book," but for the north, "[o]urs is already in our speech" (qtd. in *Of Grammatology* 226). The north, in effect, is death. This death, which need and work attempt to evade, accounts for the loss of melodious sound, of music from languages of the north where accent signs and punctuation replace intonation, that is, life and desire as sound (227). Nothing more clearly theorizes the living death of Shelley's Rousseau, whose language has been so hollowed out that it is eviscerated of anything but a haunting. Even its attempts to capture image and figure, poetry and measure disintegrate toward the forgetting that is overtaking him. The warning he represents for the Poet prepares us, and him perhaps, for the disintegration of the poem's integrity at the ending, its substitution of stuttering punctuation for poetic imagination, poetic imaging, poetic music. What does remain is measure, measure as counting, as beats, as what might be a gathering of dissipated energies rather than a dying into itself. The Mariner's insistently rhythmic wild force as he tells his tale is clearly present in the early part of *The Triumph* but dies away in the final lines as the speaker begins to question Rousseau's insight.

One such question is, what is it that can get the *Triumph* back from the edge of a vertiginous loss of meaningful vision? Another is, what can transform the spectacular triumph's mad careen from meaninglessness to Rousseau's hollow-eyed seeing? Hollow-eyed, hollowing out, and the root that is no root (of language, of origin[28]). Rousseau—the unrecognizable image of Rousseau when the speaker first encounters him—is a man after all. He provides spectral figurations for the failure of both sight and language in the poem, or rather, for the disfiguration that de Man locates there.

The problem of the poem is not that it dis-articulates figuration and narrative, or that it encapsulates frenzied motion and a kind of centrifugal force so that the center empties out—or is seen to have always been empty, although these are both at play. The problem is that the poem is about the struggle between existence and control as a drama of the All-in-All. To convey this, the poem references so many ideas that it works rather like a magnet that has attracted little metal bits that it allows to disfigure the unity of the whole. That unity and substance, disenfranchised by the hollowing out that Rousseau represents, and by the insistence on a messily chaotic history doomed to repeat itself that the triumph represents, comes to an end with the elliptical ending. There a blind seeing is required to see beyond the ending; it is the kind of sightedness poets are renowned for, but Shelley resists putting such seeing into words. Ideal light effaces words, while seeing that light is to forget how to see in normal terms. The self-actualizing power of light requires something more than human speech and the time-space of self-conscious activity. What Shelley requires is a different kind of writing capable of resisting the death of presence that Rousseau accords to writing by refusing that dichotomizing of essence/substance, and of presence/distance encoded in Enlightenment theories of language. Such binaries recall one even more pertinent to the origin of language, that of nature/culture, which asserts an ideological, ontotheological interpretation on history as powerful as that of writing itself. Without a new writing, those who have had power will again sit "like vultures" and "pla[y] / Within the crown which girt with empire / A baby's or an idiot's brow" (*Triumph* 497–99).

Describing Levi-Strauss's focus on the split between nature and culture, Derrida refers to "the originality of a scandalous suture." This might well also describe the chasm wall inscribed with hieroglyphs or wondrous rhymes in *The Triumph* (471, 480). The rhymes of wonder are both the failure of logocentric writing and its alternative possibility: it is not the rhymes that are wonderful but the wonder they strive to capture. Derrida refers to iterability as repetition with a difference;[29] rhymes of wonder would then be writing with a difference, one of immanent expression. Shelley is envisioning a different kind of writing then, one that would match the body's expression with expressive writing. This would have to be a writing that goes beyond rhythm and meter to capture immanent life itself. Perhaps this is a writing of breath, felt in the beats of the ellipses that measure out the poem's partial ending, but so that all breath is heard at the same time, along with the squirrel's heartbeat and the bud's bursting. In any case, it is wonderous: the words "wonder," "wondrous," even "wonder-winged" appear frequently in the *Triumph* as if words fall short of the revelatory. Behind each use of "wonder" is the sharp intake of breath that spells awe.

The *Triumph*'s allegorical form is also in question. Despite its clear allegiance to Dante's *Divine Comedy* and Petrarch's *Trionfi* ("Triumph"), another allegory sits behind the poem, Plato's allegory of the cave: " 'Figures ever new / Rise . . . paint them how you may; / We have but thrown, as those before us threw, / Our shadows on it,' " Rousseau explains to the speaker as he points out, "All that is mortal of great Plato there" "chained to the triumphal chair" with the rest (*Triumph* 248–51, 254, 52). Shelley's Platonism is well-known, but I believe that in his last major poem he overleaps Plato's vision just as he does Dante's. Derrida's analysis of Plato's allegory in *Memoirs of the Blind* is helpful here because it reveals the difficulty at the heart of the cave analogy: human passivity as the condition for seeing differently.

Plato describes his allegorical cave as peopled by humans chained to the walls by their various kinds of blindness, caused when opinion is valued over the logic of ideas. Unable even to move their heads, these prisoners mistake shadows for real things. They are passive while chained, but even what frees them is not due to their own agency: "A conversion will free them . . . But before this dazzling ascent, an *anabasis* that is also an *anamensis*," a journey through previous lives must take place. This "passion of memory . . . will turn the soul's gaze towards the 'intelligible place' " (*Memoirs* 15). Far from being an act of will, however, Plato's prisoners are represented as motionless through this process. Rousseau's conversion is a rewriting of this allegory, his repeated retracing of his life as a philosophe prompted by the "shape all light" rather than by his own initiative, and like the prisoners, the process produces a second kind of blindness, as Derrida notes, which Plato attributes to the exchange of dark shadows for intelligible light, where otherness might indeed be perceived otherwise and without blinding distortion. Rousseau must see through eyes hollowed out of their prior blindnesses. Part of what Rousseau, and the speaker he instructs, must forget is the blinding opinions of Cartesian thought—constrained by postulates, skepticism, and Kantian critique—which rejects any stretching out to the thing-in-itself. Clearly Rousseau's finger stretches in just such a way to point to the in-itself, the triumphal march as the essence of ideologically bound and blinded Life. Derrida notes that Plato's prisoners never stretch their hands even toward the shadows on the cave's walls; they are motionless in their inability even to touch the representations of things, let alone things-in-themselves. Shelley rejects such rejection, insisting that Rousseau *can* see blindly, *can* point to verities and intelligibilities. De Man disagreed with Derrida's interpretation of Rousseau's blindness, remarking in a letter that "The desire to exempt Rousseau (as you say) at all costs from blindness is therefore, for me, a gesture of fidelity to my own itinerary . . . that, on the specific question of the rhetoricity of his writing, he was not blinded."[30] The truth-tropes of poetic language, that is, for de Man, Derrida and Shelley, were accessible to Rousseau under certain conditions: when his metaphors overtook him, as does the "shape all light." The intelligible place he points to is off the map, of course, just as is Plato's ideality. Finding it requires an expedition of a different sort, one that accommodates different frames of reference than those of past lives.

Shelley's *Triumph of Life* suggests that we consider history not as something that must be erased, as in Rousseau's translation to a higher consciousness, but that must be remembered, read metaleptically, in order to absorb and sublate history's lessons into the networks of the new plane of immanence. To reverse the order of cause and effect, to overleap the ontotheological reading of historical events and their causes, requires considering a longer historical timeframe than that which shapes everyday life. It is worth noting here that, like Shelley, Schelling was also a Plato enthusiast and also found Plato's teaching on light and shape nutritive. For both poet and philosopher, reading Plato was a resistance campaign against Enlightenment Aristotelian science, with its divisive thinking and wrongheaded insistence on substance, leading to a non-progressive conception of nature that left it ripe for exploitation.[31] Shelley's dream vision, like Schelling's depiction of God's unconscious in *Ages of the World*, provides the space in which to contemplate deep time in a dynamic and evolving world, a time that extends in both directions beyond man's historiographical grasp. It is the deep time that geological and archaeological findings had recently made more objectively knowable than what the cosmological imagination could speculate, but that cosmic imaginary is nevertheless the resource (as in Dante's and Petrarch's great works) for conceiving of an evental time to come.

Comparably, pastness could be thought as inhabiting a larger, more flexible temporality in which time before memory can be traced through historical time-schemes and geological, scientific deep time, both of which Shelley seems aware of and concerned about for the tension between them and their seeming incompatibility.[32] In "Defence of Poetry," written the year before *Triumph of Life*, Shelley does accord poetry both a visionary divinity and a central role in "comprehend[ing] all science," but he then emphasizes its capacity for differential thought and action—"It is at the same time the root and blossom of all other systems of thought"—in the same paragraph in which he likens the poetic mind to a fading coal (Reiman and Fraistat 531). In the *Triumph*, "normative" time exists outside the dream vision's temporal frame, leaving open the problem of what the current time might be or mean. Shelley seems particularly concerned about the Enlightenment and its epistemology, with the rigors of its regime of empirical experience, cognition, and truth-making. Any epistemology is an intellectual and phenomenal trap in the making leading to distorted seeing without lessons learned. However grounded, any human-organized way of comprehending reality is ideological: after Hume, skepticism adds to the suffering; after Kant, resistance to dreams of the new does. The leap must be more world-shattering, more indicative of a post-Napoleonic world in which new dreams are possible. *The Triumph* gestures toward a differential time situated between geological time and ancestral time on one side, and triumphal-ideological time on the other. It neither truly belongs to the deep time of the nonhuman *chronos* nor that of the ancestors, but keeps with an evental time, an as-yet unrepresentable time to come. The yearning of its ellipses, reflecting the yearning of Shelley's essays on love and on poetry's capacity to matter, indicates an encounter with alterity that doesn't need to end. It is a yearning for immanent life as the time and reality beyond the horizon of ideologically charted conduits of the charioteer's course, and of a "reality" wherein each day is "the sick day in which we wake to weep" (*Triumph* 430).

In the *Triumph*, it is the historically fraught figure of Rousseau that points toward the plane of this differential time. Literally, Rousseau points to the spectacular triumph, but his recursive self-translation into a non-self gestures beyond the chasm wall, beyond the horizon of perception. This differential time of before the horizonal wall and beyond it opens up the chasm between ancestral time (or geological deep time, or cosmic time) and the normative time that engulfs us. Rajan argues that in Blake's early illuminated books, Urizen's body "is ejected and dejected on the border between ancestral and human time" ("Blake's Body" 357). Urizen's self-creating body is an apposite image for Rousseau's self-dissolution of ego; they both point to the border between normative time and immanent time, which is at once ancestral deep time and what underlies human time. What Shelley's poem projects is the hope that immanent time is also a new time beyond the wall, one that will resist the pull of human time's distortions by instead taking into account all things, all bodies, all ideas as existents in a world where poetry and love are generative. Rousseau points the way to this world:

> "Before the chariot had begun to climb
> The opposing steep of that mysterious dell,
> Behold a wonder worthy of the rhyme
>
> "Of him whom from the lowest depths of Hell
> Through every Paradise & through all glory
> Love led serene, & who returned to tell
>
> "In words of hate & awe the wondrous story
> How all things are transfigured, except Love . . . . (*Triumph* 469–76)

Telling of Dante's visionary achievement, Rousseau reminds us that the disfigurations and distortions that make human life hellish are rewritten by love. Dante's prophecy is of a world where Love's compassion releases bodies from their ego-driven distortions. Moreover, this world has always been available but always foreclosed to distorted seeing, as Blake's Urizen demonstrates. For Shelley, " 'The world can hear not the sweet notes that move / The sphere whose light is melody to lovers—/ A wonder worthy of his [Dante's] rhyme' " (478–80). Only a new world, a new plane of immanence is worthy of such insightful verse. To achieve it, however, Shelley's poem points toward a cataclysmic break with the past where "From every form beauty slowly waned" and human sorrow "thus stained / The track in which we moved" (517–18). With its equally cataclysmic break with language, this new time would stave off a return to the old Platonic *logos* and its effects, and allow for wondrous words.

This is a futurity worth risking if its repositioning of past histories as ephemeral mean we are not doomed to repeat them: Rousseau's erasure of self points to this. And if Shelley evinces anxiety in the "Defence of Poetry" over the distorting mirrors of futurity, surely Rousseau's hollow-eyed seeing can overcome distortions that would only return us to a recursively recycled history of error and suffering. "We let '*I dare not* wait upon *I would*,'" whereas instead "We want the creative faculty to imagine that which we know; we want the generous impulse to act that which we imagine; we want *the poetry of life*" ("Defence" 530, emphasis added). Poets have long been able to create a bridge from the past into a possible futurity ("The poetry of Dante may be considered as the bridge thrown over the stream of time, which unites the modern and antient world," 526). But "poets have been challenged to resign the civic crown to reasoners and mechanists" (528), categories to which Rousseau at first capitulated in his poetical philosophy. The imagination, action, and poetry requisite for a futurity without distortion in *The Triumph* would inaugurate the post-Anthropocene and require, as Shelley's Rousseau has demonstrated, a giving up of past words, memories of self and achievements, and therefore of the Cartesian *cogito* per se. His recursive story-making of self into non-self is a movement toward a new temporality in which past histories are forgotten or overwritten so that a new time may come into being. Similar to Rousseau's self-fragmentation, the *Triumph*'s ending ellipses—which might be a cracking or fissuring in the chasmic walls, a positive fragmenting whose leaving off opens up the potentiality of poetry rather than a breaking up of logocentric linguistic formulations—gesture toward a different realization.

A differential realizing is also the vision of philosophers of the post-Anthropocene, such as Wolfe, in arguing that nonhumanist thought must not be brought back to a concentrism that still harbors the human at its core. The nonhuman must not be a veiled concern about the future of human survival; it must not be a practice of care toward other beings and toward the environment that restores the primacy of human agency. Both of these orientations distort otherness, casting it in logocentric terms that privilege the cogito and thus human history, undoing the lessons of the *Triumph*'s allegorical vision. "Rhymes of wonder" foresees this linguistic breakthrough that could restore sight's capacity to see what is there, awaiting a resolution into recognizable patterns whose interpretation need not privilege the logos, its theology, or its human subjectivity. Just as those currently struggling to envision what such a linguistics might entail cannot do more than gesture toward such a future, so too does Shelley's great poem do no more than indicate pointedly language's dissolve in such a futurity. Nevertheless, it is a rhyme of wonder.

III. Shelley's Speed

One of the strongest contrasts in the *Triumph* is between the careening chariot and the speaker who stands with Rousseau watching from the margin. But there is another kind of speed at work in the poem that has to do with new ways of thinking. Deleuze is the twentieth-century philosopher most influenced by both Stoic and Spinozist thought, and despite inherent incompatibilities with Derrida's deconstruction is a helpful counterpart for understanding immanence in the *Triumph*. Deleuze's plane of immanence, evental idea, and the dizzying speed of thought necessary to reconfigure an epistemic translation take these elements to construe a new way to think world-making that resonates with the ending of the *Triumph*. By absorbing Leibniz's more complex geometry into his Stoic and Spinozist thought, Deleuze helps make sense of the mobile space and volatile movement of Shelley's dream vision.

In the *Triumph*'s allegorical spectacle, Shelley gives us not a different, potentiated world—the triumphal parade as opposed to the world of the dreaming Poet—but the painful meaninglessness of this "best" world we inhabit. Shelley suggests that an alternative world to this one is precisely what is needed. A world in which desire, passions, and free will are not attuned to self-love and self-interest; a world in which willful self-blinding is not an ideological choice, as represented by the blindfolded charioteer who with his car is "Life." Seeing must be done hollow-eyed as for both Shelley's Rousseau and Derrida's blind artist. Only then can the poet begin a different writing, one compatible with the new plane of immanence but which was not yet imaginable to Shelley.

Spinoza's geometric conception of how bodies move and affect each other corresponds to Shelley's visionary space both within the dream vision and after the horizon is broken. For him, the individual is simply the greater or lesser degree of speed its body enacts. How bodies move obeys a geometry of lines and planes. In the *Triumph*, lines and planes create the courses along which the blindfolded charioteer careens and the mob follows; they create the sidelined banks on which the speaker and Rousseau discourse; and they create the horizonal wall against which the charioteer threatens to crash. Within this geometry, the movement of bodies occurs because bodies are in motion or at rest awaiting motion; bodies are self-moved, the speed changing through affection. Affection is both the emotional register (joy moves a body faster) and encounter with other bodies, including bodies of air, thought, climate. Spinoza defines air pressure, for instance, as "a form of pressure of bodies on bodies" (IIP13L4D). In Stoic terms, corporeals and incorporeals encounter each other, press on each other: the bodies crashing against each other in the dizzying wake of Shelley's charioteer are also moved by the delusion and madness, rhetoric and lies they have encountered or that have pressed on them bodily, impressed and crushed them. Movement is also a matter of conatus, or thing-power if we conceive that to be the drive to persist. Conatus is both power and motion, that which makes movement self-caused although affected by other bodies as well.[33] Those in the charioteer's wake have been affected by the belief that persistence, the striving that is life, takes this particular course, that there is no other line of movement however blindly they are taking it. Movement and conatus are not matters of will, but of life itself—as in the daffodils dancing in the breeze that Dorothy Wordsworth witnessed and William then celebrates in his joyful lyric. But clearly Shelley's celebrants are engaged in a dance of mad frenzy, the ideas pressing on them more and more forcefully. It is unethically oriented activity; the lines and planes are awry. And it is so because these dizzied dancers have been affected by what Spinoza calls "inadequate" ideas, flawed or confused ideas that have impressed them (IVP1S). Ethical movement is the pursuit of "adequate" ideas, which reflect more accurately the relation of mind to body, reason to fancy. Adequate ideas keep the individual and its ideas on the same plane. Adequate ideas, in Deleuze's interpretation of Spinoza, get us to new planes of immanence. Adequation is the process of seeing substance (that which "is in itself and is conceived through itself" [ID3]) through and through, seeing it as what fills the energy network that is Nature.

Deleuze uses the geometry of Spinoza's contemporary Leibniz to introduce how bodies move in spaces of turbulence where the lines and planes are disturbed, flexed, or affected by high speed. For Leibniz, the pure event of the line or point is inflection, which allows curvature, the very shape of the course the charioteer races along. Inflection introduces an elasticity to the body and a flexed capacity to the line (*The Fold* 14–15). Inflection is "an interdimension," a virtual or potential dimension between line and surface (16). The interval, in these terms, can be understood as the fold-between, or as directionality as point-folds, but it promotes turbulence. It is the turbulence that opens up the differential space between two individuals in an encounter, or the space of the dream vision. Here there is the possibility of one individual's projection of its self-interest or line of movement aggressively into the zone surrounding the other individual, or of one individual's inflection or elastic point bending in such as way as to respond or accommodate the other one. The first is the aggressive line of the charioteer, what Joseph Defalco Lamperez calls "the juggernaut"; the second is the accommodation of the speaker to Rousseau's corpse.[34] Involution as a propulsive movement makes sense negatively, as in Urizen's involutions and convolutions in Blake's vision of Urizen's self-making. But for Shelley it can also make sense positively, as in the creation of new lines. The *Triumph*'s final words are Rousseau's as he says, "Happy those for whom the fold / Of . . . ." (547). This is a momentous fold, one left without the words to render it, but also pointing to new lines, new relational connections. These last words are in response to the speaker's question once again, " 'Then, what is Life?' " (544). Reading the *Triumph* through a lens of immanence, life is not a deluded "reality" but the fold in which all surfaces touch, in that all bodies, things, and ideas touch and affect each other.

Rousseau had been recounting how, in the triumph of worldly ambition, physical movement is not only the individual's propulsion by self-interest or accommodation; some " 'died, / And some grew weary of the ghastly dance / And fell' " (*Triumph* 5, 39–40). At the same time, according to Leibniz, there is also a horizontal progression produced by "secondary horizontal linkages" that accounts for waves of progression (*The Fold* 104). The progression of waves occurs in the soul *and* the body en masse. The effect of a wave on a crowd such as that following the charioteer resembles how masses in general are constantly being worked on or put in motion by second-order derivative forces. It is not the speaker who will overleap the horizontal limit alone—although he and his fellow philosophers will be at the vanguard. It will be the entire mass of the triumphal procession that will arrive at the future once the Poet has initiated, through his electrifying eventual idea, the delivery of the derivative to the plastic forces (delivery of attraction and thrust to the crowd). He can begin the initiating charge that could turn the charioteer's path away from collision with the chasmic, horizontal wall, once his spiritual folds, like those of Rousseau, have inclined toward enlightenment, for Spinoza the individual's highest calling.

But how to account for the leap over that horizontal wall to a new plane of immanence? Ocean waves provide one illustration, for a succession of waves produce swells, eventuating sometimes in a tidal wave. The masses following the charioteer are their own force, creating inflections and distortions in their volatile movement along the course whose crashing over the horizontal wall could produce new subjects whose allegiance to the ethical blindnesses of their past have been erased, just as the tidal wave erases whatever boundaries guard the land. Erasure is perhaps the only way Shelley can imagine new beginnings, as in Rousseau's self-erasure in the encounter with the "shape all light." As Andrew Warren points out, Shelley has experimented with the effects of erasure previously in poems like *Cyntha and Laon* and *The Revolt of Islam*.[35] The passages in these two poems where Cyntha attempts to read the writing that the water is erasing from the sand resonates deeply to Rousseau's memory and ego erasure in his encounters with the "shape all light." Rousseau's erasure of memory is in fact an unfolding and refolding toward the light; the actualization of his refolding is one that will motivate the rewriting of the charioteer's path.

Shelley's uses of water is always rhythmic in these poems, especially the metaphoric use of water in erasing Rousseau's self-memory, which de Man highlights as involving rhythm and counting. The question of form, of Shelley's choice of *terza rima* to make his allegiance to Dante's and Petrarch's allegorical visions clear, is a question of tightness and progression, inflection and movement, involution and progression. How do the lines, bound to their triadic progression, build to a vision of frantic movement but also to the wall inscribed with rhymes of wonder? The lines, intertwined between stanzas as they are, do function like waves; *terza rima* as undulation, folding and unfolding as the small rhythmic waves that lead up to the great leap necessary to escape life in the post-Napoleonic political present of the poem, "Fall'n as Napoleon fell" (*Triumph* 224). *Terza rima* dances here in the versification as Dante's wondrous rhyme; sound, movement, and meaning build to an overpowering sensation (471). The stanzaic form allows the poem to move from its initial darkness toward enlightenment, not as Dante's *Divine Comedy* moves toward Beatrice, but as a more fundamental relation between monadic enlightenment and a horizontal, second-order progression of waves.[36] Moreover, undulation works in the poem as murmuration. Rousseau captures the attention of the speaker first when he murmurs. When he begins to speak of the "shape all light" encounters, his bemused accounts are so allusive as to be dislocated from rational thought, yet they are highly poetic. Indeed, they are murmuration prefiguring the evental idea; murmuration, then, rather than wild rhythmic force. Paradoxically, it is the dead Rousseau who murmurs truths, but the "live" Rousseau had articulated the language of logocentrism that is dead to poetic truth, dead because logocentrism articulates via signifiers detached from their signifieds.[37] Such detachment means that the many who must suffer are a political category, a sign, rather than manifest suffering.

Murmuration, undulation and rhythm, folding and unfolding, and what Derrida calls the *repli* are related in significant ways to Shelley's understanding of the movement and effects of poetic language as incorporeal bodies, particularly those of allegory and metalepsis. To understand this relation better in terms of Shelley's poem, a few more aspects of the fold must be drawn in. The movement of the line as a curve, fold, interval can also end in a point. The ellipses, which can either terminate a line or fold it in, producing a seam between lines, implies a leap. The line of inflection and the line of poetry meet in the fold of words. But ellipses that do not seam, as in the last four lines of the *Triumph*, are much more volatile. Volatility is a force of attraction for Leibniz, and in the *Triumph* they attract attention for they represent gaps, intervals, dislocations that figure in their literalization the dislocations of Rousseau's accounts of transcendent light.

If the turbulence produced in the dimension-between by inflection is deferred until later, then two points arise for Shelley's experiment in poetic language. The first is the problem of deferral in language and as Shelley's Rousseau overtly experiences it in his encounters with light. The second is that in language inflection carries a different weight. There are two major categories of word variation: inflection (which includes case, number, gender—the terms of declension), and derivational affix (prefixes and suffixes). Inflection is the most important for Shelley's allegorical vision of human suffering: case or function (caste distinctions among those in the triumphal procession), number (the many who must suffer by the law of "necessity"), and gender. These are all terms of declension; people are declined, in other words, differentiated such that their inflected determinants position them within the auto-machine that is both reading/writing and the sociopolitical system. The problem of inflection in language is clear—how can Shelley translate his critique of the present power system into an unblinded and distortion-less futurity without resorting to inflection? And yet nonlinguistic inflection is inclination, the beginning of a fold that might express desire, motivation, change. But the larger difficulty may well be that of a deferral in language such that the present moment never takes place. That is, how to make the evental idea of the to-come resolve into a new paradigm amenable to a language without deferral, an immanent expression?

How can Shelley discover a poetic language that *can* move outside the prison house of language? To do so would elude the entrapments that had previously defeated any imagining, let alone any actualizing of a futurity that could withstand the historical recycling symbolized in the *Triumph*. Without access to the idea and plane of immanence that made Modernist poetics possible, Shelley cannot resort to the sort of opacity

Percy Shelley's Immanent Language | 181

of language and evocative figuration that Mallarmé does, for instance, or to the linguistic experimentalism of mid-twentieth-century poets. The ellipses and broken line that mark the poem's last lines become more telling the longer we consider them, for in the mathematical interval of Leibniz's universe, all numbers between two given numbers are included in the set. This provides a model for inclusion that is infinite; moreover, each interval is the site of a new folding and thus transformation. Ellipses, for Leibniz, occur in relation to what he terms "Conditionables," because they are indemonstrable, as is Shelley's vision of futurity in the poem. Therefore, they must operate by syllogisms that work by "'inner suppressions,' ellipses, and problematic shortcuts" (Deleuze, *The Fold* 45). For Shelley, the conditioned material world also works by syllogism, inner suppression of will and desire, and problematic shortcuts. Ellipses are the one aspect of the conditioned world and conditioned language that might offer a way forward, allowing a different "concatenation."

IV. Folding and Rhythm

The specular folding or *repli* Derrida theorizes as essential to the blind artist helps make sense of the charioteer's inflected course; the charioteer is blindfolded, folded into his delusions and those he projects onto others. For Derrida, the fold is one of doubling back or "falling back on itself" as a withdrawal into memory or "an impossible reappropriation or mourning" (*Memoirs of the Blind* 3).[38] But growth indicates another direction: a body might develop by unfolding, by bending outward, moving by inclination in a different direction. It is through the carrying out of such transformations of a line that changes in direction, that veering off course occurs. The *Triumph*'s speaker and his fellow philosophers and visionaries must initiate that event in the triumphal procession's course. At the vanguard, they must exert pressure on the "Speed in the van and blindness in the rear" that "little profit brings" (*Triumph* 101, 100).

Indeed, an event exceeds the bodies engaged in and transformed by it. By such a vision, Shelley's evental idea is also held in that pure reserve: an immanent now realized from its ideal version of a Spinozist world. This is an evental idea that will be eventually actualized in every self and realized in things one by one once it has come to pass. Making that transformation of the line remains the problem: how to stage it, how to imagine it, how to *speak* it. In Shelley's view of a recursive and thus cursed historical cycling, the only way out of an equally cursed future is through poetry that reveals truths capable of transcending time's bondage—but also the body's bondage to its own self-interestedness. "The cultivation of poetry," Shelley writes in the "Defence," "is never more to be desired than at periods when, from an excess of the selfish and calculating principle, the accumulation of the materials of external life exceed the quantity of the power of assimilating them to the internal laws of human nature. The body has then become too unwieldy for that which animates it" (531). But the body that yearns for a different course is also one ripe for enlightenment.

It seems singularly important that Rousseau, the key figure of *The Triumph*, appears as an enlightened idea that has reanimated its unwieldy body in order to murmur poetic truths. The fossilized corpse, appearing tree-like in its afterlife, can be reactivated because all matter, all bodies express themselves. Because expressible bodies reveal immanent life, the fossil is itself a form of language. Rousseau's fossilized body recursively speaks its own history, resolving the problem of ancestrality for Shelley. For Rousseau the fold-between is an inter-space between that of the triumphal procession and that of the Poet's dreaming self. Within the dream's interval it is a folded space from which to speak otherwise, both retrospectively and prophetically. As the poem's ancestral figure, Rousseau connects the past with futurity, pointing the way toward understanding both the possibility of a post-Anthropocene world *and* the potential for human language-making that could inhabit something other than its self-interest. Shelley's elliptical language at the *Triumph's* ending might well be a version of Kristeva's theory of poetic language: it retains the rhythms of poetry, holding its *terza rima* form despite the struggle for wording that would be adequate to blind seeing. The *terza rima* rhythm carries us along even when the logocentric words cannot convey the vision. What ties Dante's three realms together is the *terza rima*, with its rhymes of wonder. What unties *The Triumph of Life* is its boundless expression of immanence just over the horizon of solipsism and self-blinding language. The beatitude that Dante experiences through Beatrice's intervention is here just possibly over the horizonal wall; immanent life as the democracy-to-come revealed. Insight as wondrous rhymes.

When Derrida writes of blind sight in *Memoirs of the Blind*, he explains that this variant sightedness requires movement, an active incorporation of the environment. It is a sightedness that pays attention to immanent bodies, as opposed to the blindfolded charioteer's pure solipsism. Derrida's subtitle *The Self-Portrait and Other Ruins* could be applied to Shelley's Rousseau, who self-portrays the ruination of his ego in order to reveal what his transformation into blind seeing potentializes. Those "Other Ruins" might also aptly provide a concurrence between Shelley's fragmenting or elliptical text and blind seeing as a ruination of logocentric sight. The alterity Rousseau displays enables the alternative future, the alternatively compossible world, toward which Shelley's great poem gestures. Unlike Dante's *Divine Comedy* and Petrarch's *Trionfi*, Shelley's *Triumph of Life* suggests the end of the line as an earthly rather than heavenly site. As such, the *Triumph*'s last few lines hold in their ellipses the immanent alterity premised in the interval.

In the next chapter I turn to De Quincey's idiosyncratically internalized exploration of Spinozist substance and Stoic expression. There I am concerned with the incorporeals of hallucination, nightmare, transformation, expressible bodies, and incorporation. The experiencing body finds immanent encounter within itself through the mediation of drugs. How language represents that, how movement occurs, how incorporeal and corporeal meet to produce enlightenment through pure vision: these are the elements of De Quincey's immanent confession. In his ruminations De Quincey also confronts his own racial prejudices. These comes up for him as "Orientalism": the Eastern origins of opium; racial others such as the Malay sailor he encounters; his own "Orientalization" through opium use in the form of furniture with Egyptian motifs, particularly crocodiles; and the intertwined mythopoetics of ancient Eastern cultures.

5

De Quincey's Eventful Dreams

> Baudelaire et Quincey ont cherché, sous drogue [la drogue des explorateurs], à nommer les limites des capacitiés humaines.
>
> —Julia Kristeva, *Chroniques du temps sensible*[1]

Thomas De Quincey's confessional musings about his life, his opium habit, and his dreams continue to fascinate readers, as reflected in Kristeva's comment, although his writings are perhaps repetitive in the sense of Coleridge's Mariner's compulsive re-narrating of his decisive encounter with immanence. They evince a fascination with dreamworlds, a longing for those worlds that is antithetical to Shelley's speaker's horror at the nightmarish vision thrust upon him in the *Triumph of Life*. Whereas Shelley's work queried freedom and futurity, De Quincey's asks: can alterity be good for us?; is dream death any different from physical death?; and is an afterlife what we are living now?

De Quincey was supremely poised to scrutinize such questions in the most quotidian of ways because whereas Shelley's orientation in the *Triumph* is directed externally toward immanence as possibly knowable in the to-come futures and afterlives, De Quincey's orientation is inward, paralyzingly so. Immanence, in fact, scares him to death. His confessional work, unlike the Mariner's enlightening confession, is endarkening, since De Quincey's dark interpreter refuses to pronounce decisively, returning again and again only to question and doubt. Nevertheless and despite himself, De Quincey's dream visions, especially in *Confessions of an English Opium-Eater*, have a Dantesque consequence in that they depict both hell *and* heaven, with the heavenly last vision a redemptive portrait of immanence having been where he wasn't looking, since his perspective was always skewed toward substance abuse rather than toward the substance of expressible bodies. His dreams are events in that they *do* things, manifesting themselves materially in ways that eclipse De Quincey's own substance as corporeal while imagining compossible worlds.

Shelley's *Triumph* concerns the deformations of delusional seeing—Rousseau as a withered root, the triumphal procession as a dance of self-enslaved bodies—and the resulting deformation of the poem itself. The undoing of form, however, is also liberating once revealed as the "shape all light," which points to a future without distortion, where clear seeing is the ground of possibility. De Quincey is also fascinated with forms and their undoing. His confessional writing concerns the deformative capacity itself, whether material (tea, wine, opium) or hallucinatory (crocodiles, furniture, coaches). In his worst dreams, forms writhe into other forms, unseaming themselves in a nightmare version of immanent life: "All the feet of the tables, sophas, &c. soon became instinct with life: the abominable head of the crocodile, and his leering eyes, looked out at me, multiplied into a thousand repetitions" (*Confessions* 74). For De Quincey, Otherness can be experienced through a mediating agency, particularly opium, which both deforms and vivifies the seeing mind so that Otherness makes itself available. But it takes a pronounced exploration of that kind of blind seeing before Otherness can be perceived as immanence, as occurs in the final vision of the *Confessions*.

As for the Ancient Mariner, it takes strange others—the dead prostitute Ann, the Malay sailor—to disrupt De Quincey's solipsism so that he can recognize alterity when it stares him in the face. What De Quincey's work offers is an indication of why a recognition of immanence stalled after the Romantic period, whereas the sublime only gained as an experience of alterity. Perhaps a growing empire made the possibility of what immanence teaches us about human freedom and the equality of bodies too threateningly radical. In De Quincey's hands, xenophobic hallucinations describe the effects of an increasingly constricted moment in an imperial Britain wherein the unlimited becoming of immanent bodies was covered over by a prescriptive Christianity. Coleridge's supernatural naturalism as well as Schelling's Platonic-Spinozist *Naturphilosophie* fell victim to the *logos* of a strict Cartesian worldview of self and the othered, or at least went underground. A worldview of division and differentiation, rather than of the Stoic *hen kai pan* or Lessing's One and All, becomes necessary when the goal is the expanding empire. Self-defensive measures against the margins of empire include fending off immanence as antithetical to both possession and self-possession.

Finally, De Quincey's version of immanent life provides a telling counterpart to Blake's, with which I began this project. Where Blake created his mythopoetic world, De Quincey's happens to him—though it is no less *poiesis*, and no less in and of the body. De Quincey's immanent life corresponds with the despair at the center of the last decades of British Romanticism, whereas Blake's corresponds with the decades of revolutionary enthusiasm. Blake's immanent vision is that of a truly leveled social field where all life is valued; De Quincey's is one that invites in foreign bodies (opium, Malay sailors, prostitutes) even as he fears them. Thus, his dreams are as full of fear as they are of immanent engagement; it is as if Coleridge's Mariner saw redemption in the water-snakes but not enlightenment. De Quincey is unable to conceive of enlightenment without sublime transport (an experience that largely eludes him), and so he mitigates immanent transport as the stuff of dreams rather than an ontopolitical and ontoethical realization. De Quincey's works, then, are a telling account of why Romantic immanence was of less interest than the sublime in the decades that moved Britain further away from revolutionary enthusiasm and closer to an entrenched divide between haves and have-nots. For the very reason that De Quincey immerses himself in embodied life through his dreams, he makes a compelling case for how empire and capitalist disregard for quality of life—both of which overproduce categories of otherness in human terms—do not erase or contradict the fact of immanent life itself. No matter how hard De Quincey tries to transform himself into a good imperial subject, his body desires otherwise, and has its own revelations to force upon him.

Already intrigued by imperial thinking at an early age, De Quincey begins from the belief that what is non-self or external to him should remain so. But he is also open to the intimation that what is other can point to the afterlife's promise of redemption and eternal rest (a different futurity from Shelley's). His own life, so full of restlessness with so little actual movement achieved, is the restless interval minutely acted out, its Spinozist potential seeping away with each desisting from action, each fending off of any instant in which immanence could announce itself. Indeed, struggle as he might with philosophies of ideality, the ideal both frightens and eludes him. His interval of restless non-progression is the status quo of the disappointed gentleman. Yet its potential haunts him, intrudes on him, demands his participation. In most cases, such intrusion occurs in the dream state, but not always, as the case of the Malay at the door attests. For De Quincey, the interval is better described as unremitting aporia. And alterity, he discovers more often than he'd like, is not just disruptive but dehumanizing, full of disastrous possibility while refusing to resolve the aporia. Encounters with others, such as the Malay whose uninterpretability and need dehumanize De Quincey, reveal his internal self-contradiction *and* othered-ness; his own deformation. That the othered resides within him is an unnerving and unmanning truth, one he can't hide from because his hallucinogenic dreams continuously reveal it to him. Key scenes in *The Confessions of an English Opium-Eater* (1821; 1822) and other writings show him both denying this truth and attempting to rewrite it as comprehensible, even moral. His internalized alienability is his default setting, making it difficult for him to locate immanence in corporeal bodies: instead, he locates it in the incorporeal bodies of his most redemptive visions and memories.

De Quincey's internal alterity begins with a self-contradiction born of a twofold relation to cultural others: his not-unusual xenophobia and his fascination with the fantastic "Orient" of his imagination. But these aspects of his worldview do not reduce simply to xenophobic distortions of other cultures. Instead, it fuels a pathological stalemate rather than an enabling fiction. That makes his version of Romantic immanence both a catachresis in his own corpora and an inversion of Blake's and Coleridge's enabling myths. It is also in chiasmic relation to the blind seeing of Shelley's triumph and to the materially manifest immanence of Dorothy Wordsworth's nature. In De Quincey's hands, xenophobia as internalized alienation (crocodiles as parts of his own furniture, humans with crocodile features) extends substance to the free play of corporeal and incorporeal bodies. There is a fuzziness to which kind of body De Quincey narrates, encounters, and describes in each segment of the larger interlude of his extended self-delusion.

Although De Quincey was representative in mixing his Easts, confounding the essential matter of Egypt (water, mud, stone) with its spirit (Ancient Egyptian death cult), and both with the mysteries of the two other ancient cultures of common parlance, India and China,[2] as well as with the more accessible but still not fully comprehended Near East, he was at least equal-handed in his paranoia and fascination with these ancient and more modern orientations of his internal compass. Trade stimulated this indiscriminate conceptualization of all things Eastern, turning the matter into spirit through the chemical transformation of opium into laudanum, drug into intoxicant. Opium's introduction to Britain was as much through the transmigrations of Southeast Asians and Turkish trade as it was through the British trade in Chinese opium. De Quincey fastidiously footnotes these differences in the *Confessions* to prove himself a connoisseur rather than a mere imbiber. Similarly, if his intermixing of Chinese, Indian, and Egyptian monsters in his deepest nightmares was not unrepresentative, neither was the conceptualization of each as entities terrifying in their transmorphic abilities.[3]

De Quincey's *Confessions of an English Opium-Eater* illustrates three transmorphic aspects of colonial thought: the status of subjective identity, the status of epistemological knowledge, and the status of cultural forms. *The English Mail-Coach* (1849) continues many of these themes. In De Quincey's hands, subjectivity, knowledge, and material and rhetorical forms are all (and sometime simultaneously) vulnerable to decentering, transculturation, and displacement even as he assiduously shores up their centrality and controllability. But xenophobia manifest in De Quincey's confessional writing is different in kind from the encounter with human Otherness characteristic of the period. Instead, De Quinceyan xenophobia is a self-deforming and reorientation that allows for the alienation and self-contradiction that is always already within, waiting to irrupt into the event of immanent bodies. His encounters with different versions of alterity as the events of nature's self-announcement, as expressive bodies resistant to his fictions, are no less impactful for being of a piece with his psychodrama of aporia.

If Blake works toward a new Jerusalem that was always already sited in the here and now, and Dorothy Wordsworth similarly finds the here and now to be the locus of a manifest immanence, they might equally agree that such encounters require a state of mind rather than a state of affairs to be revealed. This chapter unpacks the conflict raised in De Quincey's writing when he realizes that the effects of opium, both pleasurable and painful, produce states of mind arising out of the stalled time of hallucination into the immanent moment. It is one that he invites inasmuch as Blake and Dorothy Wordsworth do, but, unlike them, he fears and regrets it in equal measure. A staunch materialist, De Quincey firmly believes in the self-apparent mental control of his world, believing also that changes in world order belong to the material world. They ought to be and can be controlled through daily regimen (as diet and regulation of laudanum drops) as much as through affairs of state, as in the Opium Wars and

Britain's control of the opium trade with China. Yet his internal experience belies such empiricism, and he finds that reason has no purchase on the body that is his own. Indeed, he must learn several times over that both form and nonbeing are states of mind or ways of seeing, a realization that he feels unmans him rather than enlightens him. With reason so violently unseated, he falls into innumerable abysses whose mythopoetics is more frightful than Blake's and less directed toward redemptive transformations. Unlike Blake, this paradox of the abyssal that intervenes as hell and/or paradise presents a terrible conflict for De Quincey; unable to absorb his xenophobia enough to be translated by his Otherly encounters, he can only endure rather than open himself up to its disclosure. Any recognition of immanence must occur from his very Freudian unconscious rather than a Spinozist experience of *Deus sive Natura*. If De Quincey doesn't succeed in fending off immanent bodies, he also does not give himself over to the interval's *chora*-like potencies; therefore, he believes, a return to the stalemate of the self-contradiction becomes mandatory. This return and repetition, unlike Coleridge's Mariner's, reveals in itself something of the repetition compulsion rather than the desire to transmit experience of enlightened being to others. How and why De Quincey chooses a compulsive return to such an unsatisfactory impasse, confessions rather than revelation, underlie much of this chapter.

I. Altered States

Opium is unlike other import commodities such as tea, to which De Quincey frequently refers as a counter agent because of its transformative qualities.[4] For him opium is cross-referenced by that other antigen, women: women who serve, women who accompany one on strange journeys, women who translate into hauntings, women who dish up tea. Unlike the ameliorating effects of feminized tea, opium when ingested operates either as a toxin, needing inoculation rather than antidote, or as a translative agent, sending the imbiber on a mental journey to the land of beginnings. De Quincey hints that it is this confrontation with beginnings that haunts his own tale, the one he cannot tell (which he begins only with his father's death as a kind of loss of authorization) and which he substitutes with a biography of his dreamworld. This confrontation skews his trans-temporal and trans-spatial visions that replace personal memory with cultural memory. He rewrites them into a strange new language that mystically produces animated furniture and other domestic horrors, none worse than the monstrous Nile crocodile. De Quincey's present is encoded with signs of another past, warping future potential: an agonized version of empire. This transfiguration of epistemological certainty into unstable forms and images reveals an evolution made alarmingly unstable, a devolving enlightenment, a return to an unknowable past.

Originally introduced to laudanum by a college friend, De Quincey became quite knowledgeable in the differences between kinds of opium, but the concerns are hobbyist and consumerist: "for in my time, East-India opium has been three guineas a pound, and Turkey eight," he notes in his *Confessions of an English Opium-Eater* in relation to a comment about bankrupts and relative truth (such as opium's color, expense, and capacity to kill in an overdose[5]). It is in consumerism and consumption, however, that the connection lies. Ingestion of opium requires the ingestion of more opium. The greater the quantity consumed, the greater the confusion of origins through the admixture of East and West, consumable and body, matter and spirit. Moreover, if opium consumption requires money, it also negates the labor to produce money; bankruptcy hovers over the scene of writing. Writing about opium is the only activity that alleviates this monstrous fear. The circular logic of this particular economy shadows the underlying fears of imperialism: that what goes around will inevitably come around. This is alterity on a global, even universal scale that nevertheless sits at home, locally sited on the tea tray. Bankruptcy has much to do with death and a state of mind linked with opium dependency in the *Confessions*. De Quincey's regular use of laudanum, he notes, began at age twenty-eight to treat "a most painful affection of the stomach, which I had first experienced about ten years before . . . originally caused by extremities of hunger, suffered in my boyish days" (6). These boyish days were those between grammar school and university, the time he spent wandering through Wales and then through the streets of London, frequently insolvent and often with nothing to eat but tea or coffee. These are, in fact, his initial drugs of choice: caffeine and hunger. Later wine enters the picture, again as one of the few food articles he can tolerate ("I had no appetite. I had, however, unfortunately [because of lack of money] at all times a craving for wine," 32). And finally, laudanum enters as an antidote to the previous drugs, which—particularly tea—continued to be part of his regimen: he depicts "an eternal tea-pot . . . for I usually drink tea from eight o'clock at night to four o'clock in the morning" (60).

Bankruptcy and consumption, two of the defining material forms of the period, haunt the beginnings of De Quincey's autobiographical narrative, revealing his attraction for the conditions of self-contradiction or internalized impasse. During the early lean months of wandering, little money and very little food produced a kind of dreamworld that presages the warping of time and space in the opiate universe that comes not long afterward. During both his hunger period and opium period, De Quincey exists in a kind of rogue state, one that is doubly in-between, for he is an escapee from grammar school, and at the same time in hiding from his guardians who will, if they find him, refuse him a university career. He embarks on a walkabout that, far from questing for self-knowledge, creates a liminal space in which he belongs nowhere and partakes of (almost) nothing. During it he is suspected (or suspects he is suspected, his paranoia growing with his hunger) of being a swindler in Wales and of counterfeiting himself in London. Instead of questing, he is enacting the role of adventurer in many travel tales: wearing the garb of another culture or condition; accepting a new diet; finding new landmarks and self-locators; realizing the impossibility of absolute return. But even if these are the marks of one who goes native, with Wales becoming a truly foreign country because the native language is unintelligible to him, he is already enacting his life as the restless interval. London is a no-man's land that he inhabits in similar fashion. But if restlessness becomes his defining trait, the non-movement of stalled time truly terrifies him.

As in a foreign land of internal impasse and restless interval, De Quincey's identity is put at risk: no one will vouch for him except as the self he has become, and his past is seemingly lost to him. To be suspected of counterfeiting himself was less a blow to his honor than being thought a swindler, since he wandered London in the guise of penury pretending not to be himself. The difficulty lay in his decision to return to his "real" life, for which he needed to borrow on his inheritance (his "real" identity). The Jewish money-lenders refused to believe him, and his Etonian friend's refusal to back his loan request meant he was no longer an avatar in a role-playing game but facing starvation and facing down death. Fear is overwhelmed by the indignity both of being examined and found wanting. This accusatory positioning haunts the *Confessions*, with De Quincey several times imagining himself the "criminal at the bar." Curiously, criminality is the psychological feature usually missing from most Europeans' activities in the Near East even when they are blatantly stealing artifacts or acting against local laws. Being a stranger in one's own land repositions the subject as self-alienated, forcing self-othering and suspect alien status. If self-alienation is not the same as loss of ego in the encounter with untimely alterity, it can nevertheless act as a precondition.

For the Ancient Mariner, that self-alienation occurred when he realized he was a mere thing: at that moment the untimely interval opened up to him. So, too, will De Quincey discover that in the self-alienation of opium-induced nightmare, the hallucinogenic effects are indistinguishable from other accounts of immanent realization. His internalized othering produces the same effect of universal self-actualizing, of participating in the great dynamic unfolding of *natura naturans*.

The two most important scenes of criminal identity in the *Confessions* occur just after scenes of edenic domesticity with its specific biblical and therefore Eastern resonance. De Quincey is barred from both kinds of edens by his sense of random guilt. Bankruptcy and cross-examination, hunger and dependency: these are the figurings of his larger sense of displacement and disinheritance. "It was strange to me to find my own self *materialiter* considered (so I expressed it, for I doated on logical accuracy of distinctions), accused, or at least suspected, of counterfeiting my own self, *formaliter* considered" (25). The material body, found wanting, cannot sustain formal identity: the self is not the subject. This distinction, indeed, sits at the heart of De Quincey's pharmacological autobiography. Too frequently neither the subject of his story nor in a subject state, he is also too often subject to something bodily or material. The bodily alteration to his core identity is derived from the thing that most displaces him from the center of his being and therefore from the native ground of his cultural identity: laudanum.

The connection between body and matter is the habit and practice of ingestion, not the necessary ingestion of food but the consumption of foreign goods, all of which are stimulants or mood-altering agents: tea, coffee, wine, and laudanum. De Quincey's preference for laudanum over opium-eating is telling but does not extricate him from his double-bind: laudanum is the liquid form of opium dissolved in a measure of distilled alcohol. The adulterated drug becomes a new substance, at once domestic "spirits" and foreign substance, an acculturated, "Englished" product requiring a cultivated tolerance and taste. Alcohol strips one's inhibitions but also, as De Quincey notes, one's pretensions: "most men are disguised by sobriety; and it is when they are drinking . . . that men . . . display themselves in their true complexion of character" (41). When inebriated, that true character is often "the merely human, too often the brutal, part of his nature: but the opium-eater . . . feels the diviner part of his nature is paramount; that is, the moral affections are in a state of cloudless serenity; and over all is the great light of the majestic intellect." In the opium-eater resides the potential for alterity-encounter. If the ratio of alcohol to opium is correct for one's capacity, clearly the best that both drugs offer can be had: an intellectual and spiritual ascendancy. This is the allure, the "pleasures of opium," that De Quincey attempts to anatomize. Why then, do the nightmares come? Why does the inoculation treatment that he devises (using laudanum in hypothetically determined amounts to build up immunity) not prevent the "pains of opium" that he must fight with "a religious zeal" to escape the "fascinating enthralment [sic]" and achieve "self-conquest"? (2). Perhaps the answer lies in the self-deception involved in dividing the animal from the opium-eater aspects of himself, but perhaps it lies—contra Shelley's speaker—in not valuing enough the immanent life revealed during the dream state.

The questions of what a present-tense afterlife (opium's "pleasures") and the horrific prophecies (opium's "pains") might mean to De Quincey are pertinent to his internal impasse and self-alienation. The "pains of opium" include the dreadful, transmorphic nightmares; the scenes of sacrificial ritual drummed up by his unconscious; the horrendous transformations of inanimate and animate matter that turn domestic objects into demons and defamiliarized scenes, estranging and displacing normative understanding. It can also point to the displacement and potential death of the self. Subjective death raises the question of resurrection, of whether in recovering his self-control over opium through "religious zeal," De Quincey recovers the possibility of a return to self. That is, is the "self-conquest" he describes an excavation of his former character, a disinterment of his buried self? Or is it a new life, an afterlife that must replace the return to origins, the Eden-land, of his dreams? Displacement and wandering, medicinal death and the afterlife are the components of De Quincey's interval, whether it manifests as the restless interval of his daily struggles or that of his hallucinogenic dreams.

II. Displacing Wandering

De Quincey's restless interval suffers from its alienating of Englishness, creating a dizzying aporia of non-identity, or too many identities randomly surfacing in the increasing globalization of his world. Walter D. Mignolo warns us in *Local Histories/Global Designs* that colonial theorists such as Bronislaw Malinowski and Fernando Ortiz have not accounted for understandings and articulations of local and world events that arise from non-European epistemological systems. In pitting Western knowledge (framed on the difference between epistemology and hermeneutics) against native knowledges (gnosis or gnoseology), Mignolo sets up a dichotomy that locates the impasse at the heart of empire. A one-sided conversation developed, revealing that such experiences came up against, and were in an alienating tension with, that which was usually thought of as the "Asiatic" unknowable. The alien as both knowable and unknowable stimulated the need to construct epistemological certitude in the face of this insoluble impasse. De Quincey, who both valued and attempted to reject such perplexity, is remarkable in his obsessive yet lucid accounts of the aporia-effect stemming from the pit of imperial not-knowing.

De Quincey's textual play with aporia indexes a larger rhetorical strategy of evasion despite his initial assurances of his ability to analyze and resolve problems. Even as his rhetorical flourishes imitate juristic or analytic gestures, his prose shape-shifts into descriptive registers and poetic flights. And even as he attempts to discipline his essays into reasoned defenses of his opiate trials by virtue of his medicalized analysis of opium's material effects, his recollections free-associate in an increasingly dreamlike manner so that form does not follow content so much as form is corrupted by content. As his body and mind are overtaken by the organic in its most persuasive, identity-shifting form, so too is his prose style. Critics have analyzed De Quincey's rhetoric variously, from M. H. Abrams's view at one end of the spectrum of an opium discourse, a kind of embodied pharmakon in which the poison is also generative, to Peter Logan's argument at the other end that De Quincey's gestural moves in the *Confessions* work against a kind of "body-talk" to define himself masculinely against the effeminizing degeneracy of Turkish and Asian opium addiction.[6] Logan maintains that De Quincey's "strategy is to rigidly police the boundary between body and voice, past and present, experience and consciousness, in order to prevent the narrator's body from entering into the narrating voice" (75, 73). This claim, however, elevates *agon* over confusion and views the narrator as heroic rather than a subject subjected, with the hero as human rather than material.[7] De Quincey is clear in positioning opium as the hero of his narrative, however, making his investigations of the incorporeal even more compelling.

De Quincey's dramatization of his failure to police the mind-body divide is prescient as a recognition and play with impasse, but he also devotes equal attention to the restless interval. Both give the *Confessions* the quality of a Freudian case study in a manner not only prescient but also different in kind from the "history" usually narrated in confessionals of contemporaneous literature.[8] Moreover, a sense of judgment rendered hovers over his clinical analysis of being estranged from himself.[9] How we want to think about the translation of personal memory into cultural memory—of case study as cultural history—poses the challenge of redirecting Foucault's definition of subjectivity as subjected experience. How might the innovative gesture of case study intersect with the acculturated subject to produce new directions in experiential "becoming" and a subjective constitution? From this perspective, De Quincey's pre-Freudian rhetoric becomes a work in progress. It is not a colonialist center-to-periphery argument between native-foreigner and consumer-import so much as an interactive and co-constitutive flow across borders. What this figural exchange produces, however, is neither medicalized knowledge nor enlightenment: Otherness continually supplements what is increasingly decentered, a subjectless confession, a talking memory that speaks from alienated ground. It is De Quincey's attempt to narrate the altered state as the ground of his own immanent becoming.

Critics like Nigel Leask, John Barrell, Barry Mulligan, and Peter Logan have taken De Quincey's confrontation with the East's "mystery" as creating a place-trading subjectivity in which self and other may swap hierarchical positions but not infiltrate. A Foucauldian subject results, who imagines himself through the commercial needs of empire. But De Quincey's mighty rhetorical struggles indicate that this is not an unreflective, unacknowledged process for him, and in this he distinguishes himself. His hallucinogenic style facilitates decoding his experience from a kind of indecipherable symbolism, a hieroglyphics, into something that can become knowable, an account of how things happened that accrues as cultural memory, as unregenerate history. Not fantasy but a dreamwork, its gestural style results from infiltration, and from balancing impossible conditions: a subtle approach, too nuanced to be either sympathy (place-swapping) or pity (speaking for another). De Quincey's achievement is to publicize a differentiating self-conception in which decenteredness is naturalized as the bodily experience of empire, yet unreassured by staunch assertions of cultural superiority. In being dislocated, in fearing rather than mastering the Other, De Quincey has descriptively mastered how things seem to be.

Crucial to this stylistic approach, in which nothing seems to be accomplished, fully analyzed or proven, is the recurrent use of aporia. De Quincey almost gives form to aporia in describing his decentered state, yet rather than confront aporia head-on, he frequently resorts to hallucinogenic digressions that sidestep the impasse set up by the frustrations of "true" knowledge. This knowledge is what Mignolo calls the "gnoseology" of the colonial Other, which for De Quincey is a mystical knowledge deriving from or influence by the East. "I shall be charged with mysticism, Behmenism, quietism, &c," he writes, "but *that* shall not alarm me" (*Confessions* 114). Yet the question of empire is accompanied by the question of the grounds of knowledge. Gnoseology is ripe ground for investigating the affective relations between corporeal and incorporeal bodies. De Quincey himself is much given to theorizing systems of knowledge, such as that of opium's effect, without feeling it necessary to concede truth to the scientists. Indeed, far from "going native" at home through opium-induced hallucinogenic experiences or from acting the flaneur in London scenes of want and alienation scarcely recognizable to his *London Magazine* readers, he conceives a self-alienating fear of the alterity brought by imported substances, rather than imported subjects. These substances force an acculturation to which he is increasingly subject. Aporia reproduces the engagement with acculturation that troubles and tantalizes De Quincey.

As Franz Boas described it at the end of the century (1888), acculturation should be merely the accommodation that one or both cultures make to each other for coexistence; it may simply be adopting certain objects and inventions of another culture. Yet acculturation that appears voluntary, as in laudanum drops, but inexplicably becomes enforced as loss of self-control, means that despite De Quincey's initiation into a rogue-state subjectivity, it is the acculturative process that has become rogue, producing a transformation of his core identity through opium use. This might be "transculturation," but that term implies a meliorating rather than dissonant effect in the changes effected. Whether acculturation and transculturation can ever be as benign as both these terms imply is called into question in De Quincey's geographical passages through Britain in which he finally lands in the Wordsworths' Dove Cottage. These passages are likewise engagements with impasse and digression. De Quincey's narrative describes his passage from native selfhood to self-loss to reconfigured identity as it is mapped onto geographical and psychological terrain. This ground cannot be restored even by occupying Dove Cottage, as De Quincey illustrates with a portrait of his parlor that emphasizes his own absence from it. Wordsworth's centering, nationalizing presence ought to hover over the cottage, but it is De Quincey's alienated presence that alters the dimensions and sanctity of this space. He could not acculturate to Dove Cottage, and it suffers from his failure. Earlier, having fled his school without leave to wander through Wales and then wandering London streets, young De Quincey sought the coordinates to establish his own local history: he is rejected here, he starves there, nowhere is home. It is in London that he believes he can control of his self-medication by rejecting the impasses that accompany his wandering, but the dislocation has settled into his psyche. Again, nowhere is home.

His transmigration of mind and soul, and the reflection of this in De Quincey's formal choices, are themes that more broadly suggest a cultural nostalgia inexorably bound to the colonial experience and its effects on the cultural stage (through imports, design influences, Asian immigration to England, and the resulting affective shifts in sensibility). This culturally imagined nostalgia became a way of understanding Englishness as a standardized British identity, mitigating the discomfort of impasse in the process. De Quincey's double knowledge of opium—both medical, as he relates in *Confessions*, and familial, through the travels and trade of his East Indian uncle—restages this nostalgia, since his knowledge of opium is both new and old, a product of psychic adventure and mental travel, and of mercantile adventure mixed, inevitably, with nostalgia for another life. His framework for believing himself superior to Asians about controlling the uses and effects of opium arises from this double ground for knowledge, as well as from his hermeneutic mastery developed from studying classical Greek, his "analytic thinking," and dabbling in philosophy. But equally it must have a bodily source, arising from his ingestion of opium as well as from his mercantile lineage in which both his deceased father and his uncle have surely passed on their trading knowledge, a knowledge that can be liminal rather than contractual.

De Quincey sets out to prove that commerce with opium need not be dangerous. Ill health might necessitate its use; inoculation should prevent immoderate use. When it doesn't, he fancies that a return to his original practice of self-control serve the purpose: pleasurable use with long interludes of abstinence will (*Confessions* 6). "I read Kant; and again I understood him, or fancied that I did," he comments after taking "only 1000 drops of laudanum" (55). Yet here fancying indicates that self-knowledge impedes hermeneutic mastery, that aporia is functioning as a better route to knowledge. Notably, the fancy of understanding Kant occurs just one and a half sentences after a quote from Wordsworth's "Resolution and Independence": "That moveth altogether, if it move at all."

De Quincey uses the quotation to illustrate how "the cloud of profoundest melancholy which rested upon my brain" one day almost inexplicably dissipated "like some black vapours that I have seen roll away from the summits of mountains, drew off," but also like a stranded ship that is "floated off by a spring tide." He is describing the return to mental health and cognitive function ("my brain performed its functions as healthily as ever before") that a decrease from 8000 to only 1000 drops of laudanum a day had effected. But the drops are corporeal bodies affecting his own. To *fancy* he is understanding Kant even if his brain is performing up to level means that a paradigm shift has occurred in his understanding. His analytic powers are now somehow illusory compared to his imaginative, creative ones. De Quincey's metaphors are strikingly more poetic than the great poet's line, which in comparison sounds self-evident, even trite. Ensconced in Dove Cottage, De Quincey differentiates his poetical fancy from Wordsworth's by locating Wordsworth not geographically but textually. He sets the Wordsworthian line off from his own text to isolate and elevate it, even as Wordsworth the man is transubstantiated into allusion, separating the quotation epistemologically by category and authority from his prose poetry. For what purpose? A clue arises from the fact that the famous Malay incident occurs toward the bottom of the paragraph that begins with fancying Kant.

"One day a Malay knocked at my door. What business a Malay could have to transact amongst English mountains, I cannot conjecture" (*Confessions* 55). Neither Wordsworth nor Kant is helpful at this intrusion of the phenomenal Other into the Lake District. The young servant who opened the door "had never seen an Asiatic dress of any sort: his turban, therefore, confounded her" (55–56). De Quincey's mocking tone, the derision of epistemological categories signified by the inferiority of the servant, the known quantity of a turban-wearing alien, and the servant's classification of the Malay as "a sort of demon" belies the serious tension wrought by the comparisons with Kant and Wordsworth. For one thing, as he composes this passage he will have already passed through a terrible period in which opium produced ocular proof that household furniture could become demonic. The passage is a commentary on his own hallucinogesis, a hallucinogenic hermeneutics. There can be no confirmation of an absolute return to cognitive health, no realization of great achievements, when hallucination puts epistemology in doubt and hermeneutics proves an unreliable aid. The Malay is surely real, although the reason for his appearance "I cannot conjecture," De Quincey notes—not I could not, but I simply cannot know or even conjure, for the necessary Kantian categories for intuition, let alone for a priori reasoning, are missing. The Malay offers readers various interpretive frames for understanding De Quincey's alienation from human Others: does it stem from possibly overdosing the Malay with opium; or from the unknowability of someone who can bolt three opium doses with no apparent ill effect; or from the transversal of imagining the Malay imagining that De Quincey might be preparing him for sacrifice to an English idol (if the native Englishman undertook to physic the Malay traveler out of his overdose)?

> On his departure, I presented him with a piece of opium. . . . I was struck with some little consternation when I saw him suddenly raise his hand to his mouth, and . . . bolt the whole, divided into three pieces, at one mouthful. The quantity was enough to kill three dragoons and their horses. . . . I could not think of violating the laws of hospitality, by having him seized and drenched with an emetic, and thus frightening him into a notion that we were going to sacrifice him to some English idol. (*Confessions* 57)

Whichever question we choose, we cannot determine the underlying cause for the defensive mockery and self-alienation of this passage; we can only note its unease and put it down to dis-ease—dis-ease both of mind and culture. There is some hint that, far from the Malay bringing contagion to De Quincey's doorstep through the cultural miscegenation he represents, De Quincey has contaminated him and thus represents the polluting factor in the cultural equation. De Quincey's self-mockery may be at the realization of how thorough his process of transculturation has been.

In elevating sacrificial imagery over the philosophical sense and commonsense that Kant and Wordsworth represent here, is De Quincey struggling to develop gnoseology as another way of knowing? After debunking the medical theory of the apothecary to Greenwich Hospital, published in 1763, in the beginning of his scientific trials with opium, De Quincey does not abandon his own attempts at medical knowledge, but his growing self-knowledge relies increasingly on a decentered self, one thrown off balance by a Malay on the threshold. This Malay will populate his dreams: he "brought other Malays with him worse than himself, that ran 'a-muck' at me" (*Confessions* 57–58). De Quincey's footnote to the Malay passage further decenters and sidelines his Western knowledge by commenting that he would be glad to publish "my projected medical treatise on opium . . . provided the College of Surgeons will pay me for enlightening their benighted understandings upon this subject" (57n.). The note clearly derides such a possibility, elevating the Malay encounter as a source of gnoseology, however uncomfortable this confrontation makes him. Opium as medical knowledge cannot translate just as English and Malay languages are mutually exclusive in this scene, not even the Turkish word for opium, which De Quincey but not the Malay knows; opium belongs, perhaps, to another knowledge system. A second footnote, to "a-muck," acknowledges this: "See the common accounts in any Eastern traveler or voyager of the frantic excesses committed by Malays who have taken opium."

Can decentering the self, rather than losing it, be a gnoseology that reconnects past to present better than biographic scenes of sentimental affect and nostalgia? As he makes his way through his self-study, De Quincey's medicalized account begins to disintegrate. When scholars focus on the lack of intellectual rigor and logic operating in the *Confessions*, are they in fact uncovering De Quincey's exploration of gnoseology through hallucination? Other questions follow: Is his inability to sustain analytic philosophy due to a search for a different mental path forward? What if an alternative past could be reconstructed through psychic experiences that is more realized and of a higher order than historiography provides?

Such a strategy would place gnoseology above epistemology, the noumenal above the phenomenal, a fuller connection to the Malay man through opium than with the ignorant English servant. Within the gnoseological view, opium and its medicative/toxic effects are corporeals that appear more substantial that the human others De Quincey encounters. Its incorporeal dream states make such others incorporeals too. Is the encounter with the Malay an immanent one in which corporeal and incorporeal have equal existential weight? De Quincey's account reveals entangled bodies as the corporeal and incorporeal dissolve into these bodies' expression. If the Malay man dies, will De Quincey's hospitality have been a death sentence? If so, will he too die for having ingested too much too often? What is the ontoethics at work here, if not to scare him to death? And to make him accountable to time. The past, whether composed of his nightmares of being a divine sacrifice to some Asian idol or his perversion of that nightmare in terms of the Malay visitor, would parallel the nightmare visions of Druidic sacrifice that Wordsworth imagines at

Stonehenge: "It is the sacrificial altar / Fed with living men" (*Salisbury Plain* st. xxi). Wordsworth's most direct reference is again most unpoetic compared with De Quincey's dream: "I ran into pagodas: and was fixed, for centuries, at the summit, or in secret rooms; I was the idol, I was the priest; I was worshipped; I was sacrificed" (*Confessions* 73).

In poetically imagining his own sacrifice, his dying-into, De Quincey substitutes the imagined history on British soil with a different form of occidentalization. If the dreams were mere fancy, they would represent cultural fantasy, but instead they touch on Jungian archetypes that suggest a connection at a deeper, more powerful, yet also more creative level. Nevertheless, this departure from knowable ground is unsettling, for uncontrollable hallucinations destabilize the verities of selfhood in the same way that untimely encounters with alterity do. If Wordsworth's imagery is frightening, De Quincey's scares him witless. Where his poetic power connects past to present in powerfully realistic terms, De Quincey struggles against the revelations of his dreams, putting them down to ill health, perhaps madness, and something that revolts. His repulsion, and his struggle to hang onto the Western order of things that he equates with mathematics and analytic philosophy, is frustrated in the *Confessions* by an inability to think clearly, that is, to organize his thoughts in epistemologically sound ways. But what he may fear in revulsion is its revolutionary nature. His logic may not be at fault; it may be othered into a gnosis of the mind-body as it is altered by Asiatic medicine through opium. His reason, that is, may be victim to the realization of alterity-encounter. The question is whether his path is truly toward immanent life or is more rightly the nostalgia of cultural fantasy predicated on constructions of human Others. Is the alien Malay really "a sort of demon," as the servant suspects, or inhumanly Other as De Quincey considers at the Malay's ability to bolt opium? Does De Quincey's forced humor in this passage cover over the encounter with immanent being that both appalls and compels him?

Yet this is an encounter that eventuates in De Quincey's darkest nightmares rather than enlightenment. The passage does not end with seeing the Malay disappear in the unknowability of his identity, his life experience, or his opium habits; it continues with a multiplication of Malays who haunt De Quincey's dreams, revealing that any self-assurances of a return to health through drug moderation are delusory. And this haunting is so unsettling that the narrative abruptly shifts to the scene of healing, "Let there be a cottage, standing in a valley . . . a white cottage, embowered with flowering shrubs" (*Confessions* 58). And yet this is the very scene of domesticity that centers on a drawing room eviscerated of De Quincey's presence. The drawing room, with its tea tray, library, and "book of German metaphysics," is a room that reveals the most dreadful aspect of De Quincey's acculturation and his decentering tactics. It is the family's room, "seventeen feet by twelve, and not more than seven and half feet high" (60): there is the book, the "eternal tea-pot," the "little golden receptacle of the pernicious drug [laudanum])," but no master of the house. "I admit that naturally I ought to occupy the foreground of the picture," but the "I" here is less the hero than "the criminal at the bar" (61). It is enough that these personal articles "will sufficiently attest my being in the neighbourhood." Whether his body is somewhere at the edges or, incriminated by his addiction, completely displaced and "had into court," it is still in a rogue state, an aporia rather than a generative interval.

Aporia, an impasse that creates a confrontation with the self, is the antithesis of the productive interval leading to immanent realization. One's assumptions, self-doubts, normal frameworks all come into question in aporia as the known is dissolved by the unknown. In Wordsworth's famous Lucy lyric, "A slumber did my spirit seal" (1800), the object of meditation was and might still be a subject but the nature of its animate qualities are unknown: "She seem'd a thing that could not feel," and "No motion has she now, no force; / She neither hears nor sees" as she rolls "round . . . With rocks, and stones, and trees." Although a few pages prior to the parlor and tea tray passage De Quincey quotes from Wordsworth's "Resolution and Independence" ("That moveth altogether, if it move at all" 55), with its rock-like leech gatherer, "A Slumber" is more resonant here. That the speaker "had no human fears" evades the question of whether he has spiritual ones or nightmarish "phantasmagoria," as De Quincey calls the surrealism of hallucinations. Human fears are pitted against "earth's diurnal course," as if this framework could sustain the unknowability of Lucy's ontological status. But as De Quincey's phantasms repeatedly reveal, even in the happiness of opium pleasure, nothing is sustainable, every vision succeeds to another in an incomprehensible sequence of suspended knowledge. As for Lucy, aporia for De Quincey becomes equated with death, and his liquid dreams become a death-in-life experience. This qualifies him to be a "last man," a remnant of what was.

Death, then, is a supreme metaphor for De Quincey's transcultural armchair activities, a term intended to capture his cultural dislocation and irredeemable angst. His own ecstatic visions involve sacrificial rites and entombment, while his worst nightmares contend with the endless death-flight from natives run amok and crocodiles: "The cursed crocodile became to me the object of more horror than almost all the rest. I was compelled to live with him . . . for centuries" (*Confessions* 74). Even his balmiest moments are linked to death, usually with female undertones. Wordsworth's Lucy poems are perhaps never far from De Quincey's romanticizing mind: he found his wife, Margaret, in Grasmere, the hamlet of Dove Cottage, as a Lucy figure ("She dwelt among the untrodden ways"); a summer day reminds him for no reason of Catherine Wordsworth, who died at age three ("Three years she grew in sun and shower; / Then Nature said. . . / This child I to myself will take"). Indeed, death and life, and death-in-life, seem nearly the same thing for De Quincey's malfunctioning galvanic battery. His own children invariably wake him from the monstrous crocodile dreams, their innocence deflecting the criminality of the visions, yet they are depicted with less vibrancy and affect than the dead Catherine. "I have had occasion to remark . . . that the deaths of those whom we love, and indeed the contemplation of death generally is . . . more affecting in summer than in any other season of the year," he remarks (*Confessions* 74). This thought leads to recounting a dream in which he is at his Dove Cottage door, early on an Easter morning, and he can somehow see to the graveyard and Catherine's "verdant" grave. The scene of resurrection leads not to a risen child, but to the lost Ann, the streetwalker companion of his London fugue: " 'So I have found you at last' . . . but she answered me not a word" (75–76).

Unsurprisingly, it is this vision that begins the concluding paragraphs of the *Confessions*. The condition of death, premised on affecting deaths of others and yoked even to the most beautiful days of the year, can provide an aesthetically curative alternative to the nightmare of a death-in-life existence, but not an articulate one. De Quincey, despite his autobiographical intentions, appears to be incapable of self-historicizing, his dreams and digressions leading instead into a self-mythologizing mode that leaves him ungrounded and lost in time as well as space. Instead, he must learn to live within the conditions of an aporia that fends off rather than resolves an irresolvable dilemma. He must learn to live in the altered-state terrain he has invited in. This is the most difficult of moves for a man allergic to the Other, resistant to the generative quality of the negative, and suspicious of the interval's restless energy. Yet it is a terrain that fascinates him, prodding him on step after step.

For De Quincey, this terrain involves living with paradoxes, indecipherability, indeterminacy. Forms of knowledge such as analytic studies, mathematics, speculative philosophy, and political economy, even his philosophical treatise, which he grandiosely titles after Spinoza (*De emendatione humani intellectûs*—the correction of human understanding [*Confessions* 150]), all dissolve into fragmentation, dream logic, and "intellectual torpor" (66). Analytic or Kantian thinking does not work for the mind-altered De Quincey: political economy and his infatuation with Ricardo dissolve into his own "physical economy" (67). Despite his claims for the intellectual elevation possible under the influence of opium, his one exemplary moment of superior analysis occurs in a passage that illustrates anything but clarity. On attending a concert in which "Grassini appeared . . . and poured forth her passionate soul as Andromache, at the tomb of Hector, &c. I question whether any Turk, of all that ever entered the Paradise of opium-eaters, can have had half the pleasure I had. But, indeed, I honour the Barbarians too much by supposing them capable of any pleasures approaching to the intellectual ones of an Englishman. For music is an intellectual or a sensual pleasure, according to the temperament of him who hears it" (45).

This passage begins by differentiating the barbarians (those who get drunk at concerts; those to whom music is "like a collection of Arabic characters"; and Turks themselves) from the civilized (those with intellectual affinity for music). Although De Quincey cites Thomas Browne's theory of music's effect on the mind, correcting the idea that musical notes must correlate to specific ideas, he does not illustrate an intellectual, theoretical, or analytic encounter with music at this concert. Rather, the "elaborate harmony, displayed before me, as in a piece of arras work, the whole of my past life—not, as if recalled by an act of memory, but as if present and incarnated in the music" (*Confessions* 45–46). This remembering of life specifically displaces analytic thinking from the opium palette. It is reincarnation that opium facilitates, and reincarnation involves a new, awakened life. But De Quincey's reincarnations are always backward-looking, to ancient civilizations such as those of Egypt, India, and China where his nightmares are placed. These will provide decipherment, whereas his wanderings through London produce "sphynx's riddles" of getting lost in "knotty problems of alleys" and "streets without thoroughfares" (47). Wandering, whether mental travel or nighttime fugues, becomes a form of limbo for De Quincey, an in-between state of neither hybridity nor transculturation, but an interval-aporia that borders on gnosis—on nearly knowing, nearly seeing. In the music passage De Quincey experiences the interval as gnosis; an incorporeal like the musical notes, it pours forth its soul and affects all who open up to it.

III. Wandering in Limbo

When De Quincey describes the three monstrosities in his confessions— the criminal at the bar, the opium-bolting Malay, and the crocodile—the numerous references to them indicate that each represents some manifestation of himself. These monstrous projections, which may or may not be real (the Malay as opposed to the Malays of the dreams) are all incidental to the confession, but they are so in the same way that alienness supplements the decentered subject striving to relocate his unreliable, wandering identity. The criminal at the bar supplements subjectivity by standing in for De Quincey in his alternative form as a swindler and the holder of forged identity, the self alienated from itself.

That swindled past is transformed through a variety of agents, many of them imports into, and then habituées of, native English culture. As these agents, whether material or human (tea, coffee, opium, wine, Malay sailors), become acculturated, it is "natural" to assume that they have become Anglicized despite ongoing cultural fears of foreign taint and toxicity. Indeed, just as tea had become an essential component of the English diet—up to 20 million pounds imported by 1789—so too had opium been domesticated, both in pill form and as laudanum, available from grocers, apothecaries, and even circulating libraries (Logan 76-82.) In being knowledgeable about the difference between laudanum as a common home remedy and opium-eating as a deliberate practice, De Quincey attempts to assert cosmopolitan expertise in being able to discern beneficial from dangerous experiences of ingestion or encounter, a faculty arising from his dislocating lifestyle, which he believes frees him from normal provincial blindnesses. Contradictorily, he also believes he is well grounded in British nativism: "I am the son of a plain English merchant" (*Confessions* 31), he notes even while describing his Grecian erudition. Attempts at inoculation were not just against opium but against the loss of native identity.

> This incident I have digressed to mention, because this Malay . . . fastened afterwards upon my dreams, and brought other

Malays with him worse than himself, that ran "a-muck" at me, and led me into a world of troubles . . . But I, who have taken happiness, both in a solid and a liquid shape, both boiled and unboiled, both East India and Turkey,—who have conducted my experiments upon this interesting subject with a sort of galvanic battery,—and have, for the general benefit of the world, inoculated myself, as it were, with the poison of eight hundred drops of laudanum per day (just for the same reason as a French surgeon inoculated himself lately with a cancer,—an English one, twenty years ago, with plague,—and a third, I know not of what nation, with hydrophobia)—I, it will be admitted, must surely know what happiness is, if anybody does. (*Confessions* 57–58)

This is a man who confounds malaise arising from the Malay at the door with pure happiness by thinking to inoculate himself against "other Malays" running "a-muck" by ingesting an Eastern poison or illness—a cancer, a plague, a mad animal's bite, all images haunted by a literal fear of water in Egypt's Nilotic death (biting crocodiles who give "cancerous kisses" [73], plague-infected waters). Building resistance to death by water means dropping liquid into one's body in "millenaries," quantities bold enough to test the mind-body relation.[10] By taking in Asian death in liquid form, De Quincey hopes to stave off cultural infection, and perhaps he had the right to think he might succeed. He was the nephew of a man who served in the East India Company, that conversionary entity whose chief commodity was opium; he received a loan from that trade for his pre-university rambles (Mulligan 59). He might think himself more immune to such influence than the common man. But as he confesses to this transformation, which shocks him with its unworldliness, De Quincey uses his account of opium eating to record history as personal memory subjected to the shifting sands of the unanticipated, unknown, and unremembered, particularly in terms of cultural encounter. His greatest fear is that, like hydrophobia, this encounter will lead to madness.

In moving from intoxicant to hallucinogen, from wine to opium, De Quincey's pharmaceutical consumerism changes his body and mind from an ingestive agency to a rehabbed domicile, a housing project for discordant constituents. "The dreamer," he notes in *The English Mail-Coach*, "finds housed within himself—occupying, as it were, some separate chamber in his brain—holding, perhaps, from that station a secret and detestable commerce with his own heart—some horrid alien nature" (*Mail-Coach* 201). West meets East through his imbibing in a perverse variant on the sacramental wine and host, such that it is not his spirit that communes at the altar, but his body and blood that are transfigured at the bar. This bar, which he describes repeatedly as one of criminal justice, appears in multiple forms as social venues of trial (such as his homeless wanderings, his encounters with alien travelers), as boundary lines whose traversal is more serious than he anticipates (such as the demarcation between the cultures of Wales and England), or as bars indeed, tea tables on which opium and wine figure each other in order to define him. Moreover, his progress is one that mobilizes contemporary ideas about the analytic mind, evolution as cultural memory, and an increasingly medicalized conception of hallucination into a tale of translated subjectivity that is simultaneously a tale of translated cultural identity.[11] How De Quincey recalls this translation in his *Confessions* produces a memorial to the transfiguration of the personal into the cultural, of private memory into a recalling of the acculturated past, of the Faustian experimenter as the British everyman.

Nigel Leask argues that De Quincey uses his description of opium's effects "as a metaphor . . . for the effects of [imperialist] capitalism upon the body politic."[12] That is, Leask sees a corollary between the private body and the body politic such that one figures the other. Although initially this appears a logical assessment of De Quincey's uneasy fascination with Asian culture and objects, it is nevertheless an odd figuration for him because he is, in his own mind, absent from his account, depleted by and taken over by the alien cultures of the East. As Leask notes, the hero of the 1821 case history essays is not the experiencing subject (or, I might add, his body) but opium itself, for it is not until the 1856 republication of the *Confessions* that the work became truly autobiographical, and its hero De Quincey himself (Leask 172). As most readers have recognized, De Quincey cannot persuasively argue his intended case for the controlled use of opium by an enlightened consumer, which would indeed have illustrated a capitalist mentality at work and aptly troped the body politic. The secondary argument he pursues is that opium eating can become a British practice despite its reception as a purely Eastern habit, and again he defeats his own analytic thinking by showing just the opposite—that Britons become hybridized by eating opium. This line of thinking does indeed trace the anxieties underlying imperialist capitalism for the national character, but in attempting to make his case by virtue of his own case history, we can see that De Quincey hopes that imperialism will be saved, as it were, by opium.

The correct use of opiates as the vehicle for intellectual supremacy would provide what Leask describes as "the means of stimulating a torpid and internally fissured national culture, and of displacing domestic anxieties onto the oriental Other" (Leask 171). That matters do not resolve in this way is revealed by the non-alleviation of domestic anxieties—bankruptcy, intellectual torpor, criminality, loss of safe haven—by opium eating. Moreover, in his own case, opium criminalizes his identity; this form of loss of character is not a factor in national anxieties over the consequences of imperialism. De Quincey does not just play out scenarios of national torpidity, he creates a hybrid land of British soil inhabited by vigilantes from the East and Near East such as amok Malays and crocodiles that hunt De Quincey down. The crocodiles continue their policing of ineffectual Britishness past the *Confessions* and on into *The English Mail Coach*:

> [T]he crocodile does not live fast—he is a slow coach"; "as the Pharaohs and the crocodile domineered over Egyptian society . . . a singular mistake . . . prevailed on the Nile. The crocodile made the ridiculous blunder of supposing man to be meant chiefly for his own eating. Man . . . viewed the crocodile as a thing sometimes to worship, but always to run away from . . . Fanny, who, being the granddaughter of a crocodile, awakens a dreadful host of wild semi-legendary animals . . . [and so] awaken[s] the pathos that kills in the very bosom of the horrors that madden the grief that gnaws at the heart, together with the monstrous creations of darkness that shock the belief, and make dizzy the reason of man. (*Mail-Coach* 198–99)

De Quincey's Britain is not an uninhabitable no-man's land; rather, it is an overpopulated dreamscape in which opium and its alien figments battle each other for possession of one's subjectivity, not one's body. The crocodile, an opiate transmorph that then morphs further into humanoid (most hideously as the mail coach driver), is the most dangerous of hallucinations. This is a time and space traveler as well as a shape changer; coming from the ancient past of Eastern matter, he effortlessly inserts himself into quotidian English life (furniture legs, coach drivers, grandfathers). "I was compelled," De Quincey recounts of the crocodile, "to live with him . . . for centuries" (*Mail-Coach* 74). It is the crocodile who references De Quincey's inadequacy as an Englishman, his criminality, whereas human innocence (his children, his wife) support him without condemnation, yet they are fleeting presences in the text and apparently absent from his dreams. The omnipresent croc represents the absolute opposite of music's intellectual challenge and demonstrates De Quincey's own fall from grace.

For Leask, it is the history of the case that provides the corollary between the individual and the body politic through the material means of psychic stimulation, but De Quincey finds the material means to be a severing and alienating of such connections. Despite the bravado of his introductory paragraphs to the *Confessions*, any sense of cultural superiority quickly dissolves into a self-alienation that predates yet foretells opium consumption. Any dismissal of colonial angst, as in the mocking tone of the Malay incident, quickly becomes self-mockery and an annihilated self-deceit. De Quincey is far more integrated into Asian subjectivity, however imaginatively rather than factually constructed, than into a representatively British colonial frame of mind. For him it is the history of the dreams that provides the key, for the material history—so many liquid drops, so many abandoned projects—proves only that nothing comes of such corollaries, for the East is untamable and implacable. Not only does De Quincey not reduce opium to a reliable aid, but opium itself consumes Britishness, eating it up like a cancer, but one that perturbs no one but himself. The Fanny of the Bath mail road becomes Fanny the granddaughter of a crocodile, transmogrified from an English rose ("roses and Fannies, Fannies and roses" [*Mail-Coach* 198]) to a nest of horrors ("griffins, dragons, basilisks, sphinxes" [199]), yet she never stops smiling.

Moving from dreams to the body at stake in the *Confessions*, his bodily housing of the West-East confrontation appears to return De Quincey to his rightful place. Although in an estranging land, his trials with opium allow him to reorient and reseat himself, to find himself properly located both in his intellectual engagement and bodily requirements as a medical intervention on the hallucinatory properties of bodily deprivation. Given this narrative line, the *Confessions* is not metaphorical so much as transfigurative, reconfiguring the cultural identity mapped onto the body into the mental terrain of the reason. Like Kant's *Critique of Pure Reason*, De Quincey attempts to relocate himself not as an exemplar of imperialist crisis, but between "I" and the constructed Other as reconceived identities through the agency of an unreal "them," a hallucinatory Other. This Other, best figured as the avenging crocodile, does not merely confront De Quincey at his doorstep as does the (non-amok) Malay; it enters his body and his dreams pharmaceutically to change how he conceives experience, and reconceives it as memory. The Other achieves this through the East's distorting or unrooting connection to indigeneity and ground, its effeminizing and enervating principle. "The Orient" stands in for the primordial on the one hand, and for a present-day East that has lost its authority on the other; these two simultaneous orientations attributed to the East mix forms in De Quincey's dreams, confusing the temporal with the allegorical.[13]

In *The English Mail-Coach*, De Quincey notes how the horror of remembering Fanny as both beauty and monstrosity revealed a "horrid reconciliation" in which human and crocodile forms enacted "the horrid inoculation upon each other of incompatible natures" (*Mail-Coach* 199, 200). Inoculation in this sense means miscegenation, true hybridity. This meeting of opposites provides "the confluence of two different keys," horror and grief (199). The affected bodies, in Spinoza's sense, are the coming together that inoculates self with "them," with the emotional affects registering the painful engendering of Britishness with monstrosity. The result is that De Quincey does not return home but relocates himself through alienated memory. This hybrid, alienated memory proves strangely authorizing and self-generating, a corollary for British imperialism.

The *Confessions* begin by way of a disorientation, thus allowing for a new direction to emerge. De Quincey places himself as the one who is falsely yet truly accused of transformed identity when, for the insinuated possibility of his Irish or English swindlerhood, he leaves the first, affordable refuge of his pre-university rambles, and so plunges into assumed poverty and his first true hallucinogen, hunger. He is manifestly *not* the hero of this story. Thereafter, hallucinogens (hunger, wine, opium, memory) trade in identity, swindling De Quincey of his presumed character. As he informs the reader, the criminal at the bar is himself, perpetually absent from the picture of cozy domesticity, with the tea tray sitting beside the decanter of wine-colored laudanum and a book of "German metaphysics" together a metaphor for his absent presence. Absence, as a form of criminality, is silence: when at the bar the criminal has no voice except when it is time to confess. Guilty before the law that accuses him, the criminal must remain silent while the witnesses may speak for or against him. Just so, the confessional requires another's intercession to regain control of the narrative; it appears that crocodiles are the witnesses for the trial of De Quincey's true identity.

To live criminally is to engage a deluded subjectivity against which inoculation may or may not prove fruitful; it is both a subjection to others and a displacement of self. Opium at first seems the proper inoculative medium but only exacerbates alienation and criminality, both of which suggest that at some level (and we see this in the Malay incident) De Quincey considers himself the plague-carrier, the polluter of native soil. With the failure of inoculation through speculative pharmacology comes a transformed identity. Like the Malay who speaks no English, like the monstrous crocodile, De Quincey is unable to speak truly because in opium-induced consciousness he is not himself. The crocodile, representing that self-loss or transmutation, comes into the English home from a place in which the earth's history remained illegible and unspeakable on its own terms. The croc is the ideal symbol for De Quincey's own unspeakable experiences in an altered state. The future can only be dreamed of in similarly hallucinatory ways, the garden gate at the end of the *Confessions* refiguring Eden's gate for the restless soul.

Unlike the untranslatable "Arabic characters" of De Quincey's non-musical friend (*Confessions* 45), the "hieroglyphics" to which De Quincey likens his opium experiences figure his Eastern transformation into a fractured and violated identity. "The dreamer finds housed within himself" not just the "duality" of his own and an alien nature, but much worse: "how, if the alien nature contradicts his own, fights with it, perplexes, and confounds it? How, again, if not one alien nature, but two, but three, but four, but five, are introduced within what once he thought the inviolable sanctuary of himself?" (*Mail-Coach* 201). Duality suggests a self and other dichotomy, but many fractures of the self suggest a colony within, a selfhood colonized by hallucinatory others, the "them" against which the violated self is posed. Is this community a stand-in for immanent life?, a way of fending off immanence as too restorative? Must the self that is tamed by opium house these other beings—increasingly they are crocodiles—who are inside the subject, colonizing him? It certainly repositions how One and All conceives the role of the individual: instead of participating in the whole, it offers itself up in open hospitality. Imperialist capitalism produces, in De Quincey's imagining, the eating of symbols of foreign conquest: opium and tea, certainly, but also hieroglyphics, the hermeneutic code. Taking these in, housing them, transforms the individual one into a combinatory All, but as a perverse version of *hen kai pan*.

As the *Confessions* and subsequently *The English Mail-Coach* make increasingly clear, ingesting foreign substances is an inoculating activity. When Spinoza discusses the motion of bodies in God's world, his concern for affecting bodies is for how their speed increases or decreases, but inoculation as the introduction of infectious agents can transform the subject in terrible ways. For De Quincey, on consumption, mysterious agents—signs with the necromantic power of hieroglyphics—come alive, their power violently transforming and bisecting the subject into a god/slave. Would eating hieroglyphs, like eating opium, translate inside of oneself, turning one into a hybrid deity, a hawk, jackal, or crocodile-headed Egyptian god? Or would it divide the self into different states, a bipolarization into the worshipped *and* the victimized? It might produce "the horrid inoculation upon each other of incompatible natures" (*Mail-Coach* 200). Would the hermeneutic code, like opium, be responsible for the resulting madness, the both/and that is characteristic of the manic depressive, the artistic genius and Faustian scientist (all of whom De Quincey aligns himself with in his memoirs), as well as the psychotic drug user? The opium eater finds himself unrecognizable (a crocodile, a hieroglyphic), transformed from a British consumer into an alienated displacement, a nobody or a pre-body. He is a pre-body awaiting his transformative substance.

The menacing crocodile, De Quincey's dream double and bailiff (the crocodile has been feared as early as his poverty-stricken time in London when his friend the Attorney lived in a seemingly haunted house, leaving each night for a strange bed in order to elude the bailiff and debtor's prison), swindles De Quincey of his identity only to forge it anew in a new tongue and new rhetorical style of comprehensible confession, a "physical economy" that replaces "intellectual philosophy" but also installs a hybrid subject (*Confessions* 49). The only alleviations of his crocodile state of alienation are, interestingly, female: Ann, Margaret (the invisible but dear "M."), his children, Catherine Wordsworth. These figures translate into each other not simply because memories do meld in such ways, but because it is through female agency that an antigen to the emasculating effects of xenophobic hallucination can be found. Through the memory of female companionship, De Quincey hopes to come back to himself, but he is never to be the same again, always finding himself even with remembered females in an "oriental scene."

Such scenes begin in immediate recognition (an Eden of beloveds) but then turn into defamiliarizing ground. There, likeness transmorphs into both same and other, multiplying into many othernesses, "not one alien nature, but two, but three, but four, but five . . . introduced within . . . the inviolable sanctuary of himself" (*Mail-Coach* 201). One nonthreatening Malay becomes many amok Malays, one crocodile morphed from a sofa leg becomes many half-human crocs. De Quincey presents himself as self-confessed victim, utilitarian sufferer for the greater good and guilty through his differential location and his scenes of sacrifice. But can he really script himself and his case into the nineteenth-century imaginary if he does so with a guilty mentality?—for there is a kind of gall about this inscribing of the criminal self. It is an emotional double-bind that reveals at once a cultural conservatism still functioning and the experiment of inverting the pain of acculturation onto British subjectivity, inviting otherness in. The cost of this trial, as much as the epistemological gall behind it, is what intrigues us about De Quincey's narrative as it tropes with unexpected verisimilitude what Kristeva calls the foreigner's "secret wound."[14] Kristeva notes that in our contemporary Western culture, the trials of acculturation have been absorbed by all of us: "Strangely, the foreigner lives within us; he is the hidden face of our identity, the space that wrecks our abode, the time in which understanding and affinity founder." What the *Confessions* provides is the experience of those experimental travelers like De Quincey, mental or physical adventurers, who were willing to explore the boundaries of subjectivity.

IV. The Afterlife

What happens when subjective exploration reveals shape-changing possibilities beyond prior imaginings? This is the problem of subjective plurality, of both/and experiences in which the subject realizes that otherness is multiple and that it affects the self's "inviolable" unity. Being singular plural, to use Nancy's term, confronts self-deception, which necessarily fades in the face of a colonized self. The inhabited self must confront the transformation of its "inviolable sanctuary" into contested ground. If the other is really "them" and not "him," as in endless Malays, endless crocodiles, then the "I" might also be not "we" but instead a varying combinatory of the multiple. Subjectivity itself becomes problematic as a category distinct from Otherness. This in itself is a giant step toward immanence. On what ground can the subject stand? Where find himself if not in the absent seat in his parlor beside the "eternal teapot"? (*Confessions* 79).

For De Quincey, his plural selves resemble Egyptian deities with their human bodies and heads of symbolically powerful animals. He essentially repositions Schelling's "subjectnature," the proposition of his *Naturphilosophie*,[15] as representable through the animal-human transmorphisms imagined by the ancients. On his explication of crocodile-coach drivers in *The English Mail-Coach*, De Quincey notes that "the fearful composition of the sphinx," the dragon that is "the snake inoculated upon the scorpion," the basilisk" all have "compound nature[s]" that are "*objectively* horrid," "but there is no insinuation that they *feel* that horror" (201). What would it *feel* like, he implicitly asks, to be inoculated with another species? Egyptian gods, like the transmorphic gods of other ancient religions such as Hinduism's Vishnu, manifest their divinity through the attributes of each face they present to their human subjects. These faces all in some way affect the conditions of life and death, the "pains" and "pleasures" of the trials that each represents. The afterlife in Egypt's necrolatrous culture is something all subjects experience if their physical bodies are preserved. The body's inviolability suggests that its transmorphism would disturb the boundaries between human and divine, and that the humanness of its form must be preserved at all costs. De Quincey's experimental play with Eastern substances confounds these finely determined differences: in his mental wanderings, human and animal grotesquely combine, divine and human identities inhabit the same (De Quinceyan) body. It is this Western interloping in Eastern affairs that perhaps inspires the seemingly unaccountable guilt, criminality, and conditions of subjective aporia that he experiences.

Because the *Confessions* are not autobiographical, the narrative's end is not the end of De Quincey's story. In many ways his story ends halfway through the work when his subjective state translates into another plane. No longer who he was, he now functions differently, and his translation—a kind of transubstantiation—is from life to the death-in-life of the opium-eater. But what happens after that is equally translative. Once De Quincey uses "religious zeal," as he tells us in the very beginning of the *Confessions*, which like the tail-in-mouth ouroboros begins at the end, he regains control of his addiction and his sanity. However, this is not a restoration; the dead cannot come back to life. Instead, he is a different man, one who is dislocated, somehow always absent from his text, always somewhere else (as he says of himself in his portrait scene of the parlor). He is living a kind of afterlife quite different from the Coleridgean Mariner's post-revelatory death-in-life behavior.

The Western imagination had room for speculation about what occurs in the Egyptian, Persian, and Zoroastrian afterlives. More archaeological and linguistic research had focused on the artifacts of Ancient

Egypt, presumably because of its biblical importance as much as its more preserved ruins, and so Egypt provided De Quincey with his most articulated ground for his metaphorical dreaming. And until the hieroglyphic and demotic scripts were decoded and the texts made widely available, casual scholars like De Quincey would have found the many narratives of pyramid and tomb excavations fruitful for conjectures about the ancient Near East's imagination. It might have seemed evident that two central features of Ancient Egyptian life—the Nile River and pyramids—would dominate visions of the afterlife. In any case, De Quincey's nightmares often included visions of pyramid entombment and Nilotic immersions, and often in this order: first architectural and then an immersion in a foreign people, then a threatening fate by water. "In the early stages of my malady, the splendours of my dreams were chiefly architectural . . . To my architecture succeeded dreams of lakes—and silvery expanses of water:— these haunted me so much, that I feared . . . that some dropsical state or tendency of the brain might thus be making itself (to use a metaphysical word) . . . *objective*; and the sentient organ *project* itself as its own object" (*Confessions* 71). Then the waters "changed their character . . . promised an abiding torment" (72). The drowning is sometimes in oceans, sometimes with the "unutterable slimy things, amongst reeds and Nilotic mud" (73). When it is the Nilotic dream, archetypally so similar to the Moses story of a gentle reed cradle set afloat on the Nile to be found by an Egyptian princess, the transformation from a hero's beginning to a criminal end, and from water to mud (the ground of crocodiles), is dramatic. With this reversal, De Quincey also reverses the movement from polytheism to monotheism that Moses enacted once he became the hero of the Exodus story. By returning to polytheism, that is, a base of religions (Chinese, Hindu, Egyptian) whose deities have attributes in common and can thus be interchanged, worshipped by many peoples, De Quincey creates the conditions for re-embracing interchangeable subjectivity. This is the "them" with which he has inoculated himself, and from the themselves thus produced comes the gnoseology, the atavistically endorsed knowledge, of his new afterlife. Such knowledge can only be released by an interpretive strategy, for like all enlightenment about immanent life in the period, immanence expresses itself but is outside, or beyond, the auto-machine of language, as we saw in chapter 4.

De Quincey's dreamwork concerning death helps to construct his afterlife in the present as a stand-in for awakening to immanence; part of this dreaming frames that strategy through the hallucinogesis he sets out to formulate. The dreamwork involved in this labor is very much fixated on antiquity. One important dream sequence begins with the pagodas of ancient China, moves to the temples of India, and ends in the Egyptian pyramids and Nile River. "I was buried, for a thousand years, in stone coffins, with mummies and sphinxes, in narrow chambers at the heart of eternal pyramids. I was kissed, with cancerous kisses, by crocodiles; and laid, confounded with all unutterable slimy things, amongst reeds and Nilotic mud" (*Confessions* 73). His psychic investment in the eternity of death as entombment—the fate of a mummy, in fact—within his hallucinogenic framework is related to this conglomerate of antique lands. The relationship, woven on a warping of time, space, and otherness, provides the hermeneutic necessary, the hallucinogesis or reading of opiate dreams.

Architectural structures in such contexts are, of course, reminders of cultural ruin, as both Volney's highly popular *Ruins* and Piranesi's equally popular *Antiquities of Rome* illustrate. But there is an important relation to dreaming, cultural memory, and the afterlife of ruins in both works. Volney's book is predicated on a dream vision that occurs from a cosmic perspective as he meditates on the ruins of civilizations; Piranesi's architectural engravings of Roman ruins (*Varie Vedute di Roma Antica e Moderna*, 1745) were then fantastically translated in his *Imaginary Prisons* (1745), which De Quincey remembers as Piranesi's *Dreams* (70). His engraving of the *Pyramid of Cestius* might have been on De Quincey's mind here as much as the *Cerceri d'invenzione*—incarceration being the proper burial for criminals. Piranesi's visions of horrible yet fascinating prisons, the general principles of which De Quincey describes in some detail, create an inversion effect. De Quincey's reversion to polytheistic imaginings and conversion (however unwilling) to a plural selfhood witness his transculturation, but Piranesi's inversion might come closest to a word De Quincey uses to describe the mysterious aspect of time, the "involute" (a word borrowed from German nature philosophy). The fantastic spaces of incarceration in Piranesi's engravings allow the viewer to inhabit those spaces, to subjectively experience them. Geometrically the involute is a continuous curve, as in a snail shell or winding staircase. Piranesi's interiors often involve involute staircases that disrupt visual orientation and imprison the viewer in irrational, dislocating space. For De Quincey, the involute traps one in time, in non-movement (movement and speed are the essential qualities of life and nature for Spinoza). Prisons that cannot be escaped become in De Quincey's hands the eternal pyramids, entombing him for a thousand years. Entombing him in non-time.

The circling in of the involute curve that traps one in static time also creates a hyper state of subjectivity, something like one would experience in the first hours of imprisonment or live burial. Different from the restless interval, the involute curve moves aporia into something else, something that gets closer to the alterity within. This inward spiral produces an oppositional effect to that of the telescope, the instrument that imaginatively structures the cosmic vision of Volney's *Ruins*. (De Quincey does use the reflector telescope metaphorically in *Suspiria de Profundis*, 1845, but for exploring dreams and "the chambers of a human brain" rather than cosmic truths.) It is as if the ruin of the self can mirror the ruin of cultures, such as ancient China, India, and Egypt, but not critique it. Alterity requires a dying into that is a ruination of the ego-self and its rationalizing propensities. For critique, by contrast, one needs an "inviolable" self, one uncontaminated by the "cancerous kisses" of opium-morphed crocodiles.

Because the experience of alterity—the human sacrifice to the gods in which he is both god and sacrifice, both human and animal, both eternal and present—terrifies rather than fully enlightens him, as it does the Ancient Mariner, De Quincey subjects his dream-vision to a cultural critique. Fending the revelation off after the fact is palliative at best, for the alterity within is always ready to re-present itself. Nevertheless, fend it off he does by transforming his digressive, associative style—the materialized form of his restless wandering in the interval—into what he calls a "palimpsest" in the *Suspiria*. The palimpsest allows the encounter with alterity to lie beneath rationalization; strata of dying-into ground and layer with a return to supposed objectivity. As Grevel Lindop notes, the palimpsest "abandons autobiography to explore a brilliantly suggestive metaphor for the human mind: the ancient manuscript whose successive layers of text correspond to the buried but recoverable deposits of memory lying below the surface of consciousness. The palimpsest may also be seen as an implicit model of De Quincey's own mode of writing."[16] This analysis of his content-formulated style reveals the archeological force behind De Quincey's case history. The dreamer experiences Asiatic-derived hallucinations through his armchair excavations of ancient ruins. The manuscript of his dreamwork can be delved, revisited, studied, and rewritten. The interval need never be departed from, yet its purpose can be endlessly deferred as long as the encounter with otherness horrifies the self rather than awakens it from its ego-needs.

Behind the palimpsest conceit lies the conflating forces of De Quincey's colonial imagination. The mysterious manuscript that must be decoded, like the Rosetta Stone, does not become yet another archeological feat in which the artifact gives up its secrets. Instead of a clinical, objective approach, his is intuitive and involved, producing "truths" such as that all ancient religions are somehow the same polytheism: "I fled from the wrath of Brama [sic] through all the forests of Asia: Vishnu hated me: Seev [sic] laid wait for me. I came suddenly upon Isis and Osiris: I had done a deed, they said, which the ibis and the crocodile trembled at. I was buried, for a thousand years, in stone coffins, with mummies and sphinxes, in narrow chambers at the heart of eternal pyramids" (*Confessions* 123). The associative style that prefigures the later palimpsest model produce a remembering of Ancient Egypt, an allegory of monumental life. This is a fantastic archeology, but one with curious tendencies toward psychological knowledge. Freud's metaphor of memory as a mystic writing pad (a kind of wax tablet) conveys a similarly anti-analytic image of human remembrance as the palimpsest conceit of De Quinceyan imaginings. If for Freud the trace of writing beneath the erased tablet proves the key, for De Quincey it is the manuscript's buried layers, yet both these images suggest burial. Living burial, death, disinterment, and the afterlife (as represented by Isis and Osiris): these are the recurrent themes of De Quincey's rhetoric. The afterlife, it seems, is a condition of constant remembering. When De Quincey remembers "The Vision of Sudden Death" in *The English Mail-Coach*, he weaves together "The Vision" and "The Dream-Fugue" to produce "an attempt to wrestle with the utmost efforts of music in dealing with a colossal form of impassioned horror" (209 n.). However, the musical "fugue" becomes yet another escape from the analytic function, another resort to the adolescent fugue-state that presaged his afterlife. The horror of sudden death, which is so opposite from the centuries-long death of the spirit that he dreams in his most important encounter with alterity, cannot be placated by superiority of intellect; it can only be uncovered and remembered. The rebirth occurs through this act of memory, just as Ann the prostitute and Fanny of the Bath Road are brought to life again and again in the remembered dreams.

If De Quincey's memories are to be anything other than a singularity, if his case is to function as a Freudian case study does by providing a key to other kinds of operations, then we have to ask what the afterlife is an afterlife of? It resembles neither the Christian paradise nor the Egyptian afterlife, but a state so self-estranged yet so continually confessional that it appears to be present tense as the remembrance and reconstitution of a life of guilt. And what crime has De Quincey truly committed? And to what is the guilt a key? It would seem that, as in the incident of the Malay's possible overdosing, De Quincey's crime is one of resisting immanence, refusing life when it stares him in the face—and mocking it instead. This is acculturation gone awry and an unintentional hybridity: the One and All becomes the transmorphed self, with its body and spirit in a state of constant impasse, an eternal aporia. It is this translation of encounter with alterity that De Quincey contends with, struggling to give it voice yet resisting its potential to take over his story, to become both its subject and its hero while he merely participates. That this is the point eludes him.

De Quincey's hybridity, as dislocating and disembodying as it proves to be, opens him up to the unwanted gnoseologies of substance and immanence. Such revelation is simply Otherly ways of recognizing the absolute. But it does battle in his dreams with imperial epistemology. In discovering how to medicate himself by what he thinks is a new method of inoculation, De Quincey realigns his mental and imaginative capacity to dreamscapes that are as powerful in their disquietude and their visceral power as Wordsworth's nostalgia-heavy spots of time. But De Quincey's version is the wrong culture, and the nostalgia is so askew that it repeatedly morphs into scenes of horror and despair. De Quincey steadfastly refuses to acknowledge the absolute's universal self-realization in the encounter with alterity, returning always to his preferred state of restless aporia. He refuses revelation and prophecy, preferring to remain mired in the past perhaps precisely because his visions are as self-horrifying as they are transformative. Or perhaps his new history of the self is frighteningly disorienting, threatening the possibility of his return to Eden so beautifully depicted at the end of the *Confessions* when he comes to the garden gate.

Inoculation prevents his immanent life, for it is, of course, a hallucinatory return, a dream vision populated by lost souls, its setting as De Quincey notes "an oriental one" (*Confessions* 76). This ending follows the theme of the tea-tray scene as domestic, native space that is an Eden barred to the fallen soul, effacing him. Eden is followed by fearful battle, "a day of crisis and of final hope for human nature," tempest, symphonies, and passions, the climax unbearable—no *Prelude* concluding vision, this is a terrible departure, a "sigh . . . [from the] caves of hell," a dreadful impasse (77). All seems inescapably lost now: the cure that isn't, the poetry that estranges, the self-knowledge that produces guilt not wisdom, the inoculation that pollutes. Gnoseology proves too uncontrollable, its truths too devastating; this can be the case with alterity's demand to give up the ego-self. What can he do but conclude with Milton's *Paradise Lost* rather than the *Prelude* with its healing wisdom: he presents its fiercest imagery: "With dreadful faces throng'd and fiery arms" (*PL* XII 644). It is an infernal version of Eden, a final refusal of immanent life. Yet his writings on opium suggest that despite his resistance, he did create the conditions of his own immanent experience. Inverted, involute, transmorphic, it inoculated him in the end.

Coda: Restorative Otherness

The works and writers I have brought into conversation in these chapters suggest that Romantic immanence, and the immanent bodies of the nonhuman world, hold a promise for the human beyond the transcendently mortal dream of a deus ex machina that will lift us up out of the fatal illness that is called "being human." De Quincey's self-absorption is a reminder that the blessedness achieved by the Ancient Mariner comes at the high cost both Blake and Percy Shelley define as self-sacrifice or dying-into. If Dorothy Wordsworth understands it more locally—as a momentary reprieve from the self-sacrifice that is woman's lot—her encounters with the self-caused nature that is *natura naturans* are no less blessed. What all the writers I have discussed share is the awareness that alterity not only comes uninvited, uninvoked, unanticipated, despite all the best efforts of a poetic age, but it also opens up the encounter with immanence and its expressive bodies. The sublime, with its one-on-one promise of a greater self-sufficiency, a transport that transforms the poet into the prophet-priest, cannot achieve this more worldly but also more important task of making the human once again into a natural being.

An important message of Romantic immanence is that human being must be torn out of its solipsistic center, a displacement that can only occur through communion with the other in a realization of the communal bond of the everything that composes the All. Since this All is literally everything, being must be realized as everywhere, as universalized, and the encounter is as likely to be within as it is to be encountered in the external world—for nature includes thought, as Spinoza tells us, or thought is the incorporeal body, as the Stoics held. The result is a blow to the sublime message of man's poetic splendor and capacity to mirror the divine rather than merely participate in the absolute as one of the myriad things co-constituting it. Hopefully the blow will prove efficacious in a potent world whose future may not have room for human efficacy. Coleridge ended his "Rime" with lines particularly descriptive of the effect of that contrast on man, represented here as the Wedding Guest: "He went, like one that hath been stunn'd / And is of sense forlorn." If he woke the next day "A sadder" man, he is also a wiser man, for even without a firsthand encounter with alterity and realization of immanence, the Guest has awakened to the now of nature's self-actualizing potency. And this is not entirely different from what De Quincey's afterlife achieves despite himself.

In the Epilogue I continue reflecting on the racial Otherness that De Quincey, in particular, is haunted by, and that may in part be responsible for why immanent alterity has continued to play a subordinate role in Western thought. If Romantic immanence is the recognition of the One and All, how does the enslaving and trading of African peoples, as the most egregious mistreatment of the particular, play a role in the elevation of the sublime over immanence in the following century? Particularity fares ill in the face of an increasing reliance on the transcendent supports on which capitalism depends, as well as empire's globalizing aspirations. But looking at immanence through a blackened lens reveals something else as well.

Section IV

Corporeal Bias: Bodies as Incorporeals

Epilogue

Immanence and Racial Alterity

Romanticism's reception of Enlightenment schemes of category and classification was multivalent. On the one hand, radical thought and radicalized attitudes toward political justice led to inquiry into other forms of a just place in which to consider the world. The world was not just Nature, though this led to an embrace of German nature philosophy and new understanding of the world as natural; the world was not just global, though this led to a renewed interest in geography, travel writing and ethnography, and foreign goods. It was this radicalized attention to the human and being in the world that reinvigorated Spinozist thought and sparked interest in his conception of immanence. On the other hand, racialization as a way of categorizing the human-animal spectrum into discrete stages of achieved "being" became more embedded even as activists called for its abolishment in terms of the human, and animal rights and vegetarianism in terms of the animal.[1] Racialization provided a rationale for the economic exploitation of parts of Africa and the Asian subcontinent for labor, while at the same time providing a national investment in racialized goods such as Caribbean sugar and Indian cotton.[2] Racialization was theorized along with speciesism by philosophers like Kant and Hegel.[3] It also put particularity up against the universal in a new way; the particular could again be relegated to that which is beneath consideration, at the same time that the universalized subject (white, male, self-possessed) was associated with the transcendent and the sublime. Bentham's utilitarianism need only benefit the latter, and had stronger proponents politically than did Spinozism or "nature."

It is one of Romanticism's characteristics that questions of Otherness and being should play out in parallel between philosophical explanations of alterity and economic justifications of subjugation. The combination of the sublime and the Otherness of ancient cultures with which De Quincey experiments in his *Confessions* is part and parcel of larger attitudes toward the unknown both in terms of transcendent Otherness and archaic wisdom. These were nearly always put in relation to an argument concerning Britain's degraded morals, loss of faith and wisdom, and inadequate knowledge. Along with many others, De Quincey agrees that despite the scientific and industrial gains of the Enlightenment, these imagined ills threatened to stall society in the march to a prosperous futurity.

At the same time, achievements in the areas of aesthetic experience (particularly of the sublime), and of affect (particularly of sympathy)—both of which arose more or less along with the revival of Spinozist immanence—provided optimism for a future of continued improvement in increasingly harmonized and just social systems. This contrasting relation between a present threatened by cultural degradation and a promising future appears in a different guise in the contrasting relation between immanent encounter as an experience of the One, and the trade in enslaved persons as that which purposely transforms bodies, robbing them of subject status. I focus on the radical othering and anti-Blackness caused by the plantation economy here but am also mindful of the egregious activities promulgated under the East India Company, whose economic interests were equally at odds with immanent life.

In *Becoming Human*, Zakiyyah Iman Jackson demonstrates how to view the self-other structure of anti-Blackness manifestly as a problem of metaphysics. Her explanation of how Blackness functioned in the transformation of free persons into laboring bodies as "human animals" provides the connective tissue of ideas that enabled immanent revelation and racialization to coexist. I do not aim here to provide Romantic poetic examples of how raciality and immanent radicality arose in parallel. One illustration exemplifies how difficult these are to disentangle: Blake's "Little Black Boy" in *Songs of Innocence and Experience* (1789) demonstrates how abolition political messaging aimed at white readers rests on the stable presence of the Black mother in a way that denies immanent expression to her. Instead, Blake's lyric resides at the political level in the same way that the two Chimney-sweeper poems in the same collection do. All three poems are illustrations of political injustice; a prescribed poetic goal such as this already heads elsewhere, having no time for the immanent encounter, for listening on the other side of silence. Yet Blake's poem, despite its uncomfortable messaging of Black suffering as a lesson for whites, is useful to illustrate why anti–anti-Blackness and immanent encounter cannot co-reside in the same poem.

In explaining how raciality became scientific "fact" in the Enlightenment, Jackson points to what has nearly always been left out of historical and philosophical accounts of race: gender. Race as a categorical term in the spectrum of animal-to-human is always used to universalize the subject as male. Jackson's formula is different: "Liberal humanism's basic unit of analysis, 'Man,' produces an untenable dichotomy—'the human' versus 'the animal,' whereby the black(ened) female is posited as the abyss dividing organic life into 'human' or 'animal'" (*Becoming Human* 12). This, she notes, is a failed metaphysics—a phrase that echoes, however unintentionally, Blake's speaker's remark to the Angel in *Marriage of Heaven and Hell*.[4] We can see this failure at work in "Little Black Boy," wherein the Black mother attempts to comfort her son with another failed metaphysics: if he can survive this life of ordeal, he will achieve God's promised afterlife of eternal peace. "She took me on her lap and kissèd me, / And, pointing to the East, began to say: / 'Look on the rising sun: there God does live . . . .'" (*Songs of Innocence and Experience* Copy L, pl. 8; 9–11). The mother's role is important because while the poem's political force is on the little boy, not the "black(ened) female," this mother plays the significant role of presenting the Black male as fully human, and fully facing his suffering to come. The reader has no choice but to sympathize with the male child and to see him as fully equal to the suffering white boys in the chimney-sweeper poems, and therefore as non-excluded from the category of human. How the mother is viewed is left open.

"Black mater" is Jackson's figure for the liminal female figure who is neither present nor absent, neither nonhuman nor human: Blake's Black mother. She is instead a translative figure who combines nature and matter with the incorporeal, transforming being into moving bodies in terms both of transport and labor. In a corruption of Spinozist terms, I interpret Jackson's theory this way: the Black mother provides causality to blackened bodies that otherwise would not be self-caused (for Spinoza all bodies are self-caused). Additionally, for Spinoza, all bodies are defined by their movement and speed; the Black mother translates Black bodies into those whose movement is that of transport and labor, acted on by the pressure of other bodies (including the chains, holds, whips they wield, which are also bodies involved in this movement). Because in Spinozist terms their blackened body's speed is stalled, so too is their temporality; their time is not "real" because it is the time of waiting, of sufferance. It is Blake's Ulro, which one scholar defines as "the internal condition of blackness, opacity, and darkness which occurs when the Divine Vision is lost." [5] It is a state that seems defined by racialization and enslavement.

Grounded in Black mater, the "blackened" body is an ideal-real construct that is figurative more than it is realized. Its structure distorts the nonduality of immanence, foreclosing immanent encounter for such bodies. Jackson analyzes this distortion based on the Black maternal figure as "the absent presence of the material metaphor of the black female as matrix-figure" (*Becoming Human* 13). She is "plastic" in the sense of being either metaphorical and translative *or* human, depending on how white subjects need to use this figure for their failed metaphysics. Theirs is a metaphysics that inherently rejects immanence because it rejects the Oneness that dissolves categories and difference. Black mater is neither a truly human mother or "Mother Nature": she is neither driven by desire like Blake's mythic female characters, the emanations, nor is she the protective spirit of nature poetry.

Neither does Spinoza's Nature, in which all corporeal and incorporeal bodies are made of the same substance and participate in the same deep interrelationality, register here. There is no correspondence because Black mater is neither incorporeal nor corporeal, but "plastic," both everything and nothing as Jackson frames it. Black mater inhabits a nonproductive interval of neither absence nor presence, neither ontological nor mystical existence—an antithesis to the interval of the generative *chora*. Yet she is absolutely necessary for the "organizational logics of racialized sexuation" (25) that makes enslaved women vulnerable to legitimized white rape and forced maternity of mixed-race children who also do not clearly fit into animal-human categories. As this logic illustrates, its intentional slowing of blackened bodies, rendering them plastic and temporally stalled for their white logicians, is the product of what Spinoza calls inadequate ideas. These confused ideas are the distortions caused by negative affects: in reducing blackened bodies to the affects of fear, anger, and pain, the failed metaphysicians are themselves affected by inadequate, confused ideas, themselves slowed in body and therefore life energy. That organizational logic and its accompanying economic justification are antithetical to immanence, precluding its encounter at every point by denying the basic commensurability of all individuals and entities as bodies whose motion is the only thing that matters.

Jackson's analysis helps clarify the vexed relation of "Black mater" to the "Mother Nature" of Romantic nature poetry, especially William Wordsworth's. Poems like book I of *The Prelude* make clear the maternal, nursing aspect of a Nature whose role is to enhance white man's poetic genius: though Nature is female, white woman's poetic aptitude, and poetic genius of any persons of color, do not qualify them to be her children in the same way. She is the opposite of Black mater: whereas Mother Nature encodes mystical transmission, Black mater translates matter into bodies that move in enslaved ways. Yet enslaved Black mothers nursed infants of mixed race, white men's children. This is the essential ground that puts immanent alterity in relation to the Otherness of Black mater, the One and All in parallel to blackened humanity. It is what makes the radical aspect of Spinozist nature and immanence a fragile source of prophecy; one that quickly dissipates, like Coleridge's opium dream of Kubla Khan, before the effects of plantation economy. The promise of immanent life, as depicted in Blake's fully realized Jerusalem, could change the direction of Shelley's triumph, or bring Dorothy Wordsworth's scenic communes into a revolutionary version of human community, but not without acknowledging the distortions perpetuated by trading in human bodies.

Notes

Introduction

1. *Coleridge's Poetry and Prose*, 181.
2. Deleuze, *Cours: Sur Spinoza*, January 1, 1978. https://www.webdeleuze.com/textes/14.
3. Johnson, "Nothing Fails Like Success," 14.
4. *The Feminine Sublime: Gender and Excess in Women's Fiction*. Freeman's examples of this literary phenomenon suggest to me that what she has identified is less a version of the sublime than a mode of alterity closer to immanence.
5. "What appears to be a theory of excess actually functions to keep it at bay" (4).
6. Levinson, "A Motion and a Spirit: Romancing Spinoza," 367–68.
7. Levinson's article, although slightly dated now, includes a compendious bibliography for British engagement with Spinoza. Dalia Nassr provides some of the strongest recent scholarship on Spinoza and German Romanticism in *The Romantic Absolute*.
8. Spinoza's use of substance is the Aristotelian one of self-grounded being. Levinson, 378.
9. Jonathan Bennett, *A Study of Spinoza's Ethics*, 41.
10. See Frederick Beiser's account in *German Idealism*, especially Jacobi's interpretation of Spinoza, 385–86.
11. Stobaeus on Cleanthes, qtd. in Grosz, 47.
12. Gilles Deleuze, *Logic of Sense*, 151; also qtd. in Grosz, 52.
13. See the *Science of Logic*. "Ground" and "grounded" change according to the moment in the thought process he is describing. Hegel's concern with the human spirit and human thought are worked through in terms of how humans metabolize the external world: how the ideal, or thought, participates in and internalizes the real, or matter.

Chapter 1

1. Schelling, *Philosophy of Art*, 73.
2. Ludwig Wittgenstein, *Tractatus Logico-Philosophicus*, proposition 6.4311.
3. Blake, "Auguries of Innocence," ll. 1–4, *The Pickering Manuscript*, pl. 13: 16–19, http://blakearchive.org/copy/bb126.1?descId=bb126.1.ms.13. Retrieved October 20, 2021.
4. Morris Eaves, Robert N. Essick, and Joseph Viscomi, eds., *Songs of Innocence and of Experience*, copy Y, pl. 47/47. William Blake Archive. Accessed 24 Oct. 2021.
5. See Orianne Smith, *Romantic Women Writers, Revolution, and Prophecy: Rebellious Daughters, 1786–1826*. Smith's argument is that Romantic prophecy has illocutionary force, but Blake prophecies immanence—which is incompatible with declaration. For this reason he rejects Swedenborg as a prophet.
6. Makdisi, *William Blake and the Impossible History of the 1790s*. See esp. 34–45.
7. Yaeger, "Of Eagles And Crows, Lions and Oxen." See esp. 5–7, "Beyond Binary Thinking."
8. Wittgenstein, *Tractatus*, proposition 6.421.
9. See my *Romantic Egypt*, esp. 2–20. Scholars treating this topic include Morton, *The Everlasting Gospel*; Yates's *Giordano Bruno and the Hermetic Tradition*; Marjorie Levinson, Jon Mee, and Alexander Regier; and for German thinkers, Magee, *Hegel and the Hermetic Tradition* and Jason Wirth on Schelling.
10. This is only a small part of Rajan's larger argument that in the Lambeth books, "the grotesque body that dis-figures these books is an autoreferential figure for Blake's projection of his own corpus as a systematic body of work" ("Blake's Bodies" 358).
11. Spinoza devotes Section IV of the *Ethics* to the affects: "On Human Bondage, or the Powers of the Affects" (Curley, 543–94). In quoting from the *Ethics* I follow the standard formula used by Curley of Roman numerals = part; Arabic numbers = axiom; D following a Roman numeral = definition; P = proposition; C = corollary; S = scholium; Exp = explanation. For example, (IIP7S) = Part II, proposition 7, scholium.
12. I refer to Derrida's exploration of the void in *Spectres of Marx* and draw on Karen Barad's use of Derrida's "hauntology" in her discussion of the void's potentiality ("Troubling Time/s," 64, 75–85).
13. See esp. *Of Grammatology*, 217–28.
14. Immanuel Kant, "The End of All Things," 221.
15. Iain Hamilton Grant, *Philosophies of Nature After Schelling*, x.
16. Hegel notes that self-consciousness is "the reflection out of the being of the world of sense and perception," and "As self-consciousness, it is movement" (*Phenomenology* 105).

17. Newton refers to the promiscuity of light in a letter to Oldenburg, February 6, 1672: "Light is a confused aggregate of Rays indued with all sorts of Colors, as they are promiscuously darted from the various parts of luminous bodies." *Newton*, ed. Cohen and Westfall, 177.

18. Goethe, *Theory of Colours*, 12.

19. Wittgenstein would much later revisit it for his philosophical study of color perception. See his *Remarks on Colour*.

20. Modern art theorists consider both the prismatic (cyan-magenta-yellow) scheme and the traditional (red-blue-yellow scheme) to be only theories of how we sense and interpret color rather than factual accounts of how color exists empirically.

21. *Athenaeum* Fragments 220, qtd. in Lacoue-Labarthe and Nancy, *Literary Absolute*, 56.

22. *Philosophical Fragments*, 52.

23. A. Schlegel had recently moved to Berlin, where Schelling visited him and maintained a heavy correspondence, borrowing Auguste's lecture notes to aid him in his own lectures. Schelling was still in the period of his identity philosophy at this time.

24. Schelling, *The Philosophy of Art*, 34.

25. David Simpson's Introduction, p. x. I am describing Schelling's thought during his identity period only.

26. A curious link between Schelling and Blake lies with Henry Crabbe Robinson, who sat in on Schelling's lectures, afterward sharing his notes with Mme. De Staël.

27. *The Aurora* (1612, unpublished); see also Magee 40–41.

28. Qtd. in Blanchot, *Space of Literature*, 45.

29. Christ as the "incarnation of God is to reconcile with God the finite that has fallen away from God by nullifying it in his own person. . . . It is as if Christ, as the infinite that has entered finitude and sacrificed it to God *in* his own human form." (*Philosophy of Art* 64).

30. Hegel explains in his *Encyclopedia of the Philosophical Sciences*, "All that is necessary to achieve scientific progress . . . is the recognition of the logical principle that the negative is just as much positive, or that what is self-contradictory does not resolve itself into a nullity, into abstract nothingness, but essentially only into the negation of its *particular* content . . . Because the result, the negation, is a specific negation it has a *content*." Introduction, *Science of Logic*, 54.

31. As Foster Damon notes in his *Blake Dictionary*, "for Generated man to enter Beulah, special gates are required" (43).

32. Until *Jerusalem*, Ulro was also the world of generation, but when the fourfold scheme of *Jerusalem* required a fourth world, Blake divided his basest world into Ulro and Generation.

33. See my discussion of Wedgwood's politicized arts industry in *Fashioning Faces*, chapter 3, "Consuming Portraits."

34. Julia Kristeva formulates two of her key concepts of subjectivity as the "subject-in-process/on-trial," that is, a subjectivity that is always already unstable, tenuous, and in process, and one that is always on trial or called into question: the unstable identity is that of the subject-in-process, but process also refers to the trial as "a legal proceeding where the subject is committed to trial, because our identities in life are constantly called into question, brought to trial, over-ruled." "A Question of Subjectivity—An Interview," 19.

35. In this debate, Being represents the continual human struggle between the antipodes of abstract positing-negation, as thesis-antithesis (an *either/or*), whereas Becoming represents a Hegelian belief in the synthesis, which dissolves the identities in a new entity, the synthesis (*both-and*). The synthesis in this model, based on Hegel's theory of historical progression but reducing it to Fichte's terminology, proves the progress to be a substantial gain.

36. See Lorraine Clark, *Blake, Kierkegaard, and the Spectre of the Dialectic*. Clark uses the term "precarious" to represent Blake's alternative to a Being-Becoming dichotomy.

37. See Makdisi's explanation of the illuminated books as interdynamic works meant to be read against each other in self-revising fashion even as these works revise each other in the shifting versions of the essential mythos. "Weary of Time," chapter 4 in *William Blake and the Impossible History of the 1790s*, 155–203.

38. See the color plate at wwww.blakearchive.org. Erdman's edition is available in copy D (http://www.blakearchive.org/exist/blake/archive/object.xq?objectid=urizen.d.illbk.01&java=yes).

39. Although there is some possibility for Urizen's redemption, when he is about to understand his own need for others, he suddenly turns back against such an event because of his continued "self deci[e]t," and proclaims himself God of the mundane world (Night the Eighth, *Four Zoas* 373, 375).

Chapter 2

1. Schelling, *Ages of the World* (1815), 44.

2. I use "speculative nature" with reference to Schelling's own term "speculative physics" to name his own nature philosophy. Nature is what endlessly becomes, and only a physics undivided from metaphysics (speculative physics) can comprehend its one-worldness.

3. Schelling's developing conceptions concerning nature's force have been likened to both Nietzsche's willing the eternal return of the world and Freud's unconscious drives. See, for instance, Judith Norman's "Schelling and Nietzsche: Willing and Time," and Odo Marquart's "Several Connections between Aesthetics and Therapeutics in Nineteenth-century Philosophy." For a discussion of the similarities and differences in Schelling's thought and early Buddhist thought,

see Michael Vater's "Schelling and Nāgārjuna: The Night Absolute, Openness, and *Ungrund*."

4. See Franklin Perkins, *Leibniz and China*. Leibniz's conception of Eastern nondualism was derived from the Confucian Tao, communicated through his Jesuit missionary correspondents. The Tao has essential similarities to earlier Indian nondualistic philosophy, so that Leibniz's absorption of the nondualistic principle holds the necessary resonance for later thinkers to see the correspondence between Eastern nondualism and Spinoza's monism in his monadic vision of the interdependence of things. Coleridge was later more interested in Leibniz than he was in the 1790s, but Leibnizian ideas concerning the monad and cosmic harmony were integrated into the renewed interest in Spinoza that characterized the reaction to Enlightenment science at the end of the eighteenth century.

5. The "Spy Nozy" affair, as it became known, took place while William and Dorothy Wordsworth resided at Alfoxden House, Somerset; Coleridge lived nearby. He and William were overheard discussing Spinoza in August 1797 by a neighbor who reported them to the Home Office, fearing they were spies for the French army and planning an impending invasion.

6. *The Notebooks of Samuel Taylor Coleridge*, I, 556; qtd. in Richard Holmes, *Coleridge: Early Visions*, 244–45.

7. See Maximiliaan Van Woudenberg's *Coleridge and Cosmopolitan Intellectualism 1794–1804: the Legacy of Göttingen University* for an account of how Coleridge's encounter with this innovative Reform university changed his thinking, making him a visionary of international philosophical and intellectual thought.

8. See also Paul Hamilton's *Coleridge and German Philosophy*.

9. Scholars have located Goethe's recurrent use of metaphor to think through issues in his writing on architecture, time, and music, among other key philosophical topics. See for instance "Season, Day, and Hour: Time as Metaphor in Goethe's *Werther*" by Frank G. Ryder; L. Purdy, "The Building in *Bildung*: Goethe, Palladio, and the Architectural Media"; Michael Spitzer's *Metaphor and Musical Thought*, chapter 6.

10. "Editor's Prolegomena," cxx, by Thomas McFarland, in *The Collected Works of Samuel Taylor Coleridge, Volume 15: Opus Maximum*. In the notes and unpublished papers that constitute the *Opus Maximum*, the late Coleridge criticizes Epicureanism (and implicitly Stoicism), pantheism, and German *Naturphilosophie*. McFarland's "Prolegomena" puts the earlier enthusiasm for these philosophical traditions in perspective with his later critiques of them.

11. Ira Profoff, trans., *The Cloud of Unknowing*, 32.

12. *Anima Poetae*, 179–80.

13. "The Earth Has Lungs. Watch Them Breathe." A blogpost by Robert Krulwich.

14. The significant passage is the "philologer" section that connects Greek, Latin, Celtic, Germanic, and even Persian to Sanskrit, creating the basis for

understanding the common roots of Indo-European languages that led to modern linguistics.

15. I use this title of the poem to maintain the distinction between Coleridge's 1798 and 1834 versions of the poem; the 1798 version articulates a more immediate revelatory experience than the highly mediated 1834 version, whose gloss indicates something of Coleridge's own modified views of German Idealism and *Naturphilosophie*.

16. I use here the identifications of the spectres given in the 1834 gloss, but the supernatural as embodied in these negating figures is clear in the 1798 version. My in-text citations to the 1798 "Rime of the Ancyent Marinere, in Seven Parts" are from *Coleridge's Poetry and Prose*, 58–98.

17. Sunday evening, 14 Oct. 1804, *Anima Poetae*, 81.

18. McFarland, "Editor's Prolegomena," cxx.

19. Even the smaller species of albatross have wingspans of more than 5.5 feet. It is most probably one of these species Coleridge was imagining, which were much more commonly encountered on sea voyages than the great whites, and thought to be an omen of good luck.

20. "Bibliological Memoranda." Entry in *Anima Poetae*, from chapter. V (Sep. 1806–Dec. 1807), 183.

21. Entry of 13 Feb. 1804, *Anima Poetae*, 67–68.

22. René Wellek, *Immanuel Kant in England*, 5, 15.

23. Paul Gordon, *Art as the Absolute*, 23.

24. Schelling later differentiates form from states of nothingness, but in this case nothingness is not the same as emptiness as this is conceptualized in Christian mysticism. There, emptiness is boundlessness or limitlessness, the alternate side of form or the limited. For Schelling's later thinking on nothingness, see Manfred Frank's "Schelling and Sartre on Being and Nothingness."

25. Editors and biographers routinely acknowledge Coleridge's borrowings, but account in different ways for them. James Engell and W. Jackson Bate insist that "Coleridge's act of reading was a perpetual state of mind, more active than passive; what he read became part of his being" (Editors' Introduction, cxxxi). Yet numerous footnotes acknowledge what Engell and Bate call a "loose paraphrase" of Schelling's words. Richard Holmes insists that Coleridge never intended to present German philosophical ideas as his own: "He specifically denied philosophical originality, stating that his aim was only to interpret and explain the system to English readers, and to apply it in a new way to poetry" (400). Michael Vater begins his Introduction to Schelling's 1800 *System* with a footnote that notes, "Schelling's System became known to the English-speaking world through Coleridge's *Biographia Literaria*, which drew heavily upon it and other early essays of Schelling for a forty-page critique of perceptual realism" (xi).

26. Fichte's reservations about Schelling's 1800 account of his ideas are most fully articulated in correspondence between himself and Schelling, collected in *The Philosophical Rupture between Fichte and Schelling*.

27. Friedrich Heinrich Jacobi's discussions with Gotthold Lessing and correspondence with Moses Mendelsohnn became the basis of his 1785 critique, popularly known as "Letters on Spinoza," in *Concerning the Doctrine of Spinoza in Letters*.

28. Wirth, *Schelling's Practice of the Wild*, 6–9. The wild "is the self-organizing, self-unfolding, self-originating, middle voice of nature" (xiv). I take the term "vestigial self" from Wirth as well: "The vestigial self, left behind in the self's movement toward self-presence, toward the pretense of autonomy, is not yet separated from nature . . . It was therefore a 'self' at the depths not only of itself, but also of nature, something like what the Zen tradition has called the 'original face'" (9).

29. Spinoza, *Ethics* V, P32, Cor: "From the third [highest] kind of knowledge there arises the greatest satisfaction of mind there can be . . . joy."

30. Among those scholars who have investigated Coleridge's indebtedness to German Romanticism and German Idealism in terms of Spinoza's philosophy I have found Richard Berkeley's *Coleridge and the Crisis of Reason* and Tim Fulford's "Pantheistic Poetry; Geological Touring; Chemical Experimentation: Coleridge and Davy in the Mountains and on the Page" especially helpful. See also Maximiliaan van Woudenberg's excellent study of Coleridge's encounter with the German university, *Coleridge and Cosmopolitan Intellectualism 1794–1804*; and Monika Class, *Coleridge and Kantian ideas in England, 1796–1817*.

31. Crabb Robinson published essays based on his lecture notes as well, largely in the *Monthly Register and Encyclopaedian Magazine*, which have been collected by James Vigus in *Essays on Kant, Schelling, and German Aesthetics*.

32. This is not too different from Jacobi's decision to recuperate a dogmatic faith in the thing-in-itself even if it remains unknowable.

33. See Moira Gatens and Genevieve Lloyd's practical application of Spinoza's concepts of freedom and responsibility for ethical life in *Collective Imaginings*, esp. 41–83.

34. See James Chandler, *Wordsworth's Second Nature*.

35. *Ethics* V, P39: "he who has a body capable of a great many things has a mind whose greatest part is eternal." Also, V, P40, Cor.: ". . . For the eternal part of the mind (by P23 and P29) is the intellect, through which alone we are said to act (by IIIP3)."

36. See his "On the Possibility of a Form of All Philosophy."

37. Vater, Introduction, System, xxii.

38. *The Tragic Absolute*: 135–48.

39. *Historical-critical Introduction to the Philosophy of Mythology*, 187 n.e. Schelling explains there that "the well-known Coleridge, the first of his fellow countrymen who has understood and meaningfully used German poetry and science, especially philosophy" stands in sharp contrast to the German response to the Samothrace lecture, which was one of non-comprehension.

40. Jason Wirth notes that "esemplasy" is Coleridge's neologism to translate Schelling's *Ineinsbildung*, a term both thinkers understood "as synonymous with the

movement of the (transcendental or productive) imagination or *Einbildungskraft* (*Ages of the World*, 146n98).

41. Schelling will later define God's freedom in these terms in *Ages of the World*, 46.

42. Qtd. in Wirth, *Practice* xiii.

43. The problem of ruination is an important element in Wirth's thesis in *Schelling's Practice of the Wild*.

44. Much of the rest of this paragraph draws from Peter Burke's account of Schelling's treatment of the hidden principle of nature in "Creativity and the Unconscious in Merleau-Ponty and Schelling."

45. *Biographia Literaria, or Biographical Sketches of My Literary Life and Opinions; and Two Lay Sermons; I—The Statesman's Manual. II—Blessed are ye that sow beside all waters* (1889).

46. *CN* II, 2546.

Chapter 3

1. Luce Irigaray, *Through Vegetal Being*, 20.

2. Qtd. in Freeman, *The Feminine Sublime*, 1.

3. Carlisle, "George Eliot and Spinoza," 591.

4. For a thorough treatment of Spinoza's reception and interpretation in the Romantic period, see Levinson's "A Motion and a Spirit: Romancing Spinoza."

5. Morris Eaves, Robert N. Essick, and Joseph Viscomi, eds., *Europe a Prophecy*, copy C, pl. 11/13: 15–17. *The William Blake Archive*. Retrieved 14 Feb. 2022.

6. Jonathan Dent, *Sinister Histories*, 154.

7. My interpretation of Wollstonecraft's nature writing has been recently influenced by Kate Singer's article " 'I feel it coming in the air tonight': Mephitical Vapors, Pestiferous Plagues, and the Psychosis of Materiality in Wollstonecraft," forthcoming in *Romantic Circles Praxis*.

8. DCMS 19, ms. pp. 37, 33. The Wordsworth Trust, Dove Cottage, Grasmere, UK.

9. In this Dorothy Wordsworth accords with women travel writers of the period who, according to Elizabeth Bohl, generally tended to eschew the disinterested, "generic perceiver," of masculinist aesthetics, as well as the (male) perceiver's equally disinterested contemplation, which is "the paradigm of reception that strips the subject's relation to the aesthetic object of any practical stake in that object's existence." Finally such a writer rejects "the autonomy of the aesthetic domain from moral, political, or utilitarian concerns and activities." *Women Travel Writers*, 7.

10. For Spinoza, bodies are made of other bodies all the way down; the human body is a conglomerate of bodies incorporating smaller bodies until the most minute level is reached. There is a convenience to this theory in that "atoms"

are always the most basic, minute level, but bodies are incorporative and so align with Stoic corporeals better.

11. See my *Becoming Wordsworthian* for Dorothy Wordsworth's investment in her brother's poetry-making and poetic project.

12. For a detailed study of vitalism in the period see Catherine Packham, *Eighteenth-Century Vitalism*. Her coverage of the "vitality debates" of the 1810s, particularly between the London surgeons William Lawrence and John Abernethy, is very helpful.

13. I use Kristeva's theory of poetic language extensively in *Becoming Wordsworthian*, and believe Kristeva is crucial to understanding Dorothy Wordsworth's relation to *poiesis*.

14. "Substance expresses itself, attributes are expressions, and essence is expressed." Gilles Deleuze, *Expressionism in Philosophy: Spinoza*, 27.

15. The attributes "are predicated of God who explicates himself in them, and of modes which imply them . . . Spinoza sees no contradiction between the assertion of a community of form and the positing of a diction of esssences," that is, a particularity of corporeal forms. "The attributes are, according to Spinoza, univocal forms of being which do not change their nature in changing their 'subject'—that is, when predicated of infinite being and finite beings, substance and modes, God and creatures." Deleuze, *Expressionism* 48, 49.

16. This is my paraphrase of Deleuze's interpretation of Spinozist revelation, an interpretation that strikes me as particularly apt for Dorothy Wordsworth studies.

17. Dorothy Wordsworth's posthumously published *George and Sarah Greene: A Narrative* details the dangers of snowstorms in the Lake District.

18. The development of more reliable thoughts or "facts" from initial perceptions involves a movement back and forth the subject and object it thinks, each in turn become the "ground" for the other that is then grounded. When the difference between ground and grounded is resolved so that difference disappears from the posited idea/thing it is "simple essential immediacy." The fact then becomes "unconditioned" or groundless, pure (*Logic* 417). Hegel develops this theory at length in *The Science of Logic*.

19. Radical liberal subjectivity is paradoxically restrictive. The liberal subject predicates its subjectivity on the concept of a unified self and an essence underlying that self. Such a subjective consciousness, whether defined as radical or the more staid Whiggish liberal, has walled itself off from either radical encounter with otherness or indeed, even the human-to-human encounter that Levinas details.

20. I am drawing on concepts in Derrida's *Rogues*, and *Of Hospitality*, as well as his discussions of the problem of homeostasis and the neighbor/stranger.

21. Haraway defines "sympoiesis" as a mutually accomplished becoming between species largely speaking, as in the human and the ecological. See her *Staying with the Trouble*.

22. Rhapsodies belong to the transportive, transcendent self of liberal subjectivity, whereas ethnography belongs to the newly imperial self of 1790s England. See Daniel O'Quinn's *Entertaining Crisis in the Atlantic Imperium, 1770–1790* and Makdisi's *Making England Western* for detailed analyses of the transformative turmoil of a rapidly expanding empire during the Romantic period.

23. Her letters and journal entries document this refusal, as does her acceptance of her role in the making of poetry as one of field-notetaker and amanuensis.

24. In *Anonymous Life*, Jacques Khalip provides a reading of the individual not privileged by a sense of autonomy and moral purpose in the Romantic Period; the "anonymous" model of subjectivity suggestively reveals the self-deception underlying both the liberal subject and the transcendently self-assertive (or morally purposive) subject.

25. Bohl finds the same disharmony in Dorothy Wordsworth's travel journal for their tour of Scotland in her chapter "Dorothy Wordsworth and the Cultural Politics of Scenic Tourism."

26. Karen Barad asks, "How can we not trouble time? Nothing less than the nature of and possibilities for change and conceptions of history, memory, causality, politics, and justice are conditioned by it. At the very core . . . are questions of time and being. The indeterminacy of untimely time-being opens up the nature of matter to a dynamism of the play of being and nothingness." "Troubling Time/s and Ecologies of Nothingness," 64.

27. Bennett participated in the early stages of object-oriented ontology's development, but her research for *Vibrant Matter* led her to consider objects in greater philosophical correspondence with Stoic thought. See her article "Systems and Things: A Response to Graham Harman and Timothy Morton."

28. The increasing literature on plant philosophy makes the case for this intersubjective possibility.

29. I treat this aspect of "Tintern Abbey" at length in *Becoming Wordsworthian*.

30. Eighteenth-century landscape writing spoke of the writing and feeling self rather than the environment. See Bohl for a discussion of the way in which landscape writing was a felicitous genre for women struggling to work through their sense of social and personal dispossession.

31. Mary Moorman, "Introduction," *Journals of Dorothy Wordsworth*, xiii.

32. Nietzsche, *Unpublished Fragments*, 350 #99.

33. See also Peter J. Burgard's edited volume *Nietzsche and the Feminine* on Nietzsche's misogyny.

34. The subject-object or subjective-object is something like what Fichte terms the Not-I.

35. *The Philosophy of Art*, 121, 118, 116.

36. Studies of plant neurobiology have aroused heated debates in the scientific community, but speak directly to the analysis I am developing in this chapter. See "Plant Neurobiology: An Integrated View of Plant Signaling" by Eric D. Brenner

et al. in the journal *Trends in Plant Science*, for both an overview and an instance of this kind of research and findings; see also "Plants and Animals: Convergent Evolution in Action?" by Frantisek Baluska and Stefano Mancuso for a strong argument for not differentiating humans and animals from plants. Mancuso's focus on plant intelligence drives much of this research. Additionally, Paco Calvo and Fred Keijzder's "Plant Cognition" treats plant neurobiology from the perspective of embodied cognition, a mental facility traditionally associated with the human only.

37. "But the woman and the mother are not mirrored in the same fashion. A double specularization in and between her/them is already in place. And more. For the sex of woman is not one" (Irigaray, *Speculum of the Other Woman*, 239). If such doubled specularization is firmly in view for women of this period, Dorothy Wordsworth is freed from it in the vegetal passages of her Alfoxden and Grasmere journals. Man's oneness and woman's plurality are not at stake here in these immanent instants of the surrounds that are an envelope or *chora* without a temporal horizon.

Chapter 4

1. Introduction, "Romanticism and the New Deleuze," ed. Ron Broglio.
2. The version of *Triumph of Life* used herein is Reiman and Fraistat's edition *Shelley's Poetry and Prose*, 483–500.
3. Faflak, "The Difficult Education of Shelley's 'Triumph of Life,'" 54.
4. It is this kind of sightedness that I believe Derrida is after in both *Memoirs of the Blind* and *The Animal That Therefore I Am*, and that Shelley is after with his confessional and self-erasing portrait of Rousseau in *The Triumph*.
5. "Shelley's 'Compelling Rhyme Schemes' in *The Triumph of Life*," 76.
6. Balfour, "Singularities: On a Motif in Derrida and Romantic Thought (Kant's Aesthetics, Rousseau's Autobiography)"; see esp. 356–360.
7. Paul de Man, using Don Reiman's archival work on the manuscripts for the poem, finds the reduction of philosopher-guides to a single one, Rousseau, a significant revision in the poem. Donald H. Reiman, *Shelley's 'The Triumph of Life': A Critical Study*; de Man, "Shelley Disfigured," in *The Rhetoric of Romanticism*, 93–123.
8. Christopher Johnson unpacks the concept of articulation further in *System and Writing in the Philosophy of Jacques Derrida*, 127–30; quoted phrase is from 128.
9. "Essay on the Origin of Language in Which Something Is Said about Melody and Musical Imitation," in *The First and Second Discourses Together with the Replies to Critics and Essay on the Origin of Languages*, 240–41.
10. Rousseau uses this phrase to describe writing's supplementation of both speech and music, quoted in *Of Grammatology*, 199.

11. I refer to both Rousseau's *Confessions* and to his confessionary narrative that consumes Shelley's poem. On the intimacy of sound and metaphor, and their relation to the idea, see Donald H. Reiman's *Shelley's "The Triumph of Life,"* 9–10.

12. In Derrida's discussion of Rousseau in "The Written Being/The Being Written," he analyses Rousseau's conception of *ousia* as "substantiality" rather than being (*Of Grammatology*, 18–26). Substantiality is what casts shadows and what lies in shadow; substantiality in the sense of the dancers in the frenzied crowd (deluded, enshadowed) is a denial of Spinozist substance, which names both shadow and the enshadowed.

13. "Shelley's Antimasques of Life: Re-Visioning 'The Triumph,'" 1195.

14. Immanuel Kant, *Critique of Judgment*, §51.

15. *Before the Law: Humans and Other Animals in a Biopolitical Frame.* Wolfe helpfully engages with the concept of auto-immunity that Derrida analyzes in *Rogues*.

16. That is, before line 373 (Reiman and Fraistat, 480 n.1).

17. This is Reiman's reading of Shelley's use of metaphor: idea corresponds analogously to impression, but not to object or to thing-in-itself (*Shelley's "Triumph"* 10).

18. "A Defence of Poetry," Reiman and Fraistat, 531.

19. Kir Kuiken, *Imagined Sovereignties*, 171.

20. For Deleuze, the event is epiphenomenal, spoken in the proposition; "The concept speaks the event, not the essence or the thing." Deleuze and Guattari, *What Is Philosophy?*, 20. See esp. 35–60.

21. Derrida, *Memoirs of the Blind* 2–4, emphases his. David Farrell Krell's meditation on Derrida's meditation, *The Purest of Bastards*, has informed my understanding of blindness as having a different knowledge structure.

22. See Ross Wilson, *Shelley and the Apprehension of Life*.

23. In *Rogues*, Derrida defines the chora politically, designating "spacing, interval . . . another 'taking-place,'" but also a beforehand, "a spacing from 'before' the world" (xiv).

24. I refer here to Deleuze's reading of Leibniz's system in *The Fold: Leibniz and the Baroque*.

25. This is de Man's phrase, *Rhetoric of Romanticism* 103.

26. As de Man notes in "Anthropomorphism and Trope in the Lyric," "truth is a trope." Quoted in Cynthia Chase, "Double-Take. Reading De Man and Derrida Writing on Tropes," *Praxis* (May 2005). The reference is to truth-statements as philosophemes, but for Shelley truths are poetic tropes, comprehensible only through the multidimensionality of metaphoricity.

27. Derrida discusses these ideas on 229–55 in *Of Grammatology*.

28. Derrida mediates on the nature of roots and entangled or intertwined roots in language and writing in *Of Grammatology* in an early passage in the section on Rousseau (101–2).

29. Derrida defines iterability as a concept in "Signature Event Context," *Margins of Philosophy*, 307–30.

30. Quoted from private correspondence in Andrzej Warminski, "Machinal Effects: Derrida With and Without de Man," 1073. See de Man, "The Rhetoric of Blindness: Jacques Derrida's Reading of Rousseau," in *Blindness and Insight*, 102–41.

31. See Grant's *Philosophies of Nature After Schelling*, ch. 1–2, for a summary of Schelling's Platonism in his nature philosophy.

32. See Meillassoux, *After Finitude*. Meillassoux classifies all post-Kantianism as correlationism, and though Shelley is not correlationist in his philosophical thought, he is skeptical as much as idealist, developing ideas about the relation between ideas and things in ways not dissimilar from Kant's. Reiman points to several Kantianisms in Shelley's mature thought in *Shelley's "The Triumph of Life"* (see his chapter 1 in particular).

33. Leibniz's monad differs from Spinoza's concept of the individual and mind: Leibniz theorizes the motivating spirit as a mechanism, whereas for Spinoza movement is a matter of the body and will as separate, an idea with movement of its own.

34. Defalco Lamperez, "'Strong Hold and Fountain-Head of Their Idolatry': The Juggernaut in the Work of Claudius Buchanan and Shelley's *The Triumph of Life*."

35. *The Orient and the Young Romantics*. Warren remarks on the similarity of the act of writing and erasure of Rousseau's memory by the Shape all light to Cyntha's writing in the sand and its erasure by the water five years earlier in *Revolt of Islam* (1817).

36. See chapter 3, "Materialism of the Beautiful" of Simon Jarvis's *Wordsworth's Philosophic Song*, 84–107.

37. Foucault understands the murmur as what hovers under the discourse of an episteme as an immanent manifestation of the episteme to follow in *The Order of Things*.

38. See Derrida's discussion of Foucault in *Writing and Difference*, "Cogito and the History of Madness," 31–63.

Chapter 5

1. Kristeva, *Chroniques du temps sensible*, 9.

2. Too little was known about ancient Mesopotamia until the excavations in Assyria beginning in the 1840s for these cultures to be included in the mix.

3. In analogical reasoning, biological entities are seen as analogous to humans; it differs from isomorphic reasoning in which a correspondence of equivalence is set up between humans and other natural biological and nonbiological entities as "like" but not analogous. By contrast, in transmorphic reasoning, biocentrism is privileged, but the correspondence between natural entities and humans is not an equivalent one, and one thing can transform into another.

4. Perhaps because it was the counter-consumable in England's trade with China.

5. *Confessions of an English Opium-Eater and Other Writings*, 41.
6. Abrams, *The Milk of Paradise*; Logan, *Nerves and Narratives*.
7. Logan does move toward a clinical analysis in that he takes De Quincey's narrative voice to represent a distinction between the acceptable medical use of laudanum and a less familiar practice of addictive opium eating (less familiar because covered up by a state invested in large-scale illegal trade in opium to China in return for huge tea imports). In focusing on the addictive practice, De Quincey explores the nature of addiction during a period in which addiction was not scientifically understood, creating the roadmap for clinical study in the Freudian sense. *Nerves and Narratives*, 73–108.
8. Not just Hogg's *Confessions*, but also *The Confessions of Nicol Muschet of Boghall* (1818), Mary Shelley's *Mathilda* (1819), and other popular works used the confessional mode to create a first-person, sensationalized narrative that proved highly popular with readers.
9. See Joel Faflak's indispensable *Romantic Psychoanalysis*, esp. 153–98, for his discussion of De Quincey.
10. John Barrell examines this master trope in De Quincey's works, seeing inoculation as De Quincey's medicalized approach to barring and limiting all alarming shifts in his psychic world. *The Infection of Thomas De Quincey* also discusses De Quincey's fear of hydrophobia, and the death of his sister in relation to "water on the brain."
11. James Hogg would have seen newspaper accounts of "dual" personalities and sleepwalking reprinted in Edinburgh periodicals when writing *Confessions of a Justified Sinner*, such as "A Double Consciousness, or a Duality of Person in the same Individual," *Edinburgh Weekly Journal* 31 (1816): 252 (reprinted in Hogg, *Confessions of a Justified Sinner*, 286–87).
12. *British Romantic Writers and the East*, 171.
13. This is different from Mulligan's account, which conflates Egypt and East (India, Turkey, China) and argues that De Quincey believed in an "oriental" origin underlying native Englishness that recouped origination from Eastern ownership—the Westerner is always already Eastern, and in control of that aspect of his identity (48–50, 60).
14. Julia Kristeva, *Strangers to Ourselves*, 5, 1.
15. See Grant's discussion of Schelling's "subjectnature" as fundamental to all his philosophy and not just the nature philosophy in chapter 1 of *Philosophies of Nature After Schelling*.
16. Lindop, Introduction, *Confessions of an English Opium-Eater*, xvi.

Epilogue

1. See Ron Broglio's *Beasts of Burden: Biopolitics, Labor, and Animal Life in British Romanticism* for how animals, as well as land and other matter, were translated into metrics during the Romantic period.

2. I have written about Britain's attitudes toward and economic dependence on the plantation economy based on sugar in "Reformation in *Mansfield Park*: The Slave Trade and the Stillpoint of Knowledge" and about the cotton trade in *Fashioning Faces: The Portraitive Mode in British Romanticism*.

3. "Kant, like Hume, looked to 'the animal kingdom' as an analogue for humanity, but what is astonishing is the manner in which his articulations of 'species' and 'race' are interdependent and concentric epistemological constructions." Hegel, additionally, "represents perhaps the most extreme articulation of 'the African's' animality, one in which animality is thought not only to be a feature, but the *essence* of African life." Jackson, *Becoming Human*, 24–25, emphasis hers.

4. "there I found my Angel, who surprised asked / me how I had escaped? / I answered. All that we saw was owing to your / metaphysics . . . ." (*Marriage of Heaven and Hell*, Copy G, pl. 19; 12–15).

5. Ellie Clayton, "William Blake: Religion and Psychology."

Works Cited

Abrams, M. H. *The Milk of Paradise: The Effect of Opium Visions on the Works of DeQuincey, Crabbe, Francis Thompson and Coleridge*. 1934. Octagon Books, 1971.
Altizer, Thomas. "The Revolutionary Vision of William Blake." *Journal of Religious Ethics*, vol. 37, no. 1, 2009, pp. 33–38.
Anon. *The Cloud of Unknowing*. Translated by Ira Profoff, Julian Press, 1957.
Austin, John L. *How to Do Things with Words*. Oxford UP, 1975.
Balfour, Ian. "Singularities: On a Motif in Derrida and Romantic Thought (Kant's Aesthetics, Rousseau's Autobiography)." *Studies in Romanticism*, vol. 46, no. 3, 2007, pp. 337–63.
Baluska, Frantisek, and Stefano Mancuso. "Plants and Animals: Convergent Evolution in Action?" *Plant-Environment Interactions. Signaling and Communication in Plants*. Edited by Frantisek Baluska, Springer, 2009, pp. 285–301.
Barad, Karen. "Troubling Time/s and Ecologies of Nothingness: Re-Turning, Re-Membering, and Facing the Incalculable." *New Formations*, vol. 92, no. 5, 2017, pp. 56–86.
Barbauld, Anna Lætitia. "A Summer Evening's Meditation." *Poems*. Printed for Joseph Johnson, in St. Paul's Church-Yard, 1773, pp. 131–38.
Barrell, John. *The Infection of Thomas De Quincey: A Psychopathology of Imperialism*. Yale UP, 1991.
Behler, Ernst. "Note on the Texts." *Encyclopedia of the Philosophical Sciences in Outline and Critical Writings*. Continuum, 1990, xxi–xxxi.
Beiser, Frederick. *German Idealism: The Struggle Against Subjectivism 1781–1801*. Harvard UP, 2002.
———. *The Romantic Imperative*. Harvard UP, 2003.
Benjamin, Walter. *The Origin of German Tragic Drama*. Translated by John Osborne, Verso, 1998.
Bennett, Jane. "Systems and Things: A Response to Graham Harman and Timothy Morton." *New Literary History*, vol. 43, no. 2, 2012, pp. 225–33.
———. *Vibrant Matter A Political Ecology of Things*. Duke UP, 2010.

Berkeley, Richard. *Coleridge and the Crisis of Reason*. Palgrave, 2007.
Blake, William. *The Complete Poetry & Prose of William Blake*. Edited by David V. Erdman, 1965; rev. ed. Anchor Books/Random House, 1988.
The Blake Archive. Edited by Morris Eaves, Robert Essick, and Joseph Viscomi. www.blakearchive.org
Blanchot, Maurice. *The Space of Literature*. Translated by Ann Smock, U of Nebraska P, 1982.
Boehme, Jacob. *Aurora, or Day-Spring*, 1612.
Bohl, Elizabeth. *Women Travel Writers and the Language of Aesthetics, 1716–1818*. Cambridge UP, 1995.
Brenner, Eric D., Rainer Stahlberg, Stefano Mancuso, Jorge Vivanco, Frantisek Baluska, and Elizabeth Van Volkenburgh. "Plant Neurobiology: An Integrated View of Plant Signaling." *Trends in Plant Science*, vol. 11, no. 8, 2006, pp. 413–19.
Broglio, Ron. *Beasts of Burden: Biopolitics, Labor, and Animal Life in British Romanticism*. State U of New York P, 2018.
Broglio, Ron, and Robert Mitchell. Introduction. "Romanticism and the New Deleuze." *Romantic Circles Praxis*. Edited by R. Broglio, https://romantic-circles.org/praxis/deleuze/intro/intro.html. Accessed 27 Feb. 2022.
Budge, Gavin. *Medicine and the Natural Supernatural: Transcendent Vision and Bodily Spectres, 1789–1852*. Palgrave, 2013.
Burgard, Peter J., editor. *Nietzsche and the Feminine*. U of Virginia P, 1994.
Burke, Edmund. *A Philosophical Enquiry into the Origin of our Ideas of the Sublime and the Beautiful*. Edited by James T. Boulton, U of Notre Dame P, 1968.
Burke, Peter. "Creativity and the Unconscious in Merleau-Ponty and Schelling." *Schelling Now: Contemporary Readings*. Edited by Jason M. Wirth, Indiana UP, 2005, pp. 184–206.
Calvo, Paco, and Fred Keijzder. "Plant Cognition." *Plant-Environment Interactions: Signaling and Communication in Plants*. Edited by Frantisek Baluska, Springer, 2009, pp. 247–66.
Carlisle, Clare. "George Eliot and Spinoza: Philosophical Formations." *Victorian Studies*, vol. 62, no. 4, 2020, pp. 590–615.
Chandler, James. *Wordsworth's Second Nature*. U of Chicago P, 1984.
Clark, Lorraine. *Blake, Kierkegaard, and the Spectre of the Dialectic*. Cambridge UP, 1991.
Class, Monika. *Coleridge and Kantian Ideas in England, 1796–1817: Coleridge's Responses to German Philosophy*. Bloomsbury, 2012.
Clayton, Ellie. "William Blake: Religion and Psychology," https://ramhornd.blogspot.com/2016/02/ulro.html. Accessed 10 Feb. 2022.
Cohen, I. Bernard, and Richard S. Westfall, editors. *Newton*. W. W. Norton, 1995.
Colburn, Kathleen, editor. *The Notebooks of Samuel Taylor Coleridge*. Princeton UP, Bollingen Series and Routledge, 1957–73. 3 vols.

Coleridge, Samuel Taylor. *Anima Poetae, From the Unpublished Note-Books of Samuel Taylor Coleridge*. Edited by Ernest Hartley Coleridge, London: William Heinemann, 1895.

———. *Biographia Literaria: The Collected Works of Samuel Taylor Coleridge, Biographical Sketches of my Literary Life & Opinions*. Edited by James Engell and W. Jackson Bate, Bollingen Series LXXV, vol. 7, Princeton UP, 1985.

———. *Biographia Literaria, or Biographical Sketches of My Literary Life and Opinions; and Two Lay Sermons; I—The Statesman's Manual. II—Blessed Are Ye That Sow Beside All Waters*. London: George Bell & Sons, 1889.

———. *Coleridge's Poetry and Prose*. Edited by Nicholas Halmi, Paul Magnuson, and Raimonda Modiano, W. W. Norton, 2004.

Comay, Rebecca. *Mourning Sickness: Hegel and the French Revolution*. Stanford UP, 2010.

Damon, S. Foster. *A Blake Dictionary: The Ideas and Symbols of William Blake*. Rev. ed., UP of New England, 1988.

Damrosch, Leo. *Eternity's Sunrise: The Imaginative World of William Blake*. Yale UP, 2015.

Debaise, Didier. *Nature as Event: The Lure of the Possible*. Duke UP, 2017.

Defalco Lamperez, Joseph. "'Strong Hold and Fountain-Head of Their Idolatry': The Juggernaut in the Work of Claudius Buchanan and Shelley's *The Triumph of Life*." *Studies in Romanticism*, vol. 56, no. 4, 2017, pp. 423–569.

Deleuze, Gilles. *Cours: Sur Spinoza*. Edited by Emilie and Julien Deleuze, Vincennes, 1 Jan. 1978. Accessed 8 Mar. 2019.

———. *Expressionism in Philosophy: Spinoza*. Translated by Martin Joughin, Zone Books, 1992.

———. *The Fold: Leibniz and the Baroque*. U of Minnesota P, 1992.

———. *Spinoza: Practical Philosophy*. Translated by Robert Hurley, City Lights, 1988.

Deleuze, Gilles, and Felix Guattari. *What Is Philosophy?* Translated by Hugh Tomlinson and Graham Burchell, Columbia UP 1994.

De Man, Paul. "*Blindness and Insight: Essays in the Rhetoric of Contemporary Criticism*. U of Minnesota P, 1983.

———. "Shelley Disfigured." *The Rhetoric of Romanticism*. Columbia UP, 1984, pp. 93–123.

Dent, Jonathan. *Sinister Histories: Gothic Novels and Representations of the Past, from Horace Walpole to Mary Wollstonecraft*. Manchester UP, 2016.

De Quincey, Thomas. *Confessions of an English Opium-Eater and Other Writings*. Edited by Grevel Lindop, Oxford UP, 1985.

Derrida, Jacques. *Memoirs of the Blind: The Self-Portrait and Other Ruins*. Translated by Pascale-Anne Brault and Michael Naas, U of Chicago P, 1993.

———. *Of Grammatology*. Translated by Gayatri Chakravorty Spivak, Johns Hopkins UP, 1997.

———. *Rogues: Two Essays on Reason*. Translated by Pascale-Anne Brault, Stanford UP, 2005.

———. *The Animal That Therefore I Am*. Translated by David Wills, Fordham UP, 2008.

Derrida, Jacques, and Anne Dufourmantelle. *Of Hospitality*. Stanford UP, 2000.

Engell, James, and W. Jackson Bate. "Editors' Introduction." Coleridge, *Biographia Literaria*, pp. xli–cxxxvi.

Estermann, Barbara. "Shelley's Antimasques of Life: Re-Visioning 'The Triumph.'" *ELH*, vol. 81, no. 4, 2014, pp. 1193–1224.

Faflak, Joel. "The Difficult Education of Shelley's 'Triumph of Life.'" *Keats-Shelley Journal*, vol. 58, 2009, pp. 53–78.

———. *Romantic Psychoanalysis: The Burden of the Mystery*. State U of New York P, 2009.

Fay, Elizabeth. *Becoming Wordsworthian: A Performative Aesthetics*. U of Massachusetts P, 1995.

———. *Fashioning Faces: The Portraitive Mode in British Romanticism*. UP of New England, 2010.

———. "Reformation in *Mansfield Park*: The Slave Trade and the Stillpoint of Knowledge." *Transatlanticism and Literary Forms, 1780-1850*. Edited by Annika Bauz and Kathryn Gray, Routledge, 2017, pp. 19–34.

———. *Romantic Egypt: Abyssal Ground of British Romanticism*. Lexington Books, 2021.

Fichte, J. G., and F. W. J. Schelling. *The Philosophical Rupture between Fichte and Schelling: Selected Texts and Correspondence (1800–1802)*. Translated by Michael G. Vater and David W. Wood, State U of New York P, 2012.

Foucault, Michel. *The Order of Things: An Archaeology of the Human Sciences*. Random House, 1971.

Frank, Manfred. "Schelling and Sartre on Being and Nothingness." *The New Schelling*. Edited by J. Norman and A. Welchman, pp. 151–66.

Ferguson, Frances. *Solitude and the Sublime: The Romantic Aesthetics of Individuation*. Routledge, 1992.

Fulford, Tim. "Pantheistic Poetry; Geological Touring; Chemical Experimentation: Coleridge and Davy in the Mountains and on the Page." *The Coleridge Bulletin*, NS 55, pp. 27–41.

Gattens, Moira, and Genevieve Lloyd. *Collective Imaginings: Spinoza, Past and Present*. Routledge, 1999.

Gattens, Moira, editor. *Feminist Interpretations of Benedict Spinoza*. Pennsylvania State UP, 2009.

Goethe, Johann Wolfgang von. *Theory of Colours*. Translated by Charles Locke Eastlake, 1840. Dover, 2006.

Gordon, Paul. *Art as the Absolute: Art's Relation to Metaphysics in Kant, Fichte, Schelling, Hegel, and Schopenhauer*. Bloomsbury, 2015.

Grant, Ian Hamilton. *Philosophies of Nature After Schelling*. Continuum, 2006.
Grosz, Elizabeth. *The Incorporeal*. Columbia UP, 2018.
Hamilton, Paul. *Coleridge and German Philosophy: The Poet in a Land of Logic*. Continuum, 2007.
Haraway, Donna J. *Staying with the Trouble: Making Kin in the Chthulucene*. Duke UP, 2016.
Hegel, G. W. F. *Hegel's Aesthetics: Lectures on Fine Art*. Translated by T. M. Knox, Oxford UP, 1999. 2 vols.
———. *The Science of Logic*. Translated and edited by George Di Giovanni, Cambridge UP, 2015.
———. *The Phenomenology of Spirit*. Translated by A. V. Miller, Introduction by J. N. Findlay, Oxford UP, 1977.
Hogg, James. *The Private Memoirs and Confessions of a Justified Sinner*. Edited by Adrian Hunter, Broadview Press, 2001.
Holmes, Richard. *Coleridge: Darker Reflections 1804–1834*. Pantheon, 1998.
———. *Coleridge: Early Visions: 1772–1804*. Viking Penguin, 1990.
Huett, Steven, and David Goodman. "Alterity." *Encyclopedia of Critical Psychology*. Edited by Thomas Teo, Springer, 2014.
Irigaray, Luce. *Speculum of the Other Woman*. Cornell UP 1985.
———. *Marine Lover of Friedrich Nietzsche*. Translated by Gillian C. Gill, Columbia UP, 1991.
Irigaray, Luce, and Michael Marder. *Through Vegetal Being—Two Philosophical Perspectives*. Columbia UP, 2016.
Israel, Jonathan. *Radical Enlightenment: Philosophy and the Making of Modernity, 1650–1750*. Oxford UP, 2001.
Jackson, Zakiyyah Iman. *Becoming Human: Matter and Meaning in an Antiblack World*. New York UP, 2020.
Jacobi, Friedrich Heinrich. *Concerning the Doctrine of Spinoza in Letters to Herr Moses Mendelssohn. The Main Philosophical Writings and the Novel All Will*. Translated by George di Giovanni, McGill-Queen's UP, 1994, pp. 173–251.
Jarvis, Simon. *Wordsworth's Philosophic Song*. Cambridge UP, 2007.
Johnson, Barbara. "Nothing Fails Like Success." *SCE Reports*, vol. 8, 1980, pp. 7–16.
Johnson, Christopher. *System and Writing in the Philosophy of Jacques Derrida*. Cambridge UP, 1993.
Kant, Immanuel. *The Critique of Judgment*. Translated by Paul Guyer and Eric Matthews, Cambridge UP, 2001.
———. "The End of All Things." *Immanuel Kant: Religion and Rational Theology*. Translated by Allen W. Wood and George Di Giovanni, Cambridge UP, 2001, pp. 221–31.
———. *Dreams of a Spirit-Seer, Illustrated by Dreams of Metaphysics*. Translated by Glenn Alexander Magee, Swedenborg Foundation, 2003.
Keats, John. *The Complete Poems*. Edited by John Barnard, Penguin Books, 1988.

Khalip, Jacques. *Anonymous Life: Romanticism and Dispossession*. Stanford UP, 2008.
Kierkegaard, Soren. *Fear and Trembling*. Translated by Alastair Hannay, Penguin, 1985.
———. *The Concept of Anxiety*. Translated by Reidar Thomte, Princeton UP, 1980.
Klein, Terrance. "Adventures in Alterity: Wittgenstein, Aliens, Anselm, and Aquinas." *New Blackfriars*, vol. 88, no. 1013, 2007, pp. 73–86.
Krell, David Farrell. *The Purest of Bastards: Works of Mourning, Art, and Affirmation in the Thought of Jacques Derrida*. Pennsylvania State UP, 2000.
———. *The Tragic Absolute: German idealism and the Languishing of God*. Indiana UP, 2005.
Kristeva, Julia. *Chroniques du temps sensible*. Éditions de l'aube, 2003.
———. *Revolution in Poetic Language*. Translated by Margaret Waller, Columbia UP, 1984.
———. *Strangers to Ourselves*. Translated by Leon S. Roudiez, Columbia UP, 1991.
Kristeva, Julia, and Susan Sellers. "A Question of Subjectivity—An Interview." *Women's Review*, vol. 12, 1989, pp. 19–21.
Krulwich, Robert. "The Earth Has Lungs. Watch Them Breathe." *National Geographic*, 9 Mar. 2016, http://phenomena.nationalgeographic.com/2016/03/09/the-earth-has-lungs-watch-them-breathe/. Accessed 12 Mar. 2017.
Kuiken, Kir. *Imagined Sovereignties: Toward a New Political Romanticism*. Fordham UP, 2014.
Lacan, Jacques. *The Seminar of Jacques Lacan: On Feminine Sexuality, the Limits of Love and Knowledge (Encore) (Seminar XX)*. Edited by Jacques-Alain Miller and Bruce Fink, translated by Bruce Fink, W. W. Norton, 1999.
Lacoue-Labarthe, Philippe, and Jean-Luc Nancy. *The Literary Absolute: The Theory of Literature in German Romanticism*. State U of New York P, 1988.
Leask, Nigel. *British Romantic Writers and the East: Anxieties of Empire*. Cambridge UP, 2004.
Levinas, Emmanuel. *Alterity and Transcendence*. Translated by Michael B. Smith, Columbia UP, 1999.
———. *Entre Nous: Thinking-of-the-Other*. Translated by Michael B. Smith and Barbara Harshav, Columbia UP, 1998.
———. "God and Philosophy." *The Levinas Reader*. Edited by Sean Hand, Basil Blackwell, 1989, pp. 166–89.
———. *Totality and Infinity, An Essay on Exteriority*. Translated by Alphonso Lingis, Duquesne UP, 1969.
Levinson, Marjorie. "A Motion and a Spirit: Romancing Spinoza." *Studies in Romanticism*, vol. 46, no. 4, 2007, pp. 367–408.
Logan, Peter Melville. *Nerves and Narratives: A Cultural History of Hysteria in 19th-Century British Prose*. California UP, 1997.
Magee, Glenn Alexander. *Hegel and the Hermetic Tradition*. Cornell UP, 2001.

Makdisi, Saree. *Making England Western: Occidentalism, Race, and Imperial Culture*. U of Chicago P, 2014

———. *William Blake and the Impossible History of the 1790s*. U of Chicago P, 2002.

Marquart, Odo. "Several Connections between Aesthetics and Therapeutics in Nineteenth-century Philosophy." *The New Schelling*. Edited by J. Norman and A. Welchman, pp. 13–29.

McFarland, Thomas, with Nicholas Halmi, editors. *The Collected Works of Samuel Taylor Coleridge, Volume 15: Opus Maximum*. Princeton UP, Bollingen Series, 2002.

McFarland, Thomas. "Editor's Prolegomena." *The Collected Works of Samuel Taylor Coleridge, Volume 15: Opus Maximum*. Princeton UP, Bollingen Series, 2002.

Mee, Jon. *Dangerous Enthusiasm: William Blake and the Culture of Radicalism in the 1790s*. Clarendon Press, 1992.

———. "Is There an Antinomian in the House?" *Historicizing Blake*. Edited by Steve Clarke and David Worrall, Macmillan, 1994, pp. 43–58.

Meillassoux, Quentin. *After Finitude: An Essay on the Necessity of Contingency*. Continuum, 2010.

Melamed, Yitzhak Y. *Spinoza's Metaphysics: Substance and Thought*. Oxford UP, 2015.

Mignolo, Walter D. *Local Histories/Global Designs: Coloniality, Subaltern Knowledges, and Border Thinking*. Princeton UP, 2000.

Moorman, Mary. "Introduction." *Journals of Dorothy Wordsworth*. Edited by Moorman, Oxford UP, 1971, pp. xi–xx.

Morton, A. L. *The Everlasting Gospel: A Study in the Sources of William Blake*. Lawrence and Wishart, 1958.

Nancy, Jean-Luc. *Being Singular Plural*. Translated by Robert D. Richardson and Anne E. O'Byrne, Stanford UP, 2000.

———. *The Experience of Freedom*. Translated by Bridget McDonald, Stanford UP, 1993.

———. *Hegel: The Restlessness of the Negative*. Translated by Jason Smith and Steven Miller, U of Minnesota P, 2002.

Nassr, Dalia. *The Romantic Absolute: Being and Knowing in Early German Romantic Philosophy, 1795–1804*. U of Chicago P, 2014.

Newton, Isaac. *Newton: Philosophical Writings*. Edited by Andrew Janiak, Cambridge UP, 2014.

Nietzsche, Friedrich. *Unpublished Fragments from the Period of Thus Spoke Zarathustra*. Edited by Alan Schrift and Duncan Large, vol. 14, Stanford UP, 2019.

Norman, Judith. "Schelling and Nietzsche: Willing and Time." *The New Schelling*. Edited by J. Norman and A. Welchman, pp. 90–105.

Norman, Judith, and Alistair Welchman, editors. *The New Schelling*. Continuum, 2004.

O'Quinn, Daniel. *Entertaining Crisis in the Atlantic Imperium, 1770–1790*. Johns Hopkins UP, 2011.

Orsini, Gian N. *Coleridge and German Idealism: A Study in the History of Philosophy*. Southern Illinois UP 1969.

Packham, Catherine. *Eighteenth-Century Vitalism: Bodies, Culture, Politics*. Palgrave Macmillan, 2012.

Perkins, Franklin. *Leibniz and China: A Commerce of Light*. Cambridge UP, 2004.

Perry, Seamus, editor. *Coleridge's Notebooks: A Selection*. Oxford UP, 2002.

Pillow, Kirk. *Sublime Understanding: Aesthetic Reflection in Kant and Hegel*. The MIT Press, 2003.

Plato. *The Cratylus*. Translated by C. D. C. Reeve, Hackett Publishing, 1998.

———. *The Timaeus. Plato: Timaeus, Critias, Cleitophon, Menexenus, Epistles*. Loeb Classical Library No. 234. Translated by R. G. Bury, Harvard UP, 1929, pp. 1–254.

Purdy, L. "The Building in *Bildung*: Goethe, Palladio, and the Architectural Media." *Goethe Yearbook*, vol. 15, 2008, pp. 57–74.

Radcliffe, Ann. *The Romance of the Forest*. Edited by Chloe Chard, Oxford UP, 1991.

Rajan, Tilottama. "Blake's Body Without Organs: The Autogenesis of the System in the Lambeth Books." *European Romantic Review*, vol. 26, no. 3, 2015, pp. 357–66.

———. *Dark Interpreter: The Discourse of Romanticism*. Cornell UP, 1980.

Rawes, Alan. "Shelley's 'Compelling Rhyme Schemes' in *The Triumph of Life*." *Romanticism*, vol. 22, no. 1, 2016, pp. 76–89.

Regier, Alexander. *Exorbitant Enlightenment: Blake, Hamann, and Anglo-German Constellations*. Oxford UP, 2019.

Reiman, Donald H. *Shelley's 'The Triumph of Life': A Critical Study*. U of Illinois P, 1965.

Reiman, Donald H., and Neil Fraistat, editors. *Shelley's Poetry and Prose*. W. W. Norton, 2002.

Robinson, Henry Crabb. *Essays on Kant, Schelling, and German Aesthetics*. Edited by James Vigus, Modern Humanities Research Association, 2010.

Rousseau, Jean-Jacques. *The First and Second Discourses together with the Replies to Critics and Essay on the Origin of Languages*. Translated by Victor Gourevitch, Harper and Row, 1986.

Ryder, Frank G. "Season, Day, and Hour: Time as Metaphor in Goethe's *Werther*." *The Journal of English and Germanic Philology*, vol. 63, no. 3, 1964, pp. 389–407.

Schelling, F. W. J. *The Ages of the World*. Translated by Jason M. Wirth, State U of New York P, 2000.

———. *System of Transcendental Idealism (1800)*. Translated by Peter Heath, U of Virginia P, 1978.

———. *Historical-critical Introduction to the Philosophy of Mythology*. Translated by Mason Fichey and Markus Zisselsberger, State U of New York P, 2007.

---. "On the Possibility of a Form of All Philosophy." *The Unconditional in Human Knowledge: Four Early Essays (1794–6)*. Translated by Fritz Marti, Bucknell UP, 1980.

---. *The Philosophy of Art*. Translated by Douglas W. Stott, Minneapolis, U of Minnesota P, 1989.

Schlegel, Friedrich. *Philosophical Fragments*. Translated by Peter Firchow, U of Minnesota P, 1991.

Smith, Orianne. *Romantic Women Writers, Revolution, and Prophecy: Rebellious Daughters, 1786–1826*. Cambridge UP, 2013.

Spinoza, Benedict de. *Ethics*, in *the Collected Works of* Spinoza. Edited and translated by Edwin Curley, Princeton UP, 1985, pp. 408–617.

Spitzer, Michael. *Metaphor and Musical Thought*. U of Chicago P, 2004.

Van Woudenberg, Maximiliaan. *Coleridge and Cosmopolitan Intellectualism 1794–1804: The Legacy of Göttingen University*. Routledge, 2018.

Vater, Michael G. Introduction. Schelling, *System of Transcendental Idealism (1800)*, pp. xi–xxxvi.

---. "Schelling and Nāgārjuna: The Night Absolute, Openness, and *Ungrund*." *The New Schelling*. Edited by J. Norman and A. Welchman, pp. 190–208.

Vater, Michael G., and David W. Wood, editors. *The Philosophical Rupture between Fichte and Schelling: Selected Texts and Correspondence (1800–1802)*. State U of New York P, 2012.

Warminski, Andrze J. "Machinal Effects: Derrida With and Without de Man." *MLN*, vol. 124, 2009, pp. 1072–90.

Warren, Andrew. *The Orient and the Young Romantics*. Cambridge UP, 2014.

Wellek, René. *Immanuel Kant in England 1793–1838*. Princeton UP, 1931.

Wilson, Ross. *Shelley and the Apprehension of Life*. Cambridge UP, 2016.

Wirth, Jason M., editor. *Schelling Now: Contemporary Readings*. Indiana UP, 2005.

Wirth, Jason M. *Schelling's Practice of the Wild: Time, Art, Imagination*. State U of New York P, 2015.

Wittgenstein, Ludwig. *Remarks on Colour*. Translated by Linda McAlister and Margarete Schättle, Blackwell Publishing, 1977.

---. *Tractatus Logico-Philosophicus*. Translated by C.K. Ogden, Dover Publications, 1999.

Wolfe, Cary. *Before the Law: Humans and Other Animals in a Biopolitical Frame*. U of Chicago P, 2012.

Wollstonecraft, Mary. *Letters Written in Sweden, Norway, and Denmark*. Edited by Tone Brekke and Jon Mee, Oxford UP, 2009.

Wordsworth, Dorothy. *George and Sarah Greene: A Narrative*. The Clarendon Press, 1936.

---. *The Grasmere Journals*. Edited by Pamela Woof, Oxford UP, 1993.

———. *The Grasmere and Alfoxden Journals*. Edited by Pamela Woof, Oxford UP, 2008.

———. Journal manuscript DCMS 19. The Wordsworth Trust, Dove Cottage, Grasmere, UK.

Wordsworth, William. "Lines Written a Few Miles Above Tintern Abbey." *Lyrical Ballads* (1798). Edited by Michael Schmidt, Penguin, 2007, pp. 110-15.

———. *The Prelude: 1799, 1805, 1850*. Edited by M. H. Abrams et al., W. W. Norton, 1979.

———. *Poems in Two Volumes, and Other Poems, 1800-1807*. Edited by Jared Curtis, Cornell UP, 1983.

Yates, Frances. *Giordano Bruno and the Hermetic Tradition*. U of Chicago P, 1970.

Yeager, D. M. "Of Eagles And Crows, Lions and Oxen: Blake and the Disruption of Ethics." *Journal of Religious Ethics*, vol. 37, no. 1, 2009, pp. 1-31.

Zizek, Slavoj. *Less Than Nothing: Hegel and the Shadow of Dialectical Materialism*. Verso, 2013.

Index

absolute, 1, 5, 14, 26, 41, 45–46, 49, 72–73, 81–87, 90, 109, 112, 143, 157, 166, 220, 222
acculturation, 193, 196–98, 203, 206, 208, 214, 220
affection, 1–2, 5, 12–13, 15–17, 26, 28–29, 31, 37, 69, 83, 108–109, 118, 120, 124, 126–27, 136–37, 142–43, 176–78, 197, 211, 213, 228, 232n11
affects, 19, 29, 112, 115–16, 128, 193, 201, 204, 226; passions, 16, 18–19, 37, 60, 77, 82, 97, 154–56, 169, 171, 176, 219, 220; terror, 4–6, 8, 41–42, 112, 117, 118, 128; Spinozist
alterity, 1–13, 15, 18, 31, 34, 49, 57, 64, 67, 108, 188–91, 197, 202, 218–21; defined, 6; immanence, 4, 13, 69–72, 82, 90, 109–10, 117–18, 122–23, 137, 139, 142, 151, 157, 161, 183, 185; the sublime, 1–11, 18, 21, 49, 67, 80, 88, 109–10, 112–18, 122, 125, 157, 186–87, 221, 226; feminine sublime, 8–9, 109, 117, 231n4; racial alterity, 3, 6, 11, 21, 36, 183, 186, 188, 199–202, 206–207, 214, 225–28
anti-body, 124–25, 133, 134
antinomianism, 3–4, 27, 28, 34, 62
aporia, 156, 188–89, 194–98, 203–204, 206, 215, 218, 220

assemblage, 121–23, 126, 129, 132–33, 135, 137, 140, 143–44
atoms, 14, 118, 238n10

Barbauld, Anna Lætitia, 108, 110–12
beauty, aesthetic, 45–46, 80–81, 84, 95, 101, 112, 114–15, 211; spiritual beauty, 15, 54, 133–34
Behmenism. *See under* Böhme
Bennett, Jane, 121, 135–37, 140, 144, 240n27
Blackness, 21, 221, 226–28; Black mater, 227–29; anti-Blackness, 226
Blake, William, 19–30; *America a Prophecy*, 26, 39–41, 53, 62; "Auguries of Innocence," 7, 25, 30; *First Book of Urizen*, 32, 34–35, 40, 50, 58; *The Four Zoas*, 60–61, 234n39; *Jerusalem*, 19, 26, 30–32, 40, 42–43, 47, 55–58, 60–62, 65, 233n32; *Marriage of Heaven and Hell*, 27, 33, 41–42, 44, 50–55, 57, 64, 76, 227, 245n4; *Milton*, 34, 42, 49, 54–56; *Songs of Innocence and Experience*, 226–27
Blanchot, Maurice, 42, 48, 51
Boas, Franz, 197
Böhme, Jakob, 28, 46–47, 50, 72–74, 77–78; Behmenism, 197

breath, 2, 17, 73–80, 83, 107, 109, 110, 114–15, 119–20, 124, 130, 135, 140–42, 144, 164, 170
Browne, Thomas, 205
Bruno, Giordano, 28, 72, 232n9
Burke, Edmund, 1, 3, 6–7, 9, 113–14

Cartesianism. *See under* Descartes
catachresis, 188
chora, 32–33, 35–36, 50, 121, 136, 162, 190, 228, 241n37, 242n23
Cleanthes, 16, 231n11
Cloud of Unknowing, 74
Coleridge, S. T., 8, 14–15, 67–70, 72, 108–10, 116–17, 119, 126, 135, 137–39, 144, 155, 186; *Biographia Literaria*, 70–71, 87–89, 92, 95–96, 98–100, 101–103, 236; "Kubla Khan," 1, 72, 84, 87–88, 96–97, 229; "Religious Musings," 3; "Rime of the Ancient Mariner," 5, 16, 67–73, 75–76, 78, 82–85, 87–88, 90, 96, 99, 103, 222
conatus, 12, 32, 56, 68–69, 177
corporeals, 135, 144, 176, 201, 239n10

Deleuze, Gilles, 5, 17, 149, 160–61, 175–77, 181
de Man, Paul, 63, 164–65, 167–69, 172, 179, 241n7, 242n26
democracy, 11, 20, 39–42, 159, 163, 182
De Quincey, Thomas, 8, 11, 13, 15, 126, 137, 150–51, 183, 185–90, 226, 244n7, 244n10, 244n13; *Confessions of an English Opium-Eater*, 19, 154, 185–86, 188–93, 195, 197–202, 205–208; *The English Mail-Coach*, 189, 207–15, 219, *Suspiria de Profundis*, 218
Derrida, Jacques, 36, 38–40, 42, 154–68, 160–62, 164–66, 170–72, 176, 179, 181–83, 232n12, 239n20, 241n4, 242n12, 242n23, 242n28
Descartes, René, 8, 14, 32, 45, 165; Cartesianism, 6, 8, 12, 14, 33, 110, 165, 171, 175, 186
dualism, 6, 32, 34, 46, 58, 68, 83, 128, 141

Eckhart, Meister, 72
Eden, 20, 30–32, 34, 42, 55–57, 64–65, 193–94, 212–13, 220–21
Eliot, George, 6, 8–9, 107–108
ellipsis, 39, 164–66
enantiodromia, 33
Enlightenment, 2–4, 6, 8, 11–14, 20, 48, 68, 71, 92, 153, 170, 172–73, 225–27, 235n4; universal subject, 4, 164
entre nous, 128–29, 131–33, 135–38, 140, 142–43
eternity. *See under* temporality
ethics, 15–17, 25, 27, 30, 58, 69, 124; ontoethics, 69, 102, 121, 126, 139, 201
expression, 5, 14–15, 19–20, 26–27, 30, 33–35, 42, 46, 68–69, 74–75, 77–79, 82, 84–87, 93, 98, 100, 111, 118–19, 121–22, 136, 143; defined, 239n14

fancy, 52, 111, 119, 177, 198–99
Fichte, Johann Gottlieb, 71, 78, 86, 89–94, 97, 103, 139, 234n35, 236n26; Not-I, 240n34
Foucault, Michel, 196, 243n37, 243n38
freedom, 42–43, 56, 63–64, 67, 77, 82–83, 86–87, 92–94, 97–99, 108, 157–60, 162–63, 185–86, 237n33, 238n41
Freemasonry, 4, 28
future-to-come, 158, 162–63

Index | 259

geometric method, 79, 150, 176–77, 217
gnosis, 195, 197, 200–202, 206, 216, 220–21
Goethe, Johann Wolfgang von, 44, 47–48, 73, 76, 89–90, 101, 235n9
Gothic, 2–6, 11, 13, 18, 70–71, 90, 112, 118

Haraway, Donna, 123, 239n21
Hegel, G. W., 3, 8, 11, 15, 17, 35, 36, 41, 43, 50, 58, 63–64, 89, 94, 101, 122, 154, 225, 231n13, 232n16, 233n30, 234n35, 239n18, 245n3
hen kai pan (One and All), 4, 13–15, 19–20, 37, 59, 62, 94, 118, 153, 163–64, 186, 212, 220, 222, 229
Heraclitus. *See under* Pre-Socratics
hospitality, 80, 122, 157–59, 200, 201, 212

immanence. *See under* alterity
incorporeals, 12–13, 15, 31, 128, 135–36, 176, 183
indifference, 47, 84–85
infinition, 129, 131, 134, 140–42
infinity. *See under* space
interbeing, 2, 6, 26, 69–70
interval, 9, 17, 26, 31–42, 49–50, 53, 58, 60, 63–65, 68–70, 83, 111, 115, 119–21, 129, 135, 139, 141, 144, 150–51, 153, 161, 163–64, 177, 180–82, 187–88, 190, 192, 194, 203, 206, 218, 228, 242n23
Irigaray, Luce, 107, 135, 140–42, 144, 241n37

Jacobi, Friedrich Henrich, 14, 90, 237n27, 237n32

Kant, Immanuel, 1–3, 7–9, 41, 43, 71, 74, 77–78, 80–82, 85, 89–92, 94–95, 101, 113, 153–54, 157–59, 163, 173, 198–200, 205, 210, 225, 245n3
Kristeva, Julia, 120, 182, 185, 214, 234n34, 239n13

Leibniz, Gottfried Wilhelm, 78–79, 176–78, 180–81, 235n4, 243n33
Lessing, Gotthold Ephraim, 13–14, 72, 89–90, 186, 237n27
Levinas, Emmanuel, 124–25, 128–29, 133, 135–38, 140, 142–43, 239n19
Logos, 15, 100–102, 166, 174–75, 186
Longinus, 1, 7, 9
love, 29, 47, 50–51, 55, 62, 77–78, 83, 112, 155–56, 158–59, 168, 173–74

Mendelssohn, Moses, 14, 237n27
metalepsis, 17, 152, 159–61, 166–67, 169, 172, 180
metaphor, 1, 20, 73, 75–76, 78, 80, 82–84, 86–87, 107, 114, 155–56, 159, 166, 168, 172, 179, 199, 203, 208, 210, 211, 216, 218–19, 228, 235n9, 242n11, 242n17, 242n26
Mignolo, Walter D., 194–95, 197
music, 83, 155–56, 168–69, 205–206, 210, 219, 235n9
mythopoetics, 26, 30–31, 47, 67, 82–83, 111, 149, 183, 187, 190

Nancy, Jean-Luc, 37, 40, 135, 142–44, 214
natura naturans. *See under* Spinoza
Nature, 2, 4–5, 9–10, 15–17, 19–20, 26–27, 29, 32, 35, 37, 43, 46, 55, 67–72, 75–76, 79–80, 83–90, 93, 96–102, 107–109, 112–20, 122–27, 129–31, 141–44, 168, 170–72, 177, 189, 204, 217, 221–22, 225, 227–29, 234n2, 234n3, 237n28, 238n44, 244n15
Neoplatonism, 10, 14, 46–47, 95

nondualism, 7, 13, 31, 44, 60, 109, 235n4

object-oriented ontology (OOO), 135–36, 139
occidentalization, 202
ontoethics. *See under* ethics
ontology, 13, 15, 30, 65, 87, 119, 131–32, 137–39, 142, 240n27
ontopolitics, 27, 58, 187
opium, 1–2, 20–21, 183, 185–87, 189–95, 197–203, 205–13, 218, 221, 229, 244n7; laudanum, 3, 11, 97, 189, 191, 193–94, 197–99, 206–207, 211, 244n7; Opium Wars, 189
Otherness. *See under* alterity

pantheism controversy, 10, 14, 62, 72, 90, 92, 142
picturesque, 114, 118–19, 127
Piranesi, Giambattista, 217
Plato, 36–37, 46, 74, 78 98, 136, 154, 165–66, 171–72, 186
Plotinus, 78, 95
pneuma, 120
poiesis, 45, 47–48, 187, 239n13
potentia, 33, 36–37, 39–40, 46–47
potestas, 40, 48
pre-Socratics, 14, 17; Heraclitus, 100

Radcliffe, Ann, 108, 110, 112–16, 143
restlessness, 26, 35, 37, 40, 43, 44, 60, 192
revelation, 6, 14–15 17, 38–39, 43, 53–54, 77–79, 81–82, 94, 98–100, 122, 139, 142, 220, 226
revolution, 8, 11–12, 27, 29, 39–40, 54, 58, 71, 112–13, 149–50, 158, 187
Rousseau, Jean-Jacques, 150, 155, 170, 242n11; as figure, 151–52, 154, 156–58, 160–67, 169–76, 178–80, 182–83, 186, 241n7; *The Essay on the Origins of Language*, 168–69, 241n10, 242n28; *The Second Discourse*, 155, 168; *The Social Contract*, 158

Sanskrit, 75, 235–36n14
Schelling, F. W. J., 8, 11, 15, 28, 42, 45–46, 49, 51, 78, 81, 87, 89, 100, 233n23, 233n26, 236n24, 237n39, 237–38n40; *The Ages of the World*, 67, 96, 99–100, 102, 172, 238n41; "Deities of Samothrace," 96, 237n39; *Naturphilosophie*, 70–71, 98–99, 186, 215, 234n2, 234–35n3, 243n41, 244n15; *Philosophy of Art*, 25, 45–46, 82, 92, 94–96, 144, 165–67, 233n29; *System of Transcendental Philosophy*, 71–72, 81–87, 89–95, 97–98, 100–101, 143, 160, 236n25, 236n26
Schiller, Friedrich, 89, 101
Schlegel, Auguste Wilhelm von, 8, 45, 233n23
Schlegel, Friedrich von, 8, 45–47
Shelley, Percy Bysshe, 13, 15, 179, 221; "Defence of Poetry," 159, 172, 174–75, 182; "Ode to the West Wind," 49; *The Triumph of Life*, 17, 145, 149–53, 155–56, 159, 161, 163, 166, 168, 170–74, 176, 178–83, 185–86, 242n11, 242n17, 243n32
space, 5, 7, 9, 16, 31–36, 42, 50, 68, 111, 120–21, 124–25, 129, 133, 135–36, 150–51, 165, 170, 176–77, 182, 192, 217; infinity, 5, 7, 25, 36, 41, 84, 94, 99, 139
spark, 47–48, 49, 73–80, 83, 119
Spinoza, Baruch, 1, 3–6, 8, 11–18, 28, 29–30, 35, 40, 68–69, 72, 76, 78, 81–82, 89–90, 93–94, 102, 107, 110, 118, 120–21, 123, 126, 136, 139, 166, 168, 205, 213, 217, 222, 228, 231n8, 235n4, 235n5, 238–39n10, 239n15; *Deus sive Natura*,

5, 10, 198, 35, 71, 98, 142, 153; *natura naturans*, 70, 85, 90; *natura naturata*, 85; radical thought, 12; *The Ethics*, 5–6, 10, 31–32, 37, 40, 55–56, 77, 92, 94, 97, 108, 176–77, 232n11; *Theological-Political Treatise*, 40
Spinozists, 12, 90, 99
Stoics, 12, 15, 16, 18, 30, 40, 97, 100, 108, 120, 124, 136, 142, 221
Strabo, 74
subjectivity, 37, 48, 57, 58, 61–62, 98, 101, 121, 124, 166, 175, 189, 196–87, 206, 208–10, 212, 214, 216, 218, 234n34, 239n19, 240n22; subjective-object, 103, 118, 136, 142, 240n34
subjectnature, 215, 244n34
sublime. *See under* alterity
sympathy, 118, 196, 226
sympoiesis, 123, 239n21

temporality, 14, 17, 25, 32, 33, 36, 76, 78, 90, 127, 141, 152, 172–73, 175, 190, 211, 228, 241; eternity, 6–7, 25, 33–37, 39, 41, 52, 56–57, 94, 99, 217

Unitarianism, 4

vitalism, 74, 118, 239n12

Wittgenstein, Ludwig, 25, 27, 36, 37, 233n19
Wolfe, Cary, 158, 175, 242n15
Wollstonecraft, Mary, 15, 20, 27, 108, 110, 140, 143; *Letters Written During a Short Residence in Sweden, Norway and Denmark*, 6, 114–16
Wordsworth, Dorothy, 15, 16, 20, 108–10, 177, 188, 189, 221, 229, 235n5, 238n9, 239n11, 239n13, 239n16, 239n17, 240n25; *Alfoxden and Grasmere Journals*, 115–43, 241n37
Wordsworth, William, 88, 103, 108, 110, 117–18, 119, 125, 126, 128, 131–33, 135, 137, 141–43, 144, 177; *Lyrical Ballads*, 67; "Nutting," 10, 17; *The Prelude*, 1, 103, 138, 142, 229; "Tintern Abbey," 116, 131–32, 134, 139

xenophobia, 13, 21, 186, 188–90, 213